Human Dignity and Law

This book argues that human dignity and law stand in a privileged relationship with one another. Law must be understood as limited by the demands made by human dignity. Conversely, human dignity cannot be properly understood without clarifying its interaction with legal institutions and legal practices. This is not, then, a survey of the uses of human dignity in law; it is a rethinking of human dignity in relation to our principles of social governance. The result is a revisionist account of human dignity and law, one focused less on the use of human dignity in our regulations and more on its constitutive implications for the governance of the public realm.

The first part conducts a wide-ranging moral, legal, and political analysis of the nature and functions of human dignity. The second part applies that analysis to three fields of legal regulation: international law, transnational law, and domestic public law.

The book will appeal to scholars in both philosophy and law. It will also be of interest to political theorists, particularly those working within the liberal tradition or those concerned with institutional design.

Dr Stephen Riley is a lecturer in the law school of the University of Leicester, UK. He previously worked as a postdoctoral researcher in philosophy at Utrecht University.

This book develops an original revisionist understanding of human dignity. Under this understanding, dignity does not exist prior to or independently of law. Human dignity should be analyzed as a value which lies at the intersection of morality, law, and politics. This valuable approach challenges established dogmas and establishes the significance of law as a value-sustaining institution.

Alon Harel, Mizock Professor of Law,
The Hebrew University Law Faculty and
the Federmann Center for the Study of Rationality.

In place of conceptions of human dignity that suffer from normative indeterminacy, regulative redundancy or constitutive incoherence, Stephen Riley elaborates an account that focuses on the basic status of humans and their entitlements in a network of obligations that ranges across law, politics, morals, and justice. This is a truly impressive work, beautifully written and compellingly argued.

Roger Brownsword, King's College London and
Bournemouth University.

Human Dignity and Law

Legal and Philosophical Investigations

Dr Stephen Riley

Routledge
Taylor & Francis Group
LONDON AND NEW YORK

First published 2018 by Routledge

2 Park Square, Milton Park, Abingdon, Oxfordshire OX14 4RN
52 Vanderbilt Avenue, New York, NY 10017

Routledge is an imprint of the Taylor & Francis Group, an informa business

First issued in paperback 2019

British Library Cataloguing-in-Publication Data
A catalogue record for this book is available from the British Library

Library of Congress Cataloging-in-Publication Data
Names: Riley, Stephen, 1977–, author.
Title: Human dignity and the law : legal and philosophical investigations / Stephen Riley.
Description: New York, NY : Routledge, 2017. | Includes bibliographical references and index.
Identifiers: LCCN 2017022609 | ISBN 9781138287587 (hardback) | ISBN 9781351975254 (adobe reader) | ISBN 9781351975247 (epub) | ISBN 9781351975230 (mobipocket)
Subjects: LCSH: Respect for persons—Law and legislation. | Law—Philosophy. | Dignity.
Classification: LCC K3249 .R55 2017 | DDC 340/.11—dc23
LC record available at https://lccn.loc.gov/2017022609

ISBN: 978-1-138-28758-7 (hbk)
ISBN: 978-0-367-88585-4 (pbk)

Typeset in Galliard
by Apex CoVantage, LLC

To Ella and Joe

Contents

Preface ix
Acknowledgements x
Introduction xi
Outline xiv

PART I

1 Human dignity and law 3
Introduction 3
1.1 Three jurisprudential problems 4
1.2 Three jurisprudential questions 6
1.3 Dignitarian principles 10
1.4 A general jurisprudence of human dignity 14
1.5 Between justice and virtue 18
1.6 Directions and desiderata *24*

2 Human dignity as status 31
Introduction 31
2.1 The normative core of human dignity 32
2.2 Human dignity as status 36
2.3 Juridical necessity 40
2.4 The normative implications of human dignity 45
2.5 Human rights 50
2.6 Status and value 57

3 Human dignity, justice, and institutions 66
Introduction 66
3.1 The institutional implications of human dignity 68
3.2 The limits of justice 69
3.3 The human condition 74

3.4 Democratic institutions 81
3.5 The morality of governance 88
3.6 Moral cosmopolitanism 90

PART II

4 International law 101
Introduction 101
4.1 The contradictions of international law 103
4.2 Global constitutional principles 109
4.3 International human rights law 114
4.4 Warfare 119
4.5 Humanitarian intervention 125
4.6 International criminal justice 130

5 Transnational law 138
Introduction 138
5.1 Defining transnational law 139
5.2 Lex mercatoria *144*
5.3 Human rights and globalisation 149
5.4 Social and economic rights 153
5.5 Constitutionalising Europe 157
5.6 Subsidiarity 163

6 Public law 171
Introduction 171
6.1 The responsibilities of the state 172
6.2 The rule of law and public reason 178
6.3 The public-private divide 183
6.4 Criminal law 189
6.5 Criminal justice 193
6.6 Punishment 200

Index 209

Preface

This book argues that human dignity and law stand in a privileged relationship with one another. Law must be understood as limited by the demands made by human dignity. Conversely, human dignity cannot be properly understood without clarifying its interaction with legal institutions and legal practices. We therefore need to undertake a philosophical investigation into the links between human dignity and justice. That investigation must in turn be applied to our most important legal practices. The result is a revisionist account of human dignity and law, one focussed less on the use of human dignity in our regulations and more on its constitutive implications for the governance of the public realm.

Any scholarship on human dignity must be conscious of two vices to which discussions of human dignity are prey. This first is over-reaching. Human dignity has become an all-encompassing but vague token of collective aspirations. One of the consequences of putting human dignity and law into dialogue is, I hope, exchanging human dignity rhetoric for normative precision.

The second vice is under-estimation of human dignity's consequences. Human dignity is tamed by legal our institutions. Law can reduce human dignity to its breaches, to degradation or instrumentalisation. I take the implications of human dignity to lie in our very conception of obligations and by extension in the very idea of law itself. It is necessary, then, to think again about how it is we orientate our social world to human dignity. Whether this study ultimately under- or over-reaches will be for the reader to determine.

Acknowledgements

This book was written as part of the research project 'Human Dignity as the Foundation of Human Rights' at Utrecht University, financed by the Netherlands Organisation for Scientific Research (NWO).

The chapters were read and commented upon by Patrick Capps, Catherine Dupré, Adam Etinson, Robert Fine, Machiko Kanetake, Gavin Kerr, Mary Neal, Elena Pribytkova, Phil Riley, David M. Seymour, Dina Townsend, and Elaine Webster. I am very grateful indeed for their time and constructive comments; I would have made significantly more errors without their efforts. All remaining faults are, alas, my own.

The project team at Utrecht University provided a wonderful group of scholars to work with. They have read countless drafts and given scholarly support in every imaginable way. My thanks to Gerhard Bos, Dascha During, Marie Göbel, Jurriën Hamer, and Frederike Kaldewaij. My especial thanks are owed to the project leader, Marcus Düwell, for steering me into a different engagement with human dignity than the one I had planned and for being an inspiring scholar to work with throughout my time in Utrecht.

Special thanks are owed to Ruth who made considerable sacrifices to allow me to get to this point. I want to express a deep gratitude for her support and kindness.

Introduction

This study is not a survey of the uses of human dignity in law. It is a rethinking of human dignity in relation to law. It argues that human dignity, properly understood, demands a coherent vision of law and of our principles of social governance. Human dignity demands that the basic status of every individual should form the ultimate framework of our obligations, regardless of the settled practices of our legal and political institutions. To accept, alternatively, the current contradictory manifestations of human dignity in law (and to accept its various rhetorical functions in the political realm) is to abandon human dignity to its critics: legally efficacious at times but ultimately vacuous, the 'shibboleth of all empty-headed moralists' as Schopenhauer put it with vicious relish.

I take human dignity to be an assertion of the basic status of every human. Put this way, human dignity is simpler but more demanding than some philosophies of human dignity suggest. Human status means equality between every person we encounter; it means every person whoever, and wherever, they are is presumed to have certain moral and legal entitlements. This does not require any special theories of human nature. It demands status for each individual regardless of context. That 'regardless of context' is not indifference to the specific but rather an assertion of basic entitlements existing irrespective of special local sources of obligation. That, then, is the especially demanding part: to follow the implications of the idea that human status can exist irrespective of conventional obligations.

This places human dignity in confrontation with not only positive law but with justice itself. To show that human dignity and justice are distinct but nonetheless compatible ideas is the Gordian Knot that makes this area of enquiry so important but also perplexing. We need to understand how it is that human dignity requires law but is not reducible to it. And we need to understand how justice can maintain a critical function in our thinking without subsuming it into either positive law or human dignity.

The solution to these puzzles lies in two related ideas. The first is that if we take human dignity seriously as a status idea with stringent principled consequences then we must adopt something like the 'natural law' view of law itself, i.e. we must accept, at the very least, certain kinds of principles determining whether certain laws should be accepted as laws regardless of their social source and pedigree. The second is that we must see human dignity as a cluster of principles that have no respect for our systemic practices, no respect for the putative 'closure' of law as a self-contained normative system. Together these mean that human dignity demands something like the rule of law in its most expansive sense, i.e. the good governance of human affairs through stable legislative and adjudicative practices.

Where, then, should we expect to find a coherent or defensible relationship between human dignity and law? I argue that we should look for the implications of human dignity in public law – in the governance of our public realms – but that we should look for its distinctive normative applications *between* our legal, moral, and political systems. Examples might include civil disobedience, humanitarian intervention, prosecutions of heads of state in international criminal justice, regulation of transnational actors, and migration crises. What do these have in common? One thing they have in common is normative complexity. These phenomena do not admit simple moral or legal analysis and the related political discourse is highly contested. Second, and more specifically, these sit between the moral, political, and legal; they are resistant to 'ownership' by a single normative perspective. Law will be politically contested; politics will be morally contested. As 'interstitial' problems – problems sitting between our normative orders, between our sources of obligation – these are precisely where human dignity has its paradigmatic function. Human dignity must be thought to imply interstitial principles maintaining the status of each individual despite competing sources of normativity. Put more forcefully, human dignity is distinctive because, if taken seriously, it means our systems do not condition our status; our status conditions our systems. No amount of legal or political tradition, or legal and political pragmatism, can defeat the primary importance of protecting the individuals who are subject to those systems.

In contrast to a significant proportion of legal scholarship on human dignity, these conclusions about the proper scope and application of human dignity appear 'revisionist'. The foundational nature of human dignity is given more critical attention (and the regulative uses of human dignity are much less important) than in comparison to other scholarship. What is distinctive, then, is an especial attention paid to the proper scope of dignitarian claims and, by extension, engagement with the full range of concerns that fall under practical philosophy rather than attention to jurisprudential debates alone. These claims are the focus of Part I of the book. But they have two implications that should be acknowledged from the outset. The first is my denying special significance to biolaw and bioethics in understanding human dignity. The ideas of dignity found in biolaw are, I maintain, largely separable from the idea of human dignity defended here. Where they concern the *integrity* of the person, they have some connection with human dignity; where they concern the *sanctity* of the human, they have none. This points to a second implication or presupposition, one concerning taking degradation as a starting point in dignity scholarship. While it would be churlish to deny that important advances have been made, using the discourse of human dignity in the protection of individuals at the mercy of the state, I argue that ideas like degradation, dehumanisation, and objectification should not be central to our understanding of the concept. We can understand the historical reasons why human dignity has been associated with a collective commitment to avoid atrocity; and we can value the phenomenological richness that has been invited into law through the gateway of 'violations of human dignity'. Nevertheless, distortions arise from excessive focus on the breach of bodily integrity. And there is a conceptual dead end produced by trying to draw out a systematic theory of human dignity through tracing the negation or breach of human dignity. We have to work towards a positive account of human dignity that respects, but is not beholden to, the body of positive human rights law that has arisen in the post-war world. This requires us to take hold of and explore human dignity's *general function* in human rights law – to be a foundational commitment to status – not, in contrast, to be over-awed by its effective but specific function to prohibit degradation.

This is certainly not the first study to be revisionist in these senses. There has been a considerable amount of good recent scholarship that delineates a 'modern' conception of human dignity, one tied to human rights but giving it wider political and constitutional significance. Indeed, there are studies looking to find a deeper philosophical link between human dignity and legality itself. Erin Daly has produced one such account and she points to the kind of enquiry required to make sense of their relationship:

> In one way or another, most courts must confront the relationship between dignity and law. But once they begin to notice each other, what happens? Does the very notion of dignity threaten the hegemony of law? Or does the ever-expanding reach of the law threaten primordial human dignity? Or can they sit side by side, like two restless children on a park bench, enduring or provoking occasional skirmishes over the boundary lines, but basically leaving one another intact? Or, perhaps, do they have not an antagonistic relationship, but rather an interdependent obligation to nurture one another to their mutual benefit? The answers to these questions depend in large part on how courts, in the context of specific cases, characterize the multiple qualities of individual dignity, beyond its basic inherence in human existence.
> (Daly 2012, 31)

This suggestive sketch is useful, but I would qualify it in two ways. As part of our legal investigations we must ask, prior to any questions of *adjudication*, whether and how we are to *legislate* for human dignity and make it part of positive law. We can treat human dignity as vitally important to understanding law, and yet we could also deny that it should form part of our legislation. And, as part of our philosophical investigations, we should ask precisely how it is that human dignity and *justice* interact. The jurisprudence of human dignity will always have an autonomous life of its own as long as there are variations between courts and legal cultures. But the concept of human dignity must be presumed to have a relationship with justice and with law as such. We need to know, in essence, whether law and human dignity inhabit two competing normative 'worlds' with each unable to acknowledge the superior authority of the other. We cannot expect courtrooms to give us answers to these questions. These questions require weaving together the law and the philosophy of human dignity.

Outline

Part I (Chapters 1–3) presents a general jurisprudence of human dignity. Part II (Chapters 4–6) applies that analysis to three fields of legal regulation. Chapter 1 looks to pin-point the *desiderata* of an account of human dignity's relationship with law. It commences with a critique of existing accounts of human dignity and law paying especial attention to the problems produced in the interaction of human dignity and legal decision-making. It emphasises some of the ways in which these problems are under-analysed in legal and philosophical accounts of human dignity. It argues, in response, that we should focus on the concept of human dignity associated with human rights, an association that requires us to treat human dignity as a status concept. This approach to the concept connects the existing positive law of human dignity with the natural law tradition, and it places emphasis on a division between constitutive and regulative use of human dignity. The implications of human dignity as a status concept are predominantly constitutive, meaning the proper application of human dignity lies in public law broadly construed. Human dignity as status concerns, more specifically, the protection of individuals' natural equality and natural liberties where competing moral, legal, and political obligations threaten to attenuate or negate them. It is in the light of this more specific set of functions that human dignity's relationship with positive law should be understood.

Chapter 2 builds upon the critique of Chapter 1 and systematically reconstructs the concept using (*inter alia*) the work of Kant. A focus on 'innate right' is used to defend the coherence of a status conception of human dignity, and this in turn justifies seeing human dignity as having its core normative implications in three 'status principles'. These principles – concerning human dignity's relationship with 'sovereignty', 'permission', and 'obligation' – are constitutive in a double sense: they work as constitutional principles for governance of public law, but they are also constitutive of our obligations more generally. This reconstruction therefore encompasses human dignity's foundational relationship with human rights law and its relationship with practical reason as a whole.

Chapter 3 explores what this means for our understanding of justice and institutions. We must separate the demands of human dignity from those of justice where justice denotes reasonable variations in governance and reasonable variation in legal judgment. We can, by contrast, identify those instances in which human dignity does have decisive implications for legal and political decision-making. These include the familiar phenomenon of bringing human rights claims against the state, but also in broader judgments based on moral cosmopolitanism and a 'morality of governance'. These are applications of the dignitarian principles such that we are able to determine the demands on, and permissible limits of, public law.

Chapter 4 explores a number of ways in which human dignity is said to represent or articulate a new, post-war, form of international law. In contrast to many recent accounts connecting human dignity with an especially progressive understanding of international law, I argue that human dignity has a narrower but distinctive obligation-distributing role for the international community. Human dignity has a role in articulating basic deficiencies of states and a role in understanding the permissibility of violating the rules of positive international law to enhance the international rule of law. Thus, the core role of human dignity in relation to international law lies at the limits of legality: where the rule of law has failed at a domestic level, and where the international rule of law has failed such that unilateral action is morally permitted. Attention to these core implications also allows us to make sense of the perceived dignitarian underpinnings of international criminal justice as a response to legal, moral, and political failures.

Chapter 5, concerning transnational law, argues for a form of subsidiarity-based constitutionalism, taking subsidiarity – the movement of power 'downwards' towards individuals – as essential to any defensible conception of this field of law. Subsidiarity connects the constitutive and regulative in a way consistent with human dignity. At a constitutive level we should be defending only transnational legal arrangements that are capable of being brought within institutions of accountability at a state or inter-statal level (democratic subsidiarity). This also means that at a regulative level we should be allocating competences amongst state and non-state actors with special expertise (epistemic subsidiarity) only if they can guarantee democratic oversight for processes and practices. Thus, the 'interactionism' that is commonly used to analyse transnational law is here challenged by a dignitarian defence of democratic accountability.

Chapter 6 considers the public law of states and its relationships with public reason and the rule of law. Given that the rule of law is rightly held to be a necessary condition of human dignity, we need precision over what this entails at both the constitutive and regulative levels; at a constitutive level this means a permissive orientation in our governance, and at a regulative level it means coherent and independent adjudication of human rights law. And, given the state's central but not unchallenged ability to draw distinctions between the public and the private, we have to consider the conflicting claims of public and private authority in contemporary societies. This also means considering the normative justification of punishment and criminal justice as well as the normative bases of criminalisation in the light of human dignity. Our sovereignty, our basic status, provides a right to be held responsible and to fully discharge debts of legal guilt. That status also requires, however, that state-based retribution carefully excludes moral guilt, thereby challenging over-criminalisation and over-incarceration.

Reference

Daly, E. (2012) *Dignity Rights: Courts, Constitutions, and the Worth of the Human Person*. Philadelphia, University of Pennsylvania Press.

Part I

1 Human dignity and law

> As I understand the concept of human dignity, it is not a metaphysical property of human beings. Rather, it consists in relationships among human beings in which they do not humiliate and degrade each other. Respectful relationships honor human dignity; humiliating relationships violate it; and institutions honor human dignity when they do not humiliate people. Lawmaking that violates Fuller's canons offends against human dignity by subjecting people to an especially humiliating condition: that of perpetual uncertainty and fearfulness because one's fate lies in the hands of official whim, which can choose at will to stigmatize conduct as criminal.
>
> (Luban 2010, 10–11; footnotes removed)

> [T]he multi-functional role of human dignity, in which it serves at once as a ground for all human rights, as a substantive right at issue in the particular case, and as a basis for legality [. . .] may lead to the suggestion that legality concerns should fall in the face of overwhelming injuries to dignity. [But] to say that certain legal principles, such as legality, are *necessary to* or *derived from* human dignity is not equivalent to saying that these principles must yield in the pursuit of human dignity.
>
> (Heath 2012, 353; emphasis in original)

Introduction

I start, as many others have, with philosophical and legal puzzles associated with human dignity, above all with the idea that human dignity might be a 'foundation'. Is human dignity a foundation for law or laws? The question immediately faces the rejoinder that law that has no need of foundations, only social sources. If *justice* is law's foundation we face a different, no less difficult, question of how human dignity and justice might encompass one another.

Note that the human dignity we find in positive law is of little assistance here. It could easily be characterised as either empty or as over-full. Human dignity is sometimes an empty placeholder marking the absence of agreement. It is also a legal norm, a legal principle, a right, and a standard. The human dignity we find in law raises more questions than it answers.

Jurisprudence offers us two immediate, but unsatisfactory, lenses or frameworks for making sense of these questions. A natural law position might defend the special moral force of human dignity. But this is far from a complete account of human dignity's proper institutional applications, especially how it is that human dignity can be legitimately shaped or conditioned by legal institutions. The legal positivist, in contrast, denatures the concept. By pressing it into the service of a system of positive laws, we make human dignity hostage to the contingencies of legal cases and cultures.

My response to this, and the focus of this chapter, will be a kind of internal critique of legal practice, finding ways in which legal problems yield *desiderata* for a coherent account of human dignity and law. I conclude that a critical choice is forced upon us by human dignity as we find it in law. If we are to take the relationship between human dignity and law seriously, we also have to adopt an account of law that is not only inclusive of, but partly defined by, human dignity as a foundational commitment. More specifically, we have to see human dignity as implying principles that govern our social systems and our normative orders. The alternative is continuing incoherence in both our practice and our theory.

1.1 Three jurisprudential problems

I want first to outline three classes of problems arising from human dignity's use in law. They are normative indeterminacy, regulative redundancy, and constitutive incoherence.

First, normative indeterminacy. 'Human dignity' possesses such lack of clarity that its normative significance is uncertain and contradictory. It can be used in courtrooms to extend the reach of our laws, often to good ends. But in the process it threatens to violate basic legal principles like *nulla crimen sine lege* (no crime without law). Sometimes the enforceability of human dignity in law allows moral concerns to displace strict doctrinal interpretations. This also entails virtue-based decisions invoking what is 'good for us'. And, whether or not we think these kinds of uses are unproblematic, human dignity has in the main tended to produce a narrowly prohibitive body of norms concerning degradation and objectification. Thus, we can say that human dignity has *some* adjudicative determinacy, but only at the level of degradation prohibitions and nowhere else. Its core remains indeterminate even if there are 'local' legal uses that are more determinate. As Christopher McCrudden puts it:

> Dignity discourse has, so far at least, done little to [find] the appropriate balance between the individual and the community, including such questions as the appropriate limits on individual freedom; the appropriateness of the use of state power to ensure basic standards of material security; what rights should be attributed at the beginning of life and at the end of life; and how far we have responsibilities to ourselves and to the community.
>
> (McCrudden 2008, 712)

The problem of normative indeterminacy will be addressed directly in Chapter 2, where we separate out its 'normative core' and its 'normative implications'.

Second, regulative redundancy. If we have a legal system containing equality legislation and a prohibition on degradation, then it is not clear what further work human dignity is needed for. That is, what place should it have in the fabric of our regulations? Human dignity implies equality, and it has also traditionally articulated the most fundamental norms and prohibitions concerning the treatment of the person. Human dignity makes our equality somehow ontological and not just formal: it means we are fundamentally, not merely conventionally, equal. And it articulates experiences of inequality (or degradation) that might not be easily captured in our regulations. Nevertheless, the ideas of equality and prohibition on degradation are the primary normative notions here, and human dignity is an invitation to enrich them, not a candidate to replace them. Put in positive, enforceable form, human dignity can be a barrier to rather than a justification of equal treatment:

> as critics have pointed out, human dignity is an abstract and subjective notion that, even with the guidance of the four contextual factors [dignity, equality, plurality, and democracy,] cannot only become confusing and difficult to apply; it has also proven to be an additional burden on equality claimants, rather than the philosophical enhancement it was intended to be.
>
> (*R v. Kapp* 2008; paragraphs 21–22)

With a stable body of clear legal norms and a developed equality jurisprudence, explicit reference to human dignity in law should be redundant. Where it is included in our regulations it is both over- and under-inclusive. Sometimes it purely prohibits egregious attacks on individuals' bodies; sometimes it encompasses every aspect of individuals' personality. Either way, explicit reference to human dignity in our positive law is liable to create more heat than light. This problem of regulative redundancy is addressed in Part II, where we look more closely at specific areas of law and at human dignity's more fundamental constitutional roles.

Finally, constitutive incoherence. Human dignity is explicitly 'foundational' in many contexts and implicitly foundational in the primary position it holds in many constitutions. This has meant some theorists positing two different concepts – a regulative norm and a constitutional principle – that function in parallel but are not obviously dependent upon each other. By extension, this also allows human dignity to appear to be foundational to constitutions in one way, and foundational to human rights in another. Human dignity may be a kind of constitutional *Grundnorm* (a basic or foundational norm). It may also be a more substantive moral commitment. But it is not clear how the two are linked. Suggestions that it is a special 'value' seem too opaque to be constitutionally useful; to treat human dignity as our ultimate social goal entails limitless possibilities for interpretation. Many societies are broadly committed to human dignity through their constitutions, and many also want to operationalise human dignity in their legal judgments. But it is enormously difficult to conjoin these two commitments. We want to use human dignity to reason, but if it is of profound constitutional importance, then it cannot be a mere norm susceptible to being defeated like any other. As Mary Neal puts it,

> any failure to realise dignity completely seems to be unconscionable. It is unlike other principles in that, although various aspects of dignity must often be weighed against one another to get the focus of the dignity picture right, dignity itself is never truly weighed against other values: no outcome can be both dignity-violating and legally acceptable.
>
> (Neal 2014, 36)

Overcoming these constitutional or constitutive problems is the focus of Chapter 3, where we consider the 'institutional implications' of human dignity. But getting a clear dissolution to this problem of constitutional incoherence can be taken to be the primary concern of this book.

While I have argued that we should take these problems seriously, they could be thought to invite much quicker dismissal. We might say that there are legitimate differences of emphasis in different legal cultures and contexts, and we would certainly expect differences, for instance, between the domestic and the international law of human dignity. Moreover, it seems relatively uncontroversial to divide a focal usage derived from the Universal Declaration of Human Rights (UDHR 1948) and foundational to human rights from various non-focal uses found in different areas of legal practice (for instance, health care law or defamation law). Ultimately (it might be argued), we should not expect to find a final coherent philosophy of human dignity within law, whose responsiveness to individual complaints and injustices is not intended to produce conceptual coherence.

It seems to me that these solutions are too quick. Too quick to accept contradictions in law. Too quick to allow human dignity to disrupt the rule of law. And, more to the point, too obscure on the meaning of 'law' as such. That is, they leave open the possibility that human dignity and law represent competing spheres or qualitatively different forms of normativity. They seem to suggest that uncertainty is the price we pay for importing a moral notion into an alien normative system.

In contrast, I want to pose three questions much closer to the concerns of general jurisprudence, questions that put pressure on the ideas of legality that we are or should be working with. Why does the law of human dignity not 'work itself pure'? In what sense could human dignity be said to be a product of law? And how is the idea of human dignity being foundational compatible with law as such?

1.2 Three jurisprudential questions

Why will the law of human dignity not 'work itself pure'? With complex or anachronistic concepts we assume that legal institutions will eventually produce, through repeated adjudication, a clear legal norm. The law abhors normative imprecision, and the courts are systems for imposing order on our normative concepts. There is no evidence that this is likely to happen for human dignity. There are certainly institutional barriers to this, namely different legal cultures with different judicial assumptions. And the genealogy of the concept mixes virtue with justice, allowing liberal and non-liberal cultures to make opposed readings. Still, even within liberal legal cultures, there is no likelihood that the concept will be given definitive expression or a single, consistent cross-constitutional function. Why?

One reason is that we do not have a single paradigmatic expression of human dignity but rather several dignities found in our discourses of human rights law, bioethics, equality law, and health care law, and in various constitutional uses. One immediate solution to this would be to demand consensus on what counts as the key articulation of human dignity. The choice then would be to accept a focal use (probably, but not necessarily, that found in the UDHR) or to reject that paradigmatic instantiation and accept a plurality of legal uses (McCrudden 2008; Rodriquez 2015). We need to decide what it is we want to work pure. Or we need to let different, local uses flourish without insisting on a common denominator.

Both of these options are problematic. If we try to reconstruct the meaning of human dignity using the normative materials and principles available in public international law (where we find the UDHR) we find reductive readings where human dignity must take its function within the narrow legal concerns of international law (e.g. Beitz 2009). By that route we find ourselves retreating to the idea that human dignity signals opposition to atrocity and is, ultimately, to be associated with egregious assaults on the bodily integrity of the individual. After all (it is argued), where we see human dignity and human rights being efficacious ideas in international law, it is when they are triggers for intervention in the context of atrocity (for critical analysis of this, see Tasioulas 2009). But we have not now worked human dignity pure. We have found a context in which it appears especially efficacious or discursively appropriate. This is very different to finding a single, clear, *foundational* role in international human rights law or domestic constitutional law.

Conversely, if we embrace plurality, we not only accept the kinds of normative ambiguities discussed above but we condemn human dignity to being a kind of 'essentially contested concept' (Gallie 1955; Baruah 2014; Rodriquez 2015). This means that the inner complexity of the concept, and the many different claims that can be made upon it, will never be resolved into a single idea. Christopher McCrudden provides the most prominent survey and analysis of the presence of human dignity in adjudication (2008). He found that a "basic minimum content of the meaning of human dignity can be discerned: that each human being possesses an intrinsic worth that should be respected, that some forms of conduct are inconsistent with respect for this intrinsic worth, and that the state exists for the individual not vice versa" (McCrudden 2008, 723). These competing 'worth', 'respect', and 'limited-state' conceptions of human dignity lie at the heart of human dignity's problematic status, and McCrudden himself insists "one cannot coherently hold all of these conceptions at the same time. Dignity appears to become other than impossibly vague only when it is tethered to a coherent community of interpretation" (2008, 723). But note that this does not quite fulfil the criteria of an essentially contested concept. Being 'impossibly vague' is not the same as necessarily imprecise. And nor is McCrudden ruling out the possibility of a 'coherent community of interpretation'. Moreover, the precise charge of an essentially contested concept relies upon the existence of a shared 'exemplar' or expression of the concept around which discourse radiates (Gallie 1955, 177). While human dignity perhaps has exemplary expression in human rights treaties, this exemplar is not universally accepted, and Kateb, for instance, insists on the greater importance of the U.S. Constitution (Kateb 2011, 28).

Neither option seems to me satisfactory and I suggest that we would do better to focus not on how legal institutions can bring unity to the concept but on capturing human dignity's characteristic *functions* in both international and domestic law. Those functions typically relate to the limits of authority. Human dignity points time and again to the limits of the positive law, the limits of the market, of scientific practice, and so on. The point here is not that human dignity is simply a reactive constraint on power or progress. The important function is the claim to limit power, even if it is authorised power. This includes executive, legislative, and judicial power. That is why, for instance, it is possible to invoke human dignity to justify a refusal to follow orders (German Military Manual 1992, Rule 154). Why, for instance, we can use human dignity to articulate the legitimacy of law-breaking, be it civil disobedience or humanitarian intervention (*Jehovah's Witnesses v. Russia* [2010]). And why human dignity is sometimes relied upon to justify judicial review (*Kindler v. Canada* [1991]). Human dignity is a principle *governing authority.* It is that function that cannot be worked pure, because no single legal norm, only a principle, can articulate the limits of legal authority. Human dignity is a point from which we can articulate the limits of law's authority.

If the uses of human dignity in law are contested, is human dignity, nonetheless, in some way a product of law? We have already noted the centrality of the UDHR (1948) as an expression, perhaps the preeminent expression, of a modern notion of human dignity. The uses of the term in that instrument are important expressions of human dignity in its modern form. 'Inherent dignity' is found in the Preamble to the UDHR: "Whereas recognition of the inherent dignity and of the equal and inalienable rights of all members of the human family is the foundation of freedom, justice and peace in the world [. . .] Whereas the peoples of the United Nations have in the Charter reaffirmed their faith in fundamental human rights, in the dignity and worth of the human person and in the equal rights of men and women [. . .]" And in Article 1 of the declaration: "All human beings are born free and equal in dignity and rights." A different way to look at these characteristic legal expressions of human dignity is not simply through the accidents of treaty drafting (and, famously, the need for a 'place-holder' in the absence of agreement; see Glendon 2001, 77) but as an irreducibly legal idea that could have been given expression only through law and legal practices.

One way of articulating this is to say that law has produced, out of its own normative resources, the 'modern' idea of human dignity. The closure of law – its structural and normative isolation from politics and morality – allowed it to rearrange its own resources in the aftermath of war to produce a new concept that is, from its inception, legal (Luhmann 2008, 484f). Compare this to the Fuller-inspired ideas of modern or procedural natural law where it is assumed that human dignity is accomplished through sound legal practices and the rule of law (Fuller 1964). This means good legal institutions and the rule of law are already sufficient conditions for the maintenance of human dignity. Together, these positions give us two conceptions of human dignity's pedigree in law: that it is self-produced by legal systems from their closed system of legal norms or it is immanent in legal systems and automatically flows from the rule of law.

Neither of these positions are defensible. Law is not a closed system (on the one hand) and (on the other) it is not possible to insist that human dignity is always and exclusively realised through the normal workings of the rule of law. The conceptions of law, of human dignity, and of normativity that are defended in the remainder of this book are incompatible with the idea that law can be 'cognitively open but normatively closed'. And in Chapter 3 we consider a more sustained analysis of how it is that the rule of law must be construed as a necessary, but not sufficient, condition of human dignity. There are nonetheless lessons to gleaned from these positions. Human dignity is rightly associated with 'eunomic' ideas, i.e. principles of good self-governance. This means we should not allow our different legal, political, and moral systems to be isolated normative practices. As individuals our obligations transcend these divides, and the very idea of the rule of law requires the harmonisation of the sources of normativity. These are important areas of dignitarian concern. But they still leave unresolved the fundamental normative relationship between human dignity and law.

How, then, is the idea of human dignity being foundational compatible with law as such? In other words, is law the kind of thing that has a foundation and, if so, is it human dignity? It is tempting to sweep many of the more difficult questions about human dignity into the idea of 'foundation'. This is sometimes articulated as human dignity being a *Grundnorm* (a basic or foundational norm), with human dignity treated as a basic source of legal validity. Or, more modestly, human dignity can be treated as foundational because it is an indispensable interpretive idea, a foundation through its being the final determinant of how we interpret the rules.

These are awkward claims from the point of view of jurisprudence. For instance, it is difficult to know how we should understand the idea of human dignity as *Grundnorm*, as the animating or validity-conferring foundation of a legal system. The German constitutional experience demonstrates that what starts out as putatively foundational quickly gets reduced to a narrow prohibitive norm, a norm typically regulating objectification rather than functioning in its own right as a constitutional principle (*Peep Show Case* 1981). Or we might think of the presence of human dignity in European Union treaties. Those treaty provisions have lain more or less dormant throughout Europe's recent migration crisis. When the

European Court of Justice was called upon to operationalise the idea, it was used to prohibit certain types of laser-based computer games (*Omega* 2004). It is not far-fetched to assume that human dignity was intended to do something much more radical as a constitutional commitment.

The problem, in essence, is that legal systems themselves have tended to collapse the constitutive into the regulative. In their need to operationalise the concept, legal institutions have favoured a regulative use related to degradation (and, in time, to a distinctive kind of 'dignitarian wrong') rather finding more systematic application in the design and regulation of state institutions. This is encouraged by the assumption that defence of human dignity amounts to a political *rejection* of historical abuses in states like South Africa and Germany; the special interpretive role of human dignity is thereby assumed to be one of rejecting practices that represent, or produce slippery slopes to, degradation of individuals. However, the point of giving human dignity constitutional primacy is surely far more constructive, i.e. to give a new, positive, not merely negative foundation to a polity. And, in that position of constitutional re-construction, the implication of the concept is not merely to introduce a special symbolic norm rejecting abuses of the past. It is to claim that human status is not conditioned by the boundaries that exist between our legal, moral, and political obligations. Human dignity is not just anti-consequentialist or anti-instrumentalist, it is in an important sense anti-systemic, at least in the sense of challenging the separation of the legal, moral, and political.

In that latter sense, 'foundation' or 'foundational' should be heard not as 'symbolic' or 'a rejection of past abuses'. 'Foundation' should be read as a limit of authority and as a dynamic constitutional principle. This is very clear in its relation to human rights: human rights limit the authority of the state, and, through their connection with human dignity, those rights remain dynamic, mapping changes in our social and political landscape. In that context, 'foundation' does not mean something wholly novel, nor does it mean something timeless. Our foundations (of politics, morality, and law) are the same as they have always been (at least since the dawn of modernity), principal amongst them being a line between the public and the private, a division between forms of political authority but also a division between sources of obligation (public reason and private conscience). As those boundaries change, the threats to human status change and our understanding must change with them. Thus the search for a timeless expression of human dignity *in* law is illusory. Its function is to make our legal norms dynamic, and we should find human dignity at the limits of our normative concerns and in its most contested areas.

1.3 Dignitarian principles

I have suggested, though clearly not yet justified, a number of imputations from characteristic tensions between human dignity and law. Drawing these together, I want to convert or distil the idea of human dignity directly into two principles that I argue indissolubly bind our understanding of human dignity and law. One is a permissive principle, the second an obligation principle. These do not exhaust the normative core or normative implications of human dignity as I see it. But they point the way towards an account of how some of the existing functions of human dignity and a normative reconstruction of human dignity can be brought into agreement.

The first principle is a permissive principle imposing formal and substantive boundaries on the governance of our social systems. It entails that there should be a presumption towards permissions in the structuring of our societies and norms. Whether expressed in the language of natural liberties or of a constitutional presumption towards the legality of actions where the law is silent, human dignity is rightly connected with the permissive aspects of constitutional reasoning in liberal states (see Alexy 2010, 232f). It entails, moreover, that there should be a careful separation of the public and the private, both as spheres of activity and as forms of authority. Any maintenance of good order – order beholden to neither organic political forces nor technocracy – must draw a clear division between those demands that can be made on us by public authority, and conversely, the entitlements and obligations of the private sphere which is properly given over to self-constitution of individuals. The private sphere is characterised by actions and choices that must be immunised as far as possible from public scrutiny and intervention.

To understand this as a principle, it is noteworthy that at present we face enormous practical and philosophical difficulties with the positive law of privacy (Solove 2002; Post 2017). The problem is not just anachronism in the texts or the jurisprudence of our laws (although it is that as well). Rather, we often demand too much from our regulatory norms (the right to privacy or data protection law) when what is required is something of much greater scope: a principled core surveying social orders as a whole. These permissive and privacy-protecting dimensions of human dignity are not absent in the recent jurisprudence of human dignity (*Google Spain v. AEPD* 2014; *Obergefell v. Hodges* 2015). I argue, however, that the law has yet to find a coherent principle behind our legal conceptualisation of the private and the public. We can use human dignity to fill that gap. More specifically, we can use it as a principle that responds dynamically to changes in the public and private spheres, not simply as a norm that may or may not be engaged when the private sphere or public power are violated or abused.

The second principle is an obligation principle which ensures that our status is not compromised or negated through the interaction of legal, political, and moral systems of obligations. This concerns governance of our normative systems (i.e. the different political, moral and legal systems of obligation, discussed most extensively in Chapter 3). A principled understanding of human dignity entails that clashes between different normative systems should always be resolved in a way that secures individual status. After all, we have come to expect from modern discourses of human dignity that it is shared between (not 'owned' by) law, or morality, or politics. This is clear at a philosophical level where human dignity is the cornerstone of architectonic accounts of normativity and of social order (see Bloch 1987 or Dworkin 2011). But this transcending of systems is more than merely a by-product of over-ambitious normative theorising. It is the only way to make sense of the 'foundational' discourse of human dignity. It is incoherent to make human dignity the foundation – the 'source' or the 'animating spirit' of – law (alone), or politics (alone), or morality (alone). These claims could be made intelligible only by collapsing human dignity into the ideas of justice, virtue, or obligation, at the cost of human dignity losing its meaning altogether. What connects its contemporary functions with certain aspects of the philosophy of human dignity is the governance of our systems – of all our normative practices – in ways that are orientated towards individuals. There is certainly danger in assuming that human dignity can colonise all of our normative discourse. But it should certainly be treated as *interstitial* in our normative discourse and normative practices. It is where sources of obligation meet that we should expect to need human dignity.

This obligation principle can be subdivided into three characteristic functions; first, human dignity being used as a defence of *the limitation of morality by law*. Where we encounter the demand for a division between right and virtue (or legal and moral guilt, or political and private morality), we are encountering claims that can be usefully expressed in the language of human dignity. We encounter cognate claims relatively commonly in law: that there must be a presumption of innocence, negation of guilt by association, and constraints on other unnecessary diminutions in the standing of the individual. Indeed, the most important examples here are found in criminal law. Criminal law, its substance and procedure, comprises limitations on the enforcement of morality. We see this opaquely through the 'harm principle', which aims to limit law to other-regarding duties. But human dignity demands systemic, principled alignment between public and private obligations. This means, more generally, that human dignity has been rightly associated with the question of how we draw limits to morality and the enforcement of morality. And human dignity has been rightly associated with the drive to limit the encroachment of criminal responsibility into areas hitherto treated as questions of moral responsibility. It is not merely the creeping powers of the state that we are concerned with but also the fundamental orientation between our notions of responsibility and obligation.

Second, *the limitation of law by morality* has been a persistent theme of the natural law tradition, and I argue in Chapter 2 that certain common themes from the natural law tradition are inescapable concomitants of a commitment to human dignity. This includes the idea that, in some instances, an unjust law is not a law (*lex iniusta non est lex*), i.e. that in some instances individual conscience can and should override legal responsibility. This has a permissive form that withdraws punishment from justified law-breakers, and it has an imperative form meaning some pernicious laws should never be enforced or followed. In both instances, we are drawing a limit to law itself partially from within law, but partially from a (political and moral) perspective outside law. This helps, I argue, to make sense of the many and persistent problems with this component of the natural law tradition, be it at a legislative level (the logical impossibility of passing laws that authorise the breaking of law) and at an adjudicative level (where defensible instances of civil disobedience are judged to be both punishable and defensible). We have a much better perspective on these persistent problems if we take human dignity to be an interstitial principle sitting between our sources of obligation, and whose function is to resolve their tensions always to the advantage of the individual they are intended to serve.

Third, an obligation principle must also mean *the limitation of politics by law and morality*. This is a familiar point about the rule of law and the limits of political power. Human dignity is rightly connected to the rule of law, although much more detailed analysis is required to show their precise relationship. Commonly the restraining relationship between human dignity and politics has been expressed though the anti-utilitarian implications of human dignity and its being a means to express ideas of non-domination. I argue in the chapters that follow that we should seek more constructive, and constitutive, implications of human dignity. Through its association with democratic accountability and democratic institutions, a defence of human dignity is also a defence of public accountability and the dominance of public authority over private interest and private expertise. And through its association with human rights, a defence of human dignity can also justify entrenched constitutional commitments to sustainability even where this limits some kinds of democratic freedom.

Even assuming these principles capture some of the wider implications of human dignity, there are a number of important omissions and lacunae in my connecting of human dignity and legality that are already apparent – how, for instance, we should define 'the rule of law'. And, of course, we are in need of a coherent account of human rights and their relationship with human dignity. I argue that human rights themselves must be understood via an underlying principle, namely that of sovereignty. It is that principle which is cashed out into the claim rights that (as individual rights) protect our agency but also (as a group of rights) represent our immunity from being treated as anything less than human. The permissive and obligation principles supplement this sovereignty principle; the instantiation of human rights in our practices requires the additional buttresses provided by these principles. And, as I argue in the next chapter, some of the problems associated with the idea of human rights and their foundations can be resolved if we separate individuals' direct and specific entitlements in terms of rights (the sovereignty principle), the kinds of constitutional implications that must flow from those specific entitlements (the permissive principle), and the most general and most foundational idea associated with human dignity; namely, its universality understood in the specific sense of sitting between and conjoining all of our normative systems (the obligations principle).

What has been expressed through these principles are what can be called the 'normative implications' of human dignity. These will, in Chapter 2, be further justified and distinguished from two other central objects of analytical concern. On the one hand is the 'normative core' of human dignity, meaning the nature of human dignity and its focal meaning as reconstructed via ideas drawn from law, political thought and morality. On the other are the 'institutional implications' of human dignity, meaning the way that human dignity should interact with our institutions and how it should be related to justice. Before undertaking that reconstructive work, however, there is much more that needs to be said about the interaction between our ideas of human dignity and the philosophy of law.

1.4 A general jurisprudence of human dignity

Any encounter between human dignity and law must be on terms that fairly represent both. That is, we should seek to give free rein to human dignity's normative implications and simultaneously respect the practices and the products, the institutions and doctrines, that are necessary to understand law. The idea that there could be a 'general jurisprudence of human dignity' is an insistence that despite the complexities such an encounter will produce, a conceptually and normatively coherent reconciliation is possible, with each having implications for the other. Conceptual and normative reconciliation between the two is not, then, reduction of one to the other.

From those methodological assumptions, I believe that we can nevertheless demonstrate that human dignity and law are mutually dependent ideas. This means that the position adopted here would (putting aside the crudity of such categories) be treated as a 'natural law' position. That is, we are committed to a general account of law which is not exhausted by the practices and products of our legal and political institutions. Certain, more specific, links have already been posited. They include a link between law and justice, an insistence on the moral limits of positive law, a focus of the moral importance of certain structural or procedural commitments, and an insistence (at the heart of human dignity) that each individual should be ascribed a form of sovereignty not exhausted by formal equality. It is the last-noted point that is most important and forms the focus of Chapter 2. The 'natural juridical entitlements' of the individual are the normative core of human dignity. But they also connect contemporary jurisprudence with the natural rights tradition such that we can capture attractive elements of both discourses, elements that continue to be expressed in the language of human dignity.

Like other natural law positions this entails a repositioning, not outright falsifying, of legal positivism. As a means of isolating and analysing typical language practices concerning 'law', we should still make use of legal positivism as a tool distinguishing one normative order (law) from others (politics and morality). But, more importantly for present purposes, a distinctive challenge from inclusive positivism has to be faced. The promise of inclusive positivism is to make moral concepts standards within, *but not definitive of*, law. This approach must fail on the present account because of its resistance, in the final analysis, to understanding law itself as standing in a relationship with human dignity. Specifically, the inclusive positivist might be concerned to treat human dignity as 'moral', with 'moral' denoting that human dignity was in its origins extra-legal but is now legal. This position, and its application to human dignity, is illustrated by Shapiro.

He writes that German constitutional provisions giving positive legal force to human dignity

> seem to condition legal validity on moral considerations. Thus, according to this interpretation, provisions that violate human dignity are not legally valid in the German legal system. Inclusive positivists can explain how such phenomena are possible: because officials in these systems accept that cruelty and dignity are relevant to legal reasoning, these moral considerations are ultimately backed by social fact and hence can determine the content of the law.
> (Shapiro 2011, 270)

There are two reasons to be suspicious of this rapprochement. One is simply that this offers no solutions to the normative, adjudicative, and constitutive problems I commenced with. Inclusive positivism aims to maintain a broadly moral force to the idea while leaving the concept to be operationalised and worked pure through legal conditioning. Shapiro's specific position – that we should maintain a special place for human dignity in legal reasoning because of its contribution to our understanding of cruelty – champions regulatory stability at the price of constitutive incoherence. Constitutional interpreters are required to prohibit cruelty where they find it. But we are no clearer about what human dignity adds to that task or how that task should be thought to permeate the whole of the constitution.

The inclusive positivist Robert Alexy, conversely, champions constitutive coherence at the price of normative imprecision. Human dignity's core function lies in explicating the German Constitution's general right to liberty. "[T]he principle of human dignity is capable both of supporting and explicating the principle of negative liberty. This is possible because the principle of human dignity has to be made more precise by a bundle of sub-principles [which] in the balancing process appear alongside negative liberty and can determine its weight" (Alexy 2010, 236). These sub-principles are, Alexy concedes, contested conceptions around an opaque core concept. Thus a basic normative and constitutive connection with liberty is posited here, as it is in my association with a permissive principle. But in practice human dignity is operationalised in various other 'bundles' of entitlements that are connected only by webs of family resemblance (Alexy 2010, 233).

A second point of connection with jurisprudence and positivism concerns use of principles. I translated the normative confusions of positive law into dignitarian principles. But contemporary jurisprudence tends to sweep principles either into our general legal norms, or to give legal principles only a limited set of functional applications in law. Depending upon the theorist, legal principles (if they are to be principles) must be susceptible to being weighed (Dworkin 2011) or be the kind of thing we can optimise (Alexy 2010). We could conclude, therefore, that the principles outlined above, even if they are meaningful, cannot have the status of legal principles. They cannot be weighed against, and have no justiciable link with, other legal principles. In contrast, I deny that we must define principles as having univocal functions or, more fundamentally, that we must make a distinction between legal and moral principles at all: first because principles simply are obligations giving rise to reasons for action and to judgments, not system-specific norms (Cohen 2003); second because the distinctive function of human dignity is to be interstitial – to sit between our normative orders – and not to be conditioned by existing juridical practice. For that reason we should recall Neal's conclusion: "dignity itself is never truly weighed against other values: no outcome can be both dignity-violating and legally acceptable" (Neal 2014, 36). Jurisprudentially, there must be a compromise somewhere. Either we accept with the inclusive positivist that human dignity is a principle but one that must be conditioned by legal systems or we treat human dignity as having principled implications and assert that our general jurisprudence, i.e. our conception of law, must be made to accommodate them. Given that it is the second option that I will defend, considerably more analysis must be provided to justify the idea that human dignity has its normative implications in principles and demonstrate how these principles interact with law as such. Analysis of these normative implications must await Chapter 2. But their interaction with law can be broadly drawn.

Several threads of the classic and modern forms of natural law tradition are picked up by the human dignity principles I have outlined. First is the displacement of law by morality, at least on those occasions where deep injustices are at issue. Second, and in modern Fullerean guise, human dignity implies a thick conception of the rule of law as a moral commitment coordinating law, morality, and politics. Third, the permissive principle I have defended will be used to interrogate and partially defend the idea of the *lex permissiva*, i.e. the creation of a space of reasonable variation between legal systems (aside from the direct commands and prohibitions of natural law) and which mark the permissive character of much natural law thinking. Fourth, we need *determinatio* – the turning of principles into judgments – in the sense of accepting that our social systems and normative orders are governed by principles but that this will require judgment, and latitude, in the formation of specific legal judgments.

If we accept all of this, what does this say about law as such? We should take our idea of law to be necessarily inclusive of but also *conditioned by* the principles I have outlined. And we can call these dignitarian principles interstitial principles because they are not (for reasons already suggested) easily categorised as moral or legal principles. By extension, paradigmatic, principled use of human dignity in law is therefore something we are likely to see only in its pure form where normative orders are in dispute – for example, where executive power and executive exceptionalism is challenged by the rule of law, where legislative power is challenged by judicial review, or where the entitlements of individuals are being denied on the basis of political popularism (as in the 'management' of migration in contemporary Europe). As a consequence, we should not be looking for our paradigmatic expression of human dignity in law in the preambles of international human rights treaties but rather in those interstitial problems where the solution to clashes of law, morality, and politics can be solved only in a principled way, by making our systems fit human dignity and not the other way around.

For all of these arguments to succeed, the jurisprudential arguments here will have to be situated in relation to the considerable body of literature already linking law and human dignity at a philosophical level. Three broad themes can be found within that literature. With regard to *the concept itself*, there is an argument that law and legal practice should simply embrace the internal complexity of the concept of human dignity, seeing it a constantly evolving concept (both a political concept and a virtue concept) and accepting it as a guiding principle (Dworkin 2011) or regulative idea (Weinrib 2016). Human dignity therefore also faces regulative redundancy. We are unlikely to find circumstances where human dignity consistently makes a decisive contribution to legal discourse; rather, we would expect it to continue to be invoked broadly in constitutional jurisprudence without any special constitutive function. We could focus, in contrast, only on the ways in which the currents of legal practice and legal adjudication use and reuse the concept such that certain stable but complex implications emerge and mature (McCrudden 2008). Then, we should note, we also embrace normative imprecision. Human dignity is always plural, and as such it is not only philosophically complex but a challenge, in its unpredictability, to the rule of law itself.

With regard to its *proper place in our legal thinking and legal practice* human dignity is sometimes synonymous with some of the most important respect-conferring practices in law – indeed with the rule of law itself (Waldron 2012). This, however, recalls the charge of constitutive incoherence: if human dignity is immanent in law via the rule of law, it is unclear either what precise constitutional, or precise regulative, implications should flow from human dignity. (A more extended discussion of Waldron's conception of human dignity and law can be found at the end of Chapter 2.) Alternatively, we could give it a very specific place in our theories and practices of adjudication, seeing it as a demand to 'anthropologise' our most important judicial practices (Brugger 2009). Brugger places human dignity at the centre of adjudication in a radical way, seeking to stabilise its presence in law through a distinctive role in reasoning. However, we might question how defensible his view is if it requires a radical rethinking of the role of the judge. More acutely, we thereby lose sight of the interstitial function of human dignity because, while for Brugger there is a very clear distinction between what is 'inside' and what is 'outside' law, the import of human dignity as I have outlined it is to deny that such a distinction can be made.

Finally, concerning the *competing normative force of legal justice and human dignity*, there is an important account of human dignity and human rights in Griffin's work *On Human Rights* (2008). In his account, human dignity has normative parity with legality – both are completely equal and valid as sources of reasons and obligations – but given human dignity's connection with distinctive forms of agency, we face the task of rationalising existing (international and domestic) legal systems which have failed to draw a neat enough distinction between norms arising from human dignity and norms arising from justice. Thus, for Griffin, human dignity certainly assists us to understand and refine our existing human rights, and those human rights undoubtedly have a special importance in our legal traditions and constitutional practices. However, the practices and principles that are embodied in legal systems and constitutions have equal normative force. The resulting philosophical and legal task is a pragmatic one of finding a cut-off point between the normative implications of human dignity and the norms found in law. The cut-off point is not discerned *a priori;* it has to be discovered in difficult give-and-take between human dignity and legal systems. While Griffin provides us with an important demand for doctrinal clarity, his approach has to be challenged at its very first step: we cannot presume the normative parity of human dignity and legal justice, rather we have to consider the normative core of each and decide upon a route to their philosophical, not doctrinal, reconciliation. In contrast, Beyleveld and Brownsword (2001) see a normative harmony between human dignity and legality as *moral phenomena*. Because law itself is in a continuum with practical reasoning generally, human dignity–based law has priority over other laws in the sense that any moral theorising must produce hierarchies of obligations. Nevertheless, *qua* obligations, human dignity and law are part of the same moral space: our obligations have a common rational and moral root, and rational and moral methods will provide their reconciliation. While this seems to me closest to the broadly natural law commitments which I have suggested should be associated with human dignity, we should have concerns here about regulative redundancy. What are we to *do* with human dignity such that the generic agency claims that they use to connect the moral and the legal are clarified? What does human dignity *per se* contribute to our understanding of law as a moral judgement?

This brief survey illustrates that there is disagreement not only over how to reconcile human dignity and law but also over what question we are asking when we ask for that reconciliation. Are we asking for clarity regarding the concept itself? Are we asking how human dignity is found, or should be found, within the practices and institutions of existing legal systems? Or are we asking, What is the normative bedrock or normative paradigm – legal or moral – on which human dignity and legal practice meet, and how should we seek their reconciliation given that grounding? These questions centralise a theory of human dignity, a theory of law, and a theory of obligation respectively. I believe that all of them are necessary for a clear and coherent account of human dignity and law. Systematic answers to them are provided in the next two chapters. However, before we turn to those investigations, the first question – the nature of the concept itself – needs foregrounding. Certain genealogical and jurisprudential background discussions still need to be introduced so that later philosophical analysis can draw upon the rich, but problematic, history of the concept itself. But this is not simply of historical interest, and I begin here to justify the special relationship that exists between human dignity and rights.

1.5 Between justice and virtue

It is exceptionally difficult to tie the concept of human dignity to any single function or single register of public discourse. The context of our encounter with the concept colours its meaning, and its uses outside legal discourse are often markedly dissimilar to its uses within legal discourse. This is a problem fuelled by the history of the concept. It is overburdened with history, from Roman origins, through various linguistic and philosophical appropriations and mutations, to its being cast anew in international law. A systematic genealogy or phenomenology is not attempted here (see, respectively, Riley 2010 and Kolnai 1976; also Hunt 2004). My concern is to touch upon those characteristic conceptual tensions that are especially at issue in law and legal scholarship.

The earliest traces of the term attach to religious and social dignitaries set apart by their distinctive ritual roles (Agamben 2002; Lebech 2009). Dignity thereafter could be used for description of aristocratic practices and aristocratic comportment more generally (Cicero 2001). Here the seeds of a metaphysics or cosmology were already sown to the extent that those aristocratic practices were construed (particularly by Cicero) not merely as conventions adopted by the aristocratic but as exercises of virtue. Dignity (particularly but not exclusively amongst the aristocratic) revealed the ability to exercise and maintain as dispositions precisely those behaviours that set us apart from animals. Humans' 'upright gait' (Bloch 1987) is only one of those practices or dispositions marking a decisive split between animal and human but one, we might note, that would maintain special significance even within an age of evolutionary theory. With that conjunction of species-specific *practices* and the special species-specific *being* of humans it is not surprising that dignity became associated with humanity's being in God's image (*imago dei*). Maintaining dignified practices and comportment were evidence of our distance from animals and such distance, in a medieval Christian cosmology, entailed concomitant closeness to God.

An important turn in the concept's meaning took place in the Renaissance when Pico denied that last inference, namely that our distance from animals must mean proximity to God. Rather, for Pico the ability to move from the highest to the lowest kind of creatures by choice is humanity's special dignity, its special status (Pico 2017 [1486]). Dignity is then a status, but it is not a status that must take its meaning within a hierarchy. Humans' changeable status is what marks us out from the rest of Creation without that also meaning a single defined role in Creation, a point later reiterated by Hume (2017 [1741]). Pico, then, provides a crucial point of departure for modern conceptions of human dignity. First of all, in anticipation of autonomy-centred conceptions, it stresses self-determination, autonomy and choice as the intrinsic goods that we are defending when we defend an individual's human dignity. Second, it also retains certain kinds of virtue ideas. These are transposed from Roman and Stoic thought but altered to imply that mere comportment is less important than human self-constitution and the special vices that self-constitution brings in its wake. That is, freedom, choice, and self-determination inevitably bring the threats of excess and deficiency of self-esteem (Margalit 2009). Our self-creation permits both *hubris* and deliberate self-abasement. Kant was particularly concerned about the threat of the latter to our dignity (1996 [1797], 209f), but we also see a characteristic tension between human dignity and *hubris* where individuals fail to achieve a proper self-estimation (Aristotle 1976, 300).

The early-modern natural law tradition, particularly through the work of Grotius and Pufendorf, promised a synthesis of these ideas of self-determination with wider political and legal considerations. Given the utility of a conception of the state itself as a rational agent engaged in self-creation, and given the utility of a conception of law as a network of rational permissions supporting the rational pursuits of free citizens, there is little wonder that these theorists provided holistic visions of individual and collective obligation centred on rationally discovered and self-imposed, not commanded and heteronomous, norms. The specific value of human dignity lay, for these theorists, in expressing both the sociability of humans (as an aspect of their wider philosophical anthropology) and the natural rights of individuals arising from their natural equality (Saastamoinen 2010). Drawing upon the work of both, we have Kant to thank for the separation of these lines of thought. As we will discuss elsewhere, natural equality is important for Kant but is best explored through his idea of 'innate right', a narrower claim concerning innate juridical entitlements. 'Sociability' is substituted altogether for the rational capacity to act upon the Moral Law. Thereafter we are met with familiar lines of dignitarian thought about the special dignity that attaches to our rational nature, the ability to follow the dictates of reason, and the dignity that accrues to each individual as an end in themselves. These ideas, and their operationalising through the prohibition never to treat others as mere means, still form the predominant background or default assumptions about human dignity found in Western thinking and scholarship.

The creation of a special legal function in its connection with the Universal Declaration of Human Rights (UDHR 1948) certainly did not erase the wider connections and connotations in the concept's history (see Kolnai 1976). Pritchard (1972), for instance, surveyed the characteristic idea of self-governance associated with human dignity. A special connection with integrity is central:

> First, the various forms of personal integrity are to a large extent human achievements rather than things that merely happen to persons. This is clear in the case of being able to coordinate one's goals and activities in leading a relatively satisfying life; but it is no less true of learning to walk and talk, activities we take for granted. These achievements often give one a sense of accomplishment, enhancing self-esteem. [. . .] Second, these forms of integrity all involve some degree of autonomy, or self-regulation. The connection between autonomy and dignity is shown in the resentment often felt when one believes his autonomy is being interfered with. It is also shown in the shame one feels when he fails to maintain his autonomy under pressure, as in the case of torture.
>
> (Pritchard 1972, 303; footnote removed)

This focus on personal integrity and self-constitution maintains the experience and value of dignity that Pico established. Moreover, Kant would recognise the encompassing of self- and other-regarding duties in the language of dignity. The especial importance of the language of integrity will be returned to below. But the attempt to make torture revelatory of human dignity is a rather more modern theme. The suggestion that human dignity is especially revealed 'in the breach', that its violation reveals its distinctive phenomenology and normative implications, is a common theme in contemporary (i.e. post-war) literature (Riley 2008). Of the possible reasons for this assumption, we might posit the experiences of war and the related fuelling of the human rights movement. We might assume that in creating positive laws it is easier to articulate and enforce negative duties (against abuse) than positive duties (to achieve certain desirable ends). And we might also note that the right to freedom from torture is one of the few rights that is rarely contested as a human right, meaning there is a *prima facie* case to look closely for the foundations of human rights in that prohibition. Whatever its source, this connection with torture and degradation is important in two respects. It afforded a decisive shift away from self-regarding duties to other-regarding duties. And it moves the normative focus away from obligations to prohibitions. In other words, human dignity ceases to have its characteristic or core normative expression in duties to oneself to act in certain ways but is, rather, found in prohibition of the degradation of others. There is, no doubt, a residual implication that human dignity must also imply the possibility of self-creation and self-determination. But this can be found in weak permissions, i.e. in the absence of burdensome demands on the individual and the creation of possibilities for self-determination. Such a commitment could be expressed through human dignity but it could also be expressed through liberty, freedom, democracy, or other political principles. Human dignity's most distinctive normative implication is therefore its narrow prohibitive function, whereas its more positive implications compete, often unsuccessfully, with other principles. It is this narrow alignment with abuse and degradation (and with related regulatory prohibitions) that the present text will seek to challenge.

This all-too-brief narrative of conceptual and normative transformation indicates why human dignity might be thought to sit equivocally between justice and virtue. Human dignity is grammatically connected to dignity *simpliciter* with its connotations of comportment and Stoicism, but human dignity is irreducibly tied also to self-determination and self-constitution. The concept can therefore be used in discourses of virtue and of justice. Its political implications embrace perfectionism, liberalism, and libertarianism if the permissive aspect is emphasised. And the legal, as we have seen, tends to give especial attention to the prohibition against egregious violation of others' bodies and integrity more generally but can also be used to enforce self-regarding duties.

Having stressed this kind of tension between normative paradigms – justice and virtue – it is important to consider how they are manifest in contemporary discussion of human dignity, especially with regard to the claim that human dignity is intimately related to 'respect'. MacIntyre argues that the idea of virtue takes its meaning from three elements: "a practice, [. . .] the narrative order of a single human life, [and] what constitutes a moral tradition" (2013, 187). The force of virtue as obligation-generating lies in practical self-understanding and self-constitution against a background of established social practices, on the assumption that individual integrity is a necessary condition of a good life. Now, whatever systematicity the Stoics gave to human dignity in their thinking and practices, if human dignity is today an individual *practice* it is a limited one – and perhaps a remedial one – that sets limits to what can be done consistently with one's own self-respect and self-esteem (see Margalit 2009). This is because the *tradition* against which human dignity would be a core virtue is missing. A tradition celebrating human dignity understood as honour exists (Whitman 2003, Hennette-Vauchez 2011), but there is an irreducible tension between the social stratification characteristic of honour-focussed societies and the individual self-constitution connected with human dignity. Nonetheless, the idea of human dignity being associated with the *narrative order of a human life* seems defensible, as we have seen with Pritchard's more general association with 'integrity'. The opportunity, and perhaps the obligation (Korsgaard 2009; Dworkin 2011), to give integrity, sustained and consistent commitment to values and projects, is potentially vital enough to a human life as to warrant association with human dignity. That is, human dignity retains self-regarding implications in demanding a life lived consistent with humans' proper or necessary obligations. Such a reading of human dignity is not defended here (for reasons discussed in Chapter 2). Rather it should be seen as demanding integrity, as a virtue, from *those who exercise power*. But those exercises of power take place within a wider framework of justice and human dignity which have no need to appeal to self-regarding duties to be intelligible. This means we should also be deeply suspicious of the legal enforcement of human dignity as a virtue. This is rightly viewed with suspicion within contemporary liberal political philosophy (Brownsword 2014) and has been shown to be oppressive in practice (Cunningham 2016).

This is not an end to the significance of virtue and self-regarding duties, however. In connection to *rights* and *respect*, we salvage certain limited aspects of this virtue discourse. First, the act of exercising rights is, for Feinberg, directly related to self-esteem and self-respect, which cannot be accomplished in the absence of rights:

> People who are confident of their own rights are less likely to develop servile characters. They are not forced to secure their needs by begging 'favors' from masters who have no relational duties to them, on the one hand, or by stealing and cheating, or resorting to plain force on the other. To say they have moral rights is to say that morally they are in a position to claim what they want as their due, what they have coming, and what the other party is under a moral obligation to them (not merely regarding them) to provide. [. . .] The right-holder has more dignity than a mere beggar who is not in a position to make claim to what he wants, or a highwayman who, in abandoning the moral posture altogether, forfeits, in large part, any claim he might have had to moral respect.
>
> (Feinberg 1992, 180)

Etinson's rejoinder to this is interesting insofar as the virtue Feinberg seems to identify is neither universal nor particularly attractive: "For one, the notion that people are *owed* certain forms of treatment, as a matter of duty, seems far less culturally specific than the idea that *claiming* one's due is a virtue in itself" (Etinson 2016, 4; emphasis in original). Moreover, for Etinson it is normatively significant, at least from the point of view of virtue ethics, that we sometimes celebrate *reluctance*, rather than willingness, to rely on one's rights as a virtue (an argument propounded elsewhere by Aristotle, amongst others). Nonetheless, for both the possession of rights grants the right-holder a normative status that is impossible without rights, even if exercising rights is not a sufficient condition of our being virtuous.

Compare this to Margalit's kindred position that even just political systems with the correct distribution and enforcement of rights may be lacking the means to maintain, and in some instances may systematically violate, certain forms of respect (2009; see also Sandel 2013). Racism, bureaucracy, and unemployment may all be barriers to a 'decent society', one where rights are properly distributed but where human dignity is also consciously maintained. Certain attacks on self-respect are positively prohibited as dignity-harming. For Margalit, in opposition to Feinberg, claiming rights is never a sufficient condition for us to possess human dignity; other elements of civility have to be enforced. For Margalit, the legal enforcement of rights plus certain other-regarding duties are a sufficient condition for human dignity. Margalit does not equate human dignity with virtue (at least on MacIntyre's definition) but he does come close to insisting that a defensible account of human dignity, including its legal repercussions, must include legal enforcement of certain dignitarian virtues.

Can these justice and virtue demands be synthesised in the notion of 'respect'? The demand for respect captures some of the phenomenology associated with human dignity, i.e. showing respect for others' basic humanity, or 'recognition respect', as Darwall puts it (2006, 120). This is distinguishable from 'appraisal respect' being respect for something relative to something else. The precise nature of the demand for recognition respect is opaque; how, for example, it would differ from, say, treating someone as an equal. It can potentially be given specificity through defending certain basic modes of justification. For Forst (2011, 2012) human dignity and the human rights that flow from it are premised on a right to justification, i.e. that we should be given reasons for actions imposed upon or impinging upon us, and those reasons should be rationally justifiable (or, in O'Neill's terms, 'followable' (O'Neill 1996). The respect here is principally (but not exclusively) the respect that is due citizens from their law-makers: "Respecting human dignity means not denying anybody's moral right to justification" (Forst 2011, 971). The correlate of such respect is, principally, respect for human rights:

> The moral basis for human rights, as I reconstruct it, is the respect for the human person as an autonomous agent who possesses a right to justification,

> i.e. a right to be recognized as an agent who can demand acceptable reasons for any action that claims to be morally justified and for any social or political structure or law that claims to be binding upon him or her. Human rights secure the equal standing of persons in the political and social world, based on a fundamental moral demand of respect.
>
> (Forst 2012, 5)

By this route, however, we have returned to the importance of (human) rights as the expression, or condition, of the respect lying at the core of human dignity. And those rights are to be granted equally as part of 'equal standing'. Thus a discourse of respect, in the final analysis, presents us with a choice between equal or unequal dignity: either we have the equality owed to all persons, or we have inequality and various social dignities. If the former, this will take the form of rights regardless of whether rights exhaust our concern with respect. If the latter, then we can maintain a whole range of virtue functions for 'dignity', but we will not have secured a link between human dignity and rights. This is why, in what Weinrib calls 'comprehensive conceptions of human dignity' (conceptions which strive to maintain the virtue aspects of its genealogy), we inevitably face incommensurability with the mainstream of liberal thinking:

> This problem is that comprehensive conceptions inevitably clash with the very concept that they purport to explicate. Comprehensive conceptions of human dignity typically proceed by, first, identifying the kinds of beliefs and actions that make up a good or valuable life and, then, enlisting the coercive authority of the state to bring them about. The illiberalism of comprehensive conceptions thereby comes into conflict with the liberal commitments of the concept of human dignity to the freedom and equality of each individual.
>
> (Weinrib 2016, 5)

Conceptualisations of human dignity that commence with the presumption that virtue is of central importance cannot be reconciled with the presumption that rights, or the respect that is reflected in rights-holding, are the core of human dignity. It is the latter position that is adopted here. And to the extent that any invocation of virtue is defended, it is the virtue of law-makers and of politicians: the creation of laws and political systems that are consistent with our rational natures, or conversely, consistent with the necessary conditions of human dignity. (Related positions can be found in Forst 2011 and Waldron 2012.)

1.6 Directions and *desiderata*

The various enquiries in this chapter have sought to identify the *desiderata* of a coherent account of the relationship between human dignity and law (see Debes 2009, Düwell 2014, and McCrudden 2013 for different but kindred sets of demands). Through an internal critique of their existing legal interaction we have pinpointed the central importance of separating out the constitutive from the regulative applications of human dignity. It is in the form of principles that we are likely to find the constitutive implications of human dignity; its regulative implications, in contrast, should be applications of those principles rather than free-standing 'dignitarian commands' or 'dignitarian prohibitions'. In doing so we also must be mindful that the functions of human dignity are irreducibly cross- or anti-systemic. That is, when finding constitutive or regulative implications, we should be especially hesitant about reducing human dignity to an essentially legal, moral, or political function. Resistance to such a reduction is precisely what needs to be maintained if its critical force is to be retained.

Further analysis of the genealogy and philosophy of human dignity have yielded three further *desiderata*. The first is to clarify its link with human or natural rights such that its foundational status can be clarified (and, at the same time, ensure that such a reading does not 'subvert' human rights by introducing virtue-based implications that run contrary to the autonomy-enhancing character of human rights). The second is to clarify its link with natural law, understood as rational or moral limits to positive law (and understanding, in the process, its proper adjudicative function and legislative content). The third is the need for a more sustained, dialectical enquiry comparing the reconstructed idea of human dignity with our understandings of 'justice' and with liberal political philosophy. That is, not only is it conceptually necessary to find the ways in which justice and human dignity are mutually supportive and mutually critical, we also have to explore (but not presume) that the institutional implications of human dignity are best articulated through contemporary liberal political commitments.

The *desiderata* are then as follows: dividing the constitutive and regulative significance of human dignity, explaining and justifying its cross-systemic function, explaining its link to rights, explaining its link to natural law, and performing a dialectical comparison of human dignity with justice and with the commitments of liberal political philosophy. In what follows I explain how these are realised in the remainder of the book, identifying the further substantive and methodological commitments that are necessary to realise these *desiderata*.

The reconstruction of human dignity undertaken in the next chapter gives us 'human dignity as status'. Aside from selectively building upon (and also rejecting) elements of early modern and contemporary thought on human dignity, how does this advance the *desiderata*? In the first instance, through the idea of status we have some purchase on the genealogy of the concept of human dignity, especially those aspects of its genealogy that have links with natural rights. Second, through focus on status we can capture a certain conception of equality that is not confined to the formal equality of legal justice and therefore points towards a principle *shared* between law, morality, and politics. Third, and relatedly, because such a status is linked to juridical ideas and entitlements, we have connection with the natural law tradition, but one not beholden to a particular 'moral' function for human dignity in law; rather a deeper connection at the most basic level of obligations. It should be noted that such an analysis is not dependent on a metaphysics or a sociology of human dignity. 'Human dignity as status' is not a theory of 'species being', of 'human nature', nor is it premised on sociological changes in our conception of species being or human nature. It is a theory of human dignity as an *anthropological* concept relating our practices to our obligations through principles.

This reconstruction gives us the central group of ideas defended in this book (and fully explicated in Chapter 3): a certain reading of human dignity's 'normative core', its 'normative implications' and its 'institutional implications'. The *normative core* is humans' basic status, their natural equality, but also their innate juridical entitlements which are permissive as well as protective. The *normative implications* are found in certain principles that protect these entitlements but are, importantly, *interstitial*, i.e. they transcend our normative orders of law, morality, and politics. The *institutional implications* lie in forms of governance, in a certain kind of cosmopolitanism, and in protecting the human condition. The details of these claims are undertaken in the next two chapters. But we should note that these more detailed claims have to exhibit the kind of dialectical form demanded by our *desiderata*. These claims will not be defensible unless they can stand in a coherent relationship (even if it is a critical relationship) with our understanding of justice. And the institutional implications in particular must be compared to the democratic and liberal institutional philosophical traditions. We need to know if and how human dignity claims can displace the voluntaristic or procedural foundations the liberal tradition treats as essential to justification.

This leaves us with the application of these ideas to the different forms of public law (Part II). This means, above all, finding the constitutional implications of human dignity: how the public sphere should be structured, and determining in the light of human dignity what can be legitimated by public reason. Accordingly, the three chapters on public law are attempts to systematically work out constitutive functions for human dignity in the light of the earlier reconstruction with especial attention to the links and tensions between human dignity, justice, and democratic institutions. This encompasses concerns with natural law and the limits that morality places on law, but also as importantly the limits that law places on morality. It is this, in the final analysis, that will lead us to a clear relationship between human dignity and justice.

Those three applied chapters must also bear the burden of explicating the relationship between human dignity and rights. While there are philosophical connections posited throughout Part I, it remains for the applied concerns of Part II to work through persistent specific problems created by the linking of human rights and human dignity. These can be stated in schematic form. First, human dignity presents a *subversion* (or 'Trojan horse') problem. Given the anthropological or cosmological elements that human dignity carries over from pre-modern discourse, it is doubtful that it yields only obligations that are compatible with liberal assumptions; human dignity has anti-liberal or perfectionist consequences. Second, the *peremptory* force of human dignity appears to allow it to function as a trump in any legal context. Human dignity has such moral force that it cannot be defeated like other norms or weighed like other principles. Third, human dignity leads to rights *inflation*; human dignity seems to generate rights related to any human interest or preference. Fourth, human dignity cannot be a source of any legitimate rights claims because it does not demand *correlativity* in rights; human dignity can be associated with 'manifesto rights', or broad social objectives, and these are deficient as rights because their object or their duty-holder is uncertain. A fifth problem is *disruption*: human dignity can lead to the disruption of settled fields of norms and settled deliberative practices and leads to unpredictable adjudication. Sixth, human dignity faces a *redundancy* problem: any normative work done by human dignity can be done by other legal norms and principles already found in legal systems. Seventh, and finally, human dignity is inevitably a *contradictory* component of law. In law, human dignity is simultaneously absolute and *pro tanto*; it is, at the same time, a singular norm that can be defeated and a general principle that has absolute weight. At various points ahead we will encounter each of these problems. Some reflect the need for rationalisation of the substantive legal uses of human dignity. Some are bullets that we must bite in giving human dignity a constitutive function.

In sum, these groupings of questions and related *desiderata* provide guidance for what follows. Some will be considered more directly and in a more sustained way than others. They are, nonetheless, the questions I take to flow from the critique and the investigations already undertaken in this chapter.

References

Agamben, G. (2002) *Remnants of Auschwitz: The Witness and the Archive*. New York, Zone Books.

Alexy, R. (2010) *A Theory of Constitutional Rights*. Oxford, Oxford University Press.

Aristotle. (1976) *Ethics*. Harmondsworth, Penguin Books.

Baruah, P. (2014) 'Human Dignity in Adjudication: The Limits of Placeholding and Essential Contestability Accounts' *The Canadian Journal of Law and Jurisprudence*, 27(2), 329–356.

Beitz, C.R. (2009) *The Idea of Human Rights*. Oxford/New York, Oxford University Press.

Beyleveld, D. and Brownsword, R. (2001) *Human Dignity in Bioethics and Biolaw*. Oxford, Oxford University Press.

Bloch, E. (1987) *Natural Law and Human Dignity*. Cambridge, MA, MIT Press.

Brownsword, R. (2014) 'Chapter 1: Human Dignity from a Legal Perspective' in Düwell, M. et al eds., *The Cambridge Handbook of Human Dignity: Interdisciplinary Perspectives*. Cambridge, Cambridge University Press, 1–22.

Brugger, W. (2009) 'Dignity, Rights, and Legal Philosophy within the Anthropological Cross of Decision-Making' in Brugger, W. and Kirste, S. eds., *Human Dignity as a Foundation of Law* Germany, Franz Steiner, Verlag, 41–62.

Cicero, M.T. (2001) *On Obligations*. Oxford, Oxford University Press.

Cohen, G.A. (2003) 'Facts and Principles' *Philosophy and Public Affairs*, 31(3), 211–245.

Cunningham, S. (2016) 'Reinforcing or Challenging Stigma? The Risks and Benefits of "Dignity Talk" in Sex Work Discourse' *International Journal for the Semiotics of Law-Revue internationale de Sémiotique juridique*, 29(1), 45–65.

Darwall, S.L. (2006) *The Second-Person Standpoint: Morality, Respect, and Accountability*. Cambridge, MA, Harvard University Press.

Debes, R. (2009) 'Dignity's Gauntlet' *Philosophical Perspectives*, 23(1), 45–78.

Düwell, M. (2014) 'Chapter 2: Human Dignity: Concepts, Discussions, Philosophical Perspectives' in Düwell, M. et al eds., *The Cambridge Handbook of Human Dignity: Interdisciplinary Perspectives*. Cambridge, Cambridge University Press.

Dworkin, R. (2011) *Justice for Hedgehogs*. Cambridge, MA, Harvard University Press.

Etinson, A. (2016) 'What's So Special About Human Dignity?' Available at: www.academia.edu/14634091/Whats_So_Special_About_Human_Dignity_DRAFT_PAPER, accessed March 2017.

Feinberg, J. (1992) 'The Social Importance of Moral Rights' *Philosophical Perspectives*, 6, 175–198.

Forst, R. (2011) 'The Ground of Critique: On the Concept of Human Dignity in Social Orders of Justification' *Philosophy and Social Criticism*, 37(9), 965–976.

Forst, R. (2012) 'The Justification of Human Rights and the Basic Right to Justification: A Reflexive Approach' in Corradetti, C. ed., *Philosophical Dimensions of Human Rights: Some Contemporary Views*. The Netherlands, Springer, 81–106.

Fuller, L.L. (1964) *The Morality of Law*. New Haven/London, Yale University Press.

Gallie, W.B. (1955) 'Essentially Contested Concepts' *Proceedings of the Aristotelian Society*, 56, 167–198.

German Military Manual. (1992) Available at: https://ihl-databases.icrc.org/customary-ihl/eng/docs/v2_cou_de_rule154, accessed April 2017.

Glendon, M.A. (2001) *A World Made New: Eleanor Roosevelt and the Universal Declaration of Human Rights*. New York, Random House.

Google Spain v. AEPD. (2014) 'Case C-131/12 (ECJ, May 13, 2014)', Available at: http://curia.europa.eu/juris/document/document_print.jsf?doclang=EN&docid=152065, accessed April 2017.

Griffin, J. (2008) *On Human Rights*. Oxford, Oxford University Press.

Heath, J.B. (2012) 'Human Dignity at Trial: Hard Cases and Broad Concepts in International Criminal Law' *George Washington International Law Review*, 44(2), 317–366.

Hennette-Vauchez, S. (2011) 'A Human *Dignitas*? Remnants of the Ancient Legal Concept in Contemporary Dignity Jurisprudence' *International Journal of Constitutional Law*, 9(1), 32–57.

Hume, D. (2017 [1741]) 'Of the Dignity or Meanness of Human Nature', Available at: http://public-library.uk/ebooks/47/11.pdf, accessed March 2017.

Hunt, L. (2004) 'The 18th-Century Body and the Origins of Human Rights' *Diogenes*, 203, 41–56.

Jehovah's Witnesses of Moscow v. Russia, Application no. 302/02, [ECHR], June 10, 2010, Available at: www.refworld.org/cases,ECHR,4c2090002.html, accessed April 2017.

Kant, I. (1996 [1797]) *The Metaphysics of Morals*, translated by M. Gregor. Cambridge, Cambridge University.

Kateb, G. (2011) *Human Dignity*. Cambridge, MA, Harvard University Press.

Kindler v. Canada (Minister of Justice). (1991) 2 S.C.R. 779.

Kolnai, A. (1976) 'Dignity' *Philosophy*, 51(197), 251–271.

Korsgaard, C.M. (2009) *Self-Constitution: Agency, Identity, and Integrity*. Oxford, Oxford University Press.

Lebech, M. (2009) *On the Problem of Human Dignity: A Hermeneutical and Phenomenological Investigation.* Germany, Königshausen and Neumann.
Luban, D. (2010) 'The Rule of Law and Human Dignity: Re-Examining Fuller's Canons' *Hague Journal on the Rule of Law*, 20(1), 29–47.
Luhmann, N. (2008) *Law as a Social System.* Oxford, Oxford University Press.
MacIntyre, A. (2013) *After Virtue.* London, A and C Black.
Margalit, A. (2009) *The Decent Society.* Cambridge, MA, Harvard University Press.
McCrudden, C. (2008) 'Human Dignity and Judicial Interpretation of Human Rights' *European Journal of International Law*, 19(4), 655–724.
McCrudden, C. (2013) 'Introduction' in McCrudden, C. ed., *Understanding Human Dignity.* Oxford, Oxford University Press.
Neal, M. (2014) 'Respect for Human Dignity as "Substantive Basic Norm"' *International Journal of Law in Context*, 10(1), 26–46.
Obergefell v. Hodges 576 U.S. (2015) United States Supreme Court.
Omega. (2004) Omega Spielhallen- und Automatenaufstellungs-GmbH v. Oberbürger- meisterin der Bundesstadt Bonn, [ECJ] Judgment (First Chamber) of October 14.
O'Neill, O. (1996) *Towards Justice and Virtue: A Constructive Account of Practical Reasoning.* Cambridge, Cambridge University Press.
Peep Show Case. (1981) German Constitutional Court (BVerwGE 64, 274).
Pico della Mirandola. (2017 [1486]) 'On the Dignity of Man', Available at: http://bactra.org/Mirandola/, accessed March 2017.
Post, R. (2017) 'Data Privacy and Dignitary Privacy: Google Spain, the Right to Be Forgotten, and the Construction of the Public Sphere' *Duke Law Journal*, Available at: https://ssrn.com/abstract=2953468, accessed April 2017.
Pritchard, M.S. (1972) 'Human Dignity and Justice' *Ethics*, 82(4), 299–313.
Prosecutor v. Furundzija. (1998) 'ICTY IT-95-17/1-T', Available at: www.icty.org/x/cases/furundzija/tjug/en/fur-tj981210e.pdf, accessed March 2017.
R v. Kapp. (2008) [Supreme Court of Canada] 2 S.C.R. 483, 2008 SCC 41.
Riley, S. (2008) 'Observing the Breach: Dignity and the Limits of Political Theology' *Law and Critique*, 19(2), 115–138.
Riley, S. (2010) 'Dignity as the Absence of the Bestial' *Journal for Cultural Research*, 14(2), 143–159.
Rodriguez, P-A. (2015) 'Human Dignity as an Essentially Contested Concept' *Cambridge Review of International Affairs*, 28(4), 743–756.
Saastamoinen, K. (2010) 'Pufendorf on Natural Equality, Human Dignity, and Self-Esteem' *Journal of the History of Ideas*, 71(1), 39–62.
Sandel, M.J. (2013) *What Money Can't Buy: The Moral Limits of Markets.* London, Penguin Books.
Shapiro, S. (2011) *Legality.* Cambridge, MA, Harvard University Press.
Solove, D.J. (2002) 'Conceptualizing Privacy' *California Law Review*, 90, 1087–1155.
Tasioulas, J. (2009) 'Are Human Rights Essentially Triggers for Intervention?' *Philosophy Compass*, 4(6), 938–950.
UDHR. (1948) 'Universal Declaration of Human Rights', Adopted by General Assembly Resolution 217 A(III) of December 10, 1948.
Waldron, J. (2012) 'How Law Protects Dignity' *The Cambridge Law Journal*, 71(1), 200–222.

Weinrib, J. (2016) *Dimensions of Dignity: The Theory and Practice of Modern Constitutional Law*. Cambridge, Cambridge University Press.

Whitman, J.Q. (2003) 'From Fascist "Honour" to European "Dignity"' in Joerges, C. and Singh Ghaleigh, N. eds., *Darker Legacies of Law in Europe: The Shadow of National Socialism and Fascism Over Europe and Its Legal Traditions*. London, Bloomsbury Publishing, 243–266.

2 Human dignity as status

> To the extent that human rights documents gesture, even feebly, toward justifying the assertions about human rights they make, they tend to invoke the idea of the dignity of the individual. The notion of dignity is both murky and multifaceted. [T]he Renaissance humanist philosopher Pico thought of the dignity of human beings as what distinguishes them from all other creatures and confers a unique value on them: unlike other creatures, human beings do not have a nature that is determined in advance; they are self-creators. The idea of self-creation here is closely linked to autonomy because self-creation occurs through choices guided by reason. Human rights can be seen as protecting the dignity of human beings in this [. . .] sense: if realized, these rights shield individuals from conditions that are not fit for beings of our sort.
>
> —(Buchanan 2010, 690; footnote removed)

Introduction

The question of the relationship between law and human dignity is not a question of locating a norm within a system but rather a question of linking our social systems with the entitlements of individual humans. Or more specifically, of recognising what is juridically necessary with regard to each individual human and any legal system properly so called. In recognising a necessary link between the juridical and the individual, we acknowledge individuals' status as that of 'human person', simultaneously natural human and legal person. Thus, human dignity is understood here as status, and that status is to be found in any and all social practices where human persons' basic and inexorable juridical entitlements are maintained as morally, unquestionably, necessary.

To reach this conclusion we proceed through analysis of human dignity's normative core, then its normative implications, finally considering the meta-ethical problems raised in such an analysis. More fully: we initially address a number of incomplete or deficient positions regarding the normative core of human dignity. This leads to a focus on status (basic human status) and how this implies juridical necessity, i.e. juridical, but non-positive, entitlements. Juridical necessity is explored through two complementary ideas, Kant's idea of 'innate right' and the idea of 'natural sovereign equality'. Together these give us a rounded conception of how juridical necessity must attach to each individual and allows us to outline the normative implications of human dignity. These implications are expressible in the 'dignitarian principles' we have already encountered, principles which partly underpin the ascription of human rights and which also have wider social and systemic implications. Having reached that conclusion, the remainder of the chapter addresses some of the theoretical and meta-ethical aspects of this account vis-à-vis other philosophical understandings of human dignity.

2.1 The normative core of human dignity

The normative core of human dignity is expressible as the basic status of the human person. This basic status entails that human persons are not just subject to law but have inviolable juridical entitlements. This is because humans are sources of law: sources of obligation and sources of value. And this means that the status of the individual is properly expressed using the language of 'law', 'right', and 'sovereignty'. This does not mean that law dominates the *implications* of human dignity to the exclusion of other normative claims and normative systems. It means that law is crucial to the account of human dignity defended here, and that law is at the normative core of human dignity and not just amongst its normative implications.

This idea of status will be approached via some other unsatisfactory attempts to reach human dignity's normative core. These are through ideas of 'value', 'the right to have rights', and 'philosophical anthropology'. Value is the most important and will receive additional attention at the end of the chapter, but each of these are important basic theorisations of human dignity. We look first at philosophical anthropology.

To seek its normative core is to ask for human dignity's claim to be obligating or reason-giving. This can become confused with the question of human dignity as human ontology, an account of what humans are. It is assumed that the normative core of human dignity can be vouchsafed relatively quickly through such an anthropology. Philosophical anthropology is, in the broadest sense, a discourse of human self-understanding with emphasis on human particularity and uniqueness. A number of such anthropologies place human dignity's normative core in the species and make general claims about the distinctive properties of humanity needing or worthy of protection (valuable versions include Maritain 1946; Lebech 2009; Kateb 2011). At times such links between human dignity and philosophical anthropology can veer dramatically from the uselessly airy (mere assertions of the 'dignity of man') to the brutally concrete (protection of the body's private functions, the immediate needs of survival). Indeed, this is the least satisfactory of the routes to find human dignity's normative core because of its entanglement in a three-fold problem. First, it requires, but rarely attempts to justify, a movement from fact to value. Second, it relies for its normative force on speciesism. Third, it is inherently conservative with an emphasis on conserving our biological and social inheritances valorised as our species' proper nature or station. Modern accounts of human dignity that centralise philosophical anthropology overcome these problems with very variable success (see Lee and George 2008; Kateb 2011). Both Pico and Hume anticipated the reason for their struggles (see Chapter 1), namely the malleability of human identity and culture, and the related ability of individuals to be self-constituting. It is not human nature as such that is valued in human dignity but rather a special *dynamic* relationship between each individual and the human condition. Human dignity is not, in the sense envisaged here, a conception of human being, or the human good, from which self- and other-regarding obligations can be derived. Rather, individual humans have the capacity to determine their own good. And when it is, at root, the self-constitution of individual humans that we valorise in human dignity, there is no justification for speciesism or conservativism. Self-constitution means that values are important as products of humanity, not standards for them to reach.

In a different vein, the language of value and values have proven useful in articulating that we hold human dignity to be important ('it is one of our most important values') although it is less clear that the language of value assists in telling us *what* is being valued with the language of human dignity ('we should value humanity in ourselves and others' or 'we should value rational nature' or 'we should value every human'). The problem with the last noted – i.e. with identifying what we are being asked to value – is that sometimes we are asked to value a property or capacity which may be humans, humanity, or individual persons. I hold that we have to focus on *each individual human person as grounds or sources of value*. Failing that, value discourse either puts human dignity into competition with other values or creates other axiological difficulties where no such difficulties exist. (Rosen's 2012 study explores the many possibilities here and concludes that the concept is equivalent to 'intrinsic value' but still deeply confused.) For example (and putting aside for the moment specific Kantian arguments), the essence of value-focussed accounts of human dignity appears to be that humans have a special worth or value. The principal problem here is the ambiguity of whether we are to see the value 'inhere' in individuals or humanity, or whether human dignity can take its place amongst other values. Both cannot be true. Either we are concerned with value as a 'possession' or with value as the status of each individual (as an end in themselves). Trying to keep both options open leads to a raft of problems turning on this ambiguity. Can there be partial or must there be complete realisation of human dignity? And do we value human dignity in itself (and what this would mean? valuing humanity or valuing certain individuals?), or is it decomposable into other values, states, or properties? Second, we face problems in terms of the means by which we generate specific obligations. For instance, if human dignity is a value within political morality (like 'liberty'), we have to know both what it would be to achieve or maintain it and how human dignity should be distinguished from other values. It is understandable that we would want to assimilate human dignity within that class of things we value, but the grammar, and more importantly the basic functions, of human dignity are not well served with a discourse of value.

A third and different way to approach the core of human dignity is associated with Hannah Arendt's work, namely the 'right to have rights'. Generated by concerns about the limitations of human rights discourse and what is revealed by atrocity, statelessness, and the 'abstract nakedness' of 'mere humanity', Arendt's work is taken to treat human dignity as a right to have rights, the constituting of individuals as rights-holders prior to the ascription of any particular right (Arendt 1958, 297–298). This is sometimes taken to be a defence of a 'political' conception of human rights, the drawing of human rights discourse towards political and institutional protections and the alignment of human with constitutional rights. But we can see it rather as a formal commitment to the individual being understood as a rights-bearer. This 'moral' rather than 'political' reading of Arendt, then, would take her to be identifying a presupposition found in natural or human rights discourse. After all, Arendt herself insisted, "Man, it turns out, can lose all so-called Rights of Man without losing his essential quality as man, his human dignity" (1958, 297). This is a demand for identifying each individual as a rights-holder regardless of state or citizenship, and for institutional arrangements to track that rights-holding status. Such a condition cannot be merely the political, positive granting of rights but rather takes the status of the individual as primary and shows prevailing institutional arrangements to be deficient in contrast. Accordingly, the right to have rights can be completed, and assessed, only as an account of human dignity when connected with a more complete theory of human rights and their institutional implications. When we come to provide that theory later in this chapter, certain aspects of Arendt's account will be maintained but qualified such that 'the right to have rights' is replaced with a more fundamental linking of the moral and the juridical.

In contrast to these approaches, I argue that the normative core of human dignity should be expressed (in the first instance) as *the basic status of the human person*. But this is unilluminating without more clarity concerning the functions attributed to 'status' and 'human person'. It also demands a synthesis of the insights gained from theorists of human dignity like Arendt, Kant, and Pico, to overcome their respective limits. We first consider the nature of the 'human person'; the next section gives fuller meaning to 'status'.

Appeal to the human person is crucial to understanding the obligations at work in discourses of human dignity. It is not a 'conception of the person' in the sense that we might find a thin idea of an agent in Rawlsian theory (Rawls 2005, 29f). Rather, it is a way of capturing a normative core linking the juridical and the natural. Compared to value, philosophical anthropology, and the right to have rights, beginning with the human person emphasises what any individual must be conceived as, namely as both biological humans and as rights-bearers with personhood. Human dignity is ascribed neither to the bare natural human nor the juridical person but the conjunction of the two. Thus, the human person – to which a large range of human rights laws are attributed – is not merely a vulnerable physical human being. It presumes the basic legal capacities of the legal person.

Conjoining biological human and legal personhood gives us a distinctive perspective on the universality we would assume to be asserted in a claim of human dignity. The language of the human person is a way of insisting that human dignity be understood as the status of ***each individual***, the scope of that ascription being accomplished ***either*** by law or by biology. We are not, conversely, talking about a value that can exist apart from those individuals. That is, it is the value that ***particular, individual*** humans possess, as opposed to more free-floating claims or standards that attach to 'humanity'. That danger is anticipated in a discussion by Margalit (2011) where certain uses of humanity, and by extension certain accounts of human dignity, are criticised as 'kitsch'. They are empty but emotive conceptions of humanity that have evacuated any of the natural, indeed animal, aspects of human life in favour of glib abstraction. The extension of 'human person' is all ***biological*** humans. The intension of 'human person' is humans as a juridical, not purely biological, category. The resulting conception of status is juridical, a source of laws and a source of values.

The language of human person may have evolved distinctive meaning and function in its relation to human rights law (Maritain 1946), but the idea that we can premise our normative concerns on the existence of a complex descriptive class is common to other areas of practical reason. 'Human persons' simply overcomes implicit equivocation in normative theorising between appeal to individual human (agents), humanity, and persons (with entitlements); appeal to the human person entails that at times each idea may have to come into play. Thus its extension is crucial to understanding its intension. The centrality of the human person means that biological or juridical elements of an individual may be proper objects of concern. This means, moreover, that asserting the existence of a dignity for humans, but also possibly a dignity for other species (e.g. Lebech 2009, 21), misses the point that the normativity of the concept depends upon how it conceptualises what it is ascribed to. 'Human dignity' has the idea of the human person as its bearer; it is not one species dignity amongst other species dignities. The inexorability of human dignity is not the metaphysics of the species but a necessary postulate in conceptualisation of any encounter with, or consideration of, others.

What problems does this approach to human dignity via the human person involve? First, because of its duality or conjunctive form we produce an ongoing equivocation between human dignity as a notion defending (on the one hand) the basic bodily needs of ***individual humans*** alongside (on the other) the highest ***aspirations and ends of the species.*** In fact, the idea of the 'human person' is neither a notion emphasising human physical vulnerability nor is it a notion emphasising high human aspiration. That is, it is not already overburdened with the regulative and political functions that have attached to human dignity, particularly in the latter half of the twentieth century. Nevertheless, it is not easy to escape from the idea that human dignity equivocates between these poles.

Moreover, appeal to the human person seems to revive speciesism to the extent that any claim involving the human must draw biological boundaries either between species or, worse, within the species so that it accrues to typical or normal instances of the human. Appeal to the human person does, at least, point to a *prima facie* rejection of these commitments. The idea of personhood is not naturalistic and governs in some way our attribution of 'human' insofar as the identification of humans is never decided purely on natural grounds. However, this implies a further problem of the scope of the juridical, defining (legal) 'person' such that it is not trivial or relative. The important point to note here is that the conjunction of human and person is intended to denote a distinctive conception of the bearer of human dignity, or distinctive bearer of status. It is not 'merely' the conjunction of the biological and the juridical and need not rely upon a separate conceptualisation of each term.

Finally, there is a problem of judgment being prior to ontology (see Lebech 2009, 242f). That is, any claim we make about the human dignity (and any normative core we find in human dignity) is dependent on an act of judgment that will be necessary to determine who and what is to be brought within the scope of human person. While the category of human person might be meaningful for certain descriptive and normative purposes, it cannot exist without an act of judgement.

This final question rightly insists on us clearly identifying the normative core of human dignity. Specifically, whether some kind of dialogical foundation must be sought in a relationship between individuals wherein individuals recognise the status of another (e.g. Darwall 2006). Or whether, in the first instance, any recognition of human status must begin in the individual's understanding of their self, their agency, and their entitlements (e.g. Beyleveld 2012). A dialogical approach reaches such claims to necessity through the interaction of individuals and the progressive recognition of self- and other-entitlements through that interaction. A dialectical approach reaches such claims through individuals' own practical self-understanding as agents who must act and understanding the necessary claims that arise from action and therefore claims to the conditions of such action (see Gewirth 1981a). Some such debates will be returned to both directly and obliquely. But note both positions identify the roots of our obligations with a conceptualisation of the individual as in some way a duality of natural entity and bearer of juridical entitlements (see Darwall 2006, 258; Gewirth 1981a, 31). From this we can at least assume that the idea of the human person (or something like it) is a useful starting point in reflection upon human dignity. Moreover, it is one that does not necessarily reproduce the problems associated with value, anthropology, or 'the right to have rights' as alternative, attractive but problematic, starting points. Nevertheless, if care in identifying the 'bearer' of human dignity is important, the status that they bear must be the essence of any analysis of human dignity.

2.2 Human dignity as status

Use of 'status' requires, in the first instance, some grammatical analysis. Status is an anthropological concept, not an axiological one (a distinction taken from Alexy 2010, 87f, but derived from the work of von Wright). 'Status' describes something accomplished through human action or human interaction rather than it being a property or an end of action. 'Status' describes a place in a network of human obligations or an arrangement of entitlements. Undoubtedly, 'status' can be relative to any number of possible social practices and obligations. But when we associate status with human dignity we are describing an aspect of obligation – core obligations or basic obligations – that is non-contingent or non-relative. The accomplishment of this status is automatic by virtue of being a human person. Thus when we talk about human dignity, it is the *basic* status of the human person and concerns their entitlements in *any* network of human obligations.

This requires further analysis of our grammar of status. Our human status is one status amongst others, presenting us with the immediate challenge of showing that our normal assumptions about status (namely its contingency and relativity) do not necessarily hold true while the language of 'status' is, nonetheless, meaningful. In the first instance, because basic human status is equally possessed across the class of human persons, then there is an underlying idea of equality at work. But this need not mean that 'status' collapses into 'equality' as Buchanan insists:

> It is important to distinguish here between equality as a distributive notion and equality as a status notion. 'Equality of status' here means what Waldron calls equality of 'basic status', which is compatible with a wide range of differences and with their social recognition in the form of material inequalities. For example, properly acknowledging equal basic status for all is consistent with there being various nonfundamental distinctions regarding social status [. . .].
>
> (Buchanan 2010, 685; footnote removed)

This is where the human person becomes important, not as a theoretical 'conception of the person' but as a normative category making the biological and legal inseparable. Formal equality determines individuals' entitlements relative to a chosen characteristic (that which makes them equal) and the entitlements to be distributed amongst them. We can be equal regarding agency, or reason, or citizenship, or whatever we choose; that can produce, in a procedure, an equal distribution of whatever has been chosen. Basic status, in contrast, maps all human persons and ascribes to them their basic human entitlements – that is to say, basic status points to each individual without exception but also *as an individual.* There is not a *choice* of characteristics rendering us equal, but a basic respect for whatever and whoever an individual is in their particularity. And that is why, I suggest, we should prefer the idea of 'basic status' over that of 'moral status', which is sometimes associated with human dignity. There are various reasons why 'moral' is too narrow for the purposes to which human dignity is put, but more to the point, the status we are concerned about is 'basic' because it is unconditioned, including being unconditioned by the performance of moral acts or moral recognition.

It is useful to put this understanding of status in historical, particularly legal historical, context. It is commonly argued, and correct, to see Western civilisation as tracing a broad arc from hierarchical to democratic societies bringing with it a change in the nature of status. Status can depend upon social station, but the privileges that accrue to those in higher social stations can be distributed more fairly in a democratic society (Waldron 2007). One problem with this narrative is that there is no fundamental change or qualitative difference identified in the nature of status. Rather, the privileges of higher status are redistributed. Basic status would have to transcend rather than flatten a hierarchy, exchanging the contingency of social station for the necessity of a properly human station. Accordingly, the notion of basic status I have identified is not reducible to socio-democratic change, though it may have informed or driven it. Human dignity as status does not supervene upon social practices – rather, it is an idea that has shaped our practices. The fact that human dignity as status is *found* in practices does not mean it *depends upon* those practices.

The privileges, entitlements, or liberties attaching to any status are, nonetheless, important for understanding the significance of that status. Basic status, I will go on to argue, is juridical but not reducible to positive law and constitutional rights. To make sense of this conception of status it is useful to turn from broad sociological concerns to the slightly narrower confines of legal sociology, namely Henry Maine's *Ancient Law* (1939 [1861]). Maine traces a historical change from 'status' to 'contract' in the evolution of law and legal privileges. One's legal entitlements depended upon one's status (social station) up to and including the emergence of Roman law. Through Roman law, however, a shift to the importance of contract emerged. The importance of contract is to place legal authority squarely *in each individual* as potential legal agent. Therewith, says Maine, we find the foundations of modern law. The fact that we appear, through human dignity and human rights, to have moved back to status again should not be misunderstood as a regression. Rather, basic status, a distinctive and foundational form of status has been recognised that transcends both the contingencies of social status and the contingencies of what we are capable of contracting to do (contingent upon accidents of social station and imbalances of power). Basic status is universal and inexorable, containing but transcending social status and the mere capacity to contract with others as (actual or seeming) equals. There is an instructive pattern derivable from Maine – from status, to contract, to basic status – that also captures an aspect of the sweep of legal historical thinking appropriate to human dignity as status.

If it is basic, or general, juridical standing that we should associate with basic status, what is it to maintain or to fail to maintain that basic status? It is a recurrent challenge to discourses of human dignity that its defenders have no account of how something 'intrinsic' can be lost or violated (Statman 2000). That the loss or violation of human dignity should be a problem relies on the assumption that it is a property or aspect of philosophical anthropology that has its existence 'in' the human rather than in practices. The idea of a *total* loss of human dignity or basic status is, conversely, problematic if it is taken to mean that certain contexts (statelessness, the concentration camp) reveal the complete negation of human dignity and the reduction of the human person to mere biological human life (Agamben 2002). This is confused on two levels. First, it implies, again, a property that has be deliberately negated rather than the suspension of those practices that should maintain basic status. Second, it assumes that there is a single set of conditions under which such status can be maintained. Evidence from those in desperate or dehumanised conditions has always indicated that human dignity can be maintained through various activities – through self-respect or through work – that form part of basic status (Levi 1987). Complete negation of human dignity is never possible when some form of agency and interaction is possible.

This is usefully illustrated in Jiwei Ci's important analysis of the 'stakes' of poverty, including the idea of 'agency poverty' (Ci 2013). Ci identifies three forms of poverty – subsistence, status, and agency poverty – and analyses their differences relative to one another. He uses them to solve certain kinds of puzzling inconsistencies in our phenomenology of poverty, for instance how self-imposed poverty might mean that poverty ceasing to be objectionable. 'Status poverty' exists where there is an absence of social respect, which may or may not be accompanied by material subsistence poverty. Low social status need not always mean poverty in terms of material lack, "but a special kind of lack of status that is characteristic of a society in which money is an all-important marker of social standing. Such poverty represents a shortfall with reference not to subsistence needs but to the need for respect" (Ci 2013, 126). If status were a homogenous phenomenon, we could not make this distinction (material lack and status poverty); material lack is only a form of poverty when it is seen relative to a social structure where material lack is shameful. Status poverty, however, can be removed through remuneration or changing the mores of the society in question. Conversely, what Ci calls *agency poverty* represents a more fundamental lack of resources and capabilities necessary for social functioning and for self-respect. It is worth quoting Ci at length on this:

> In agency poverty, the material resources one lacks are those required for self-constituting activities, by some or any reasonable standard [. . .]. The significance of this material deprivation is that it leads to power deprivation, which in turn poses a threat to subjectivity, a threat whose adverse effects are registered in the epiphenomenon of lack of self-respect. Thus, what should deeply worry us about agency poverty is not material deprivation as such, though this is important up to a point, nor even power deprivation as such, though this is more directly important, but the fact that material deprivation can lead to power deprivation, which in turn can lead to subjectivity or agency deprivation. Agency poverty is nothing less than a condition in which those involved are prevented by material deprivation from engaging in self-constituting experiences of power and thus from maintaining themselves as subjects. Whenever material deprivation leads to agency deprivation, it undermines the respect for oneself that is part and parcel of a self. *More than merely debilitating and humiliating, agency poverty is positively dehumanizing. Agency poverty, thus understood, is not only bad but unconditionally bad. The same is not true of either subsistence poverty or status poverty.*
>
> (Ci 2013, 134; emphasis added)

What is important here is the existence of a difference class of wrongness, not explicable in terms of (relative) status but of basic status in one's own eyes as well as those of others. And the remedies for the existence of agency poverty lie in the conjunction of social reform, providing individual choices, but also the possession of rights *both* as capacities to make choices *and* as expressions of the value and self-determination of individuals. As such, this points towards two classes of normative implications for basic status: principles governing social practices in general, and the possession of human rights. Both of these will be returned to in full, but as part of positive, constructive concern with the principled implications of human dignity. The importance of exploring failures to maintain basic status is not to identify an exclusive route to understanding human dignity through its breach but rather to show that diminution of human dignity is meaningful even while we can talk of the entitlements that *necessarily* accrue to the individual.

Thus, this wide-ranging consideration of the grammar, sociology, and normative implications of status ends in a concern with the fundamental importance of possession of rights and of principles governing our social practices. Put negatively, status (unlike philosophical anthropology) directly implies deontic consequences, and status (unlike value) directly implies concern with practices not the pursuit of a certain set of ends. With that in mind, what core normative 'force' should we see underlying (basic) status?

2.3 Juridical necessity

If human dignity is the basic status of the human person, then that basic status has normative content. That content, I will argue, is juridical. Basic status relates to rights: it insists on the possibility of creating legal relationships, having enforceable redress related to those relationships, and having human rights protecting that basic status *per se*. We are not, therefore, looking for (moral) duties in the first instance, nor are we concerned with the good of humans or their nature. We are concerned with a non-contingent, non-positive, claim about juridical status as the essence of human dignity or status. There are two complementary ways of possibly expressing this and their contrast is instructive. My concern will be to show that 'human dignity' is synonymous with 'innate right' and with 'natural sovereign equality'.

The basic status of individuals – their status prior to the claims raised in any other normative system or framework – is their *natural sovereign equality*. This notion, to the extent that it has a clear pedigree in the history of ideas, is found in the early modern natural law tradition where theorists of right like Grotius and Pufendorf, according to Tuck (2001), used insights from the practice of international law and worked them into the novel idea of the social contract. For these theorists, "we can best understand the right which individuals possess vis-à-vis one another [. . .] by looking at the rights which sovereign states seem to possess against one another" (Tuck 2001, 85). The idea of natural sovereign equality, in other words, has its origins in our conceptualisation of the rights of states and preceded, but also animated, the social contract tradition. It is 'natural' because it assumes that such a status exists independently of any positive law. It is 'sovereignty' because it assumes no individual has a natural superior (though they may have many actual, *de facto* superiors). It is 'equality' because of its ascription to each individual and because its implications have to be sought in formal equality (a basic assumption of equality) and juridical equality (standing and capacities in law). 'Natural sovereign equality', as I will argue, entwines rights discourse, modern understandings of equality, and appeal to the 'natural' law tradition broadly construed. These three connections require brief comment.

First we should note that 'natural' here must be conceptualised in contrast to 'positive'. Natural could (for the most part) be substituted for 'non-positive', but it also connotes the idea of the pre-institutional more generally. We are not granted natural sovereign equality by positive law, albeit such status might be acknowledged by positive law. It remains a different and difficult question, however, *how* it should be manifested in positive law, if at all. It could be that it is something captured and protected in the 'minimum content of natural law' (Hart 1994). It could require a more complex set of participatory practices in law (Waldron 2012). These ideas await analysis later in this chapter and in Chapter 3. Suffice it to say, positive law cannot negate the natural normative force that is assumed in ascription of human dignity, but we have not yet clarified what this must mean in practical or doctrinal terms.

Second, the language of 'sovereignty' is significant as a means of anchoring status in obligations, not ontology (Hart 1955). Sovereignty captures the power to bind and be bound by equals. No human person is naturally deficient in the capacity to enter into agreements with others, to exercise rights, or to form legal relations with others. And all are equal in sovereign immunity – that is, an immunity from having our basic entitlements changed. We can contract to change our positive legal status, and we may forfeit the right to exercise some rights depending upon the varying social context or social contract we have entered into. But we cannot have our sovereign status – our capacity for entering into legal relations, inviolability, and having no natural superior – changed.

Third, 'equality' is already implied by the idea that this sovereignty is equally distributed and also implied by the idea of the (human) person as entitled to the formal equality flowing from legal personhood. But we are concerned with a primordial, not merely formal equality. The *capacity* to form legal relationships (regardless of equality in procedural terms) must be equal to that of others. And such equal power to enter into practices with others immediately presumes some need for, and protection of, the conditions – our embodiment – that must form the backdrop of any practices (Gewirth 1981a). Nonetheless, it must also mean juridical equality in its more familiar forms. That is, structures must be in place, independently of the parties to a dispute, to adjudicate legal questions.

The underlying assumptions here are implicit in modern liberal and libertarian theorising. The equality of persons, the equal distribution of rights, and a burden on the state to (at a minimum) enforce legitimate rights claims are familiar from the political philosophy of at least the last fifty years. Natural sovereign equality as the content of basic status focusses distinctively on law and juridical entitlements.

Formal equality is certainly part of this, as is 'rights-holding' quite broadly understood. But basic status must include privileges and immunities ensuring that formal equality is bolstered by the assumption that our status as humans – rather than animals or objects – cannot be altered by others. And our 'natural rights' are again invoked, albeit in an allusive way awaiting further theorisation. With those problems and possibilities in mind, we can retrace similar territory using Kant's discussion of 'innate right'.

Kant states its meaning as follows:

> *Freedom* (independence from being constrained by another's choice), insofar as it can coexist with the freedom of every other in accordance with a universal law, is the only original right belonging to every man by virtue of his humanity. – This principle of innate freedom already involves the following authorisations, which are not really distinct from it [. . .]: innate *equality*, that is, independence from being bound by others to more than one can in turn bind them; hence a human being's quality of being *his own master* (*sui juris*), as well as being a human *beyond reproach* (*iusti*), since before he performs any act affecting rights he has done no wrong to anyone; and finally, his being authorised to do to others anything that does not in itself diminish what is theirs, so long as they do not want to accept it [. . .].
>
> (Kant 1996 [1797], 30; emphasis in original)

An 'original right' accruing to every human as such, this is not clearly *a* right in the sense of having the general elements necessary for a right "the subject of the right, the right-holder [. . .]; the object of the right [. . .]; the respondent of the right, the person who has the correlative duty [. . .]; and the justificatory basis or ground of the right" (Gewirth 1981b). It is closer to a *state of rightfulness*, i.e. in a position to form legal relationships and gain legal redress on precisely the same footing as others. If legal justice depends, in certain circumstances, on the claimant coming to the law with 'clean hands', innate right implies that we all *start* from that position and have equal claim upon the law, regardless of what rights we acquire or faults we assume.

However, it is the coexistence of freedoms that forms the general background to a claim of innate right; Kant's claims about innate right have an empirical element. Empirical human being involves clashes and competition in the physical world. But whatever the nature of such relations, we are never naturally inferior to one another. So freedom can exist in the human world – we can coexist with others on an equal footing – if these juridical assumptions (the aspects or authorisations of innate right) are respected. These are natural liberties or permissions that can be exercised by each individual without violation of the freedom of another.

In part, 'freedom' is here potentially associated with non-domination or self-mastery. According to Ripstein, Kant's arguments "rest on the simple but compelling *normative* idea that, as a matter of right, each person is entitled to be his or her own master, not in the sense of enjoying some form of special self-relation, but in the contrastive sense of not being subordinated to the choice of any *other* particular person" (2009, 4; emphasis in original). This natural sovereignty (to use our alternative terminology) is not the idea of self-ownership found in Locke (1967 [1690]), nor is it a simple natural equality. Rather, there is no natural sovereignty to be found beyond each individual understood as capable of setting their own ends. As already acknowledged by Kant (1996 [1797]), that does not exclude but rather demands that we consider the empirical implications of human coexistence. No choice or determination of ends is ever naturally superior to our own, and our own wills are capable of binding (but also in turn of being bound) through the promises and undertakings which we form with others as equals.

'Freedom' here also has empirical components that should be distinguished from 'autonomy': we should be free from the choices of others even when our freedom, empirically, must involve coexistence and with it degrees of social and interpersonal domination. The idea of being free of the *choices* of others concerns the actual encounters between embodied individuals. This is significant in two senses: it is not a formal idea of autonomy (linked to rationality) and it also has connections with the choice or will theory of rights. As Weinrib puts it:

> Adopting the language of innate right (*angeboren Recht*), Kant argues that the right of each person to freedom – independence from the constraint of another's choice – must answer to nothing other than its own systematic requirements. In elaborating this idea, Kant creates a theory of public law that may follow from features of his comprehensive philosophical project, but that can stand independently of it.
>
> (2016, 31; footnotes removed)

The significance of this commitment becomes clearer if it is contrasted with more conventional state-of-nature and contractarian positions. On the one hand, in innate right we have no positing of natural rights existing in an actual state of nature. Rather, our natural state is one that must be characterised as equality of status irrespective of any actual historical states of affairs. On the other, our liberation from humanity's 'natural state' is not one that needs to be accomplished through renunciation of personal authority (as it would be for Hobbes), nor need it mean the direct and simple translation of natural rights to the civil condition. Innate right, as with the model of natural sovereign equality, provides the normative fundaments that must be acknowledged in any movement into society and the creation of a common authority. In essence, if this is an extension of the contractarian tradition, it is one that dispenses with historical fiction and with the primacy of a single, clear, and distinct set of natural rights. Those rights will be produced later through the application of principles, not direct reflection on our natural state.

This idea of 'rightful standing' is also a crucial link between innate right and the human person. We are not merely concerned with the formal entitlements that might be expressed through equality. We have empirical concerns with the way in which human wills can clash and how humans can claim authority of other humans. Under an idea of innate right or rightful standing, such clashes and forms of domination cannot negate (or are not more primordial than) the personhood of the individual, i.e. their rightful standing.

> Innate right entitles every person to make their freedom expressive of their own purposes rather than the purposes of others. Because self-determining beings have an innate right to act in pursuit of their own purposes, every self-determining being has a correlative duty to exercise their freedom in a manner that is consistent with the innate right of all others. Since persons pursue their purposes through their bodies, innate right encompasses the right of every person to bodily integrity and the duty of every person to respect the bodily integrity of all others. Persons are to interact on the basis of their innate right to independence rather than the physical power of any person to compel another. Any person who interferes with the bodily integrity of others wrongs them.
>
> (Weinrib 2014, 116)

There are a number of overlapping threads in this analysis pointing to the ways in which 'right' and 'rightful' as Kant understands them draw together core themes in political and legal philosophy. Bodily integrity (a recurrent theme in human dignity discourse but often reduced to a prohibition) here forms part of a wider concern with the reciprocal (or universalisable) obligations that we can place on ourselves and others. The private use of *force* and its replacement with public *coercion* represents a qualitative shift from the unjust violence of natural encounters to the just harmonisation of wills possible under public law (see Murphy 1970, 109f). And action cognisant of the innate right of others is not to conceptualise or act upon any special *value*, it is to act within bounds set by the status of others. Thus Kant's position regarding innate right touches upon common themes in human dignity discourse and the political philosophy of his time, but draws it into a more coherent link between moral and political philosophy.

With these points in mind we can briefly compare and contrast the claims made under the contrasting ideas of 'innate right' and 'natural sovereign equality'. In both instances it is intelligible to say that we are talking about humans' special status as opposed to a value. We are looking at the agency and entitlements of the individual as the source of that status. Conversely, status is not dependent upon certain capacities being exercised. With regard to innate right we are concerned with the basic status of the individual as it is found in (empirical) interaction amongst humans; with regard to natural sovereign equality this is only implicit. Under innate right we are also to assume that harmonisation of human willing is possible provided that innate right is respected; again this is implicit only with regard to natural sovereign equality. In both cases our nature is juridical, but certainly in discussion of innate right it is much clearer that this juridical being must be conjoined with our empirical being and concerns the coexistence of *real and juridical* human beings. In both cases we are also concerned with normative implications that are in the first instance juridical but are not in any simple way positive laws. Our rightful condition, and our natural sovereignty, are not to be read as the basis for commands or prohibitions. They are demands for orientation of whole systems of norms and governance towards status.

So, the most important aspect of these ideas for our understanding of human dignity (as anticipated in Chapter 1) is that these normative ideas should be thought to give rise to non-positive principles. These principles hold regardless of the institutional arrangements that contingently uphold or frustrate them. These will be expressed as 'dignitarian principles' although they could easily also be called 'status principles'. These principles move us from human dignity's normative core to its normative implications. Note, nonetheless, that drawing out these normative implications must rest upon the ideas of normative necessity outlined here, whether that is expressible in terms of innate right or natural sovereign equality. In the first instance, it is within the juridical implications of innate right that these principles can be found.

2.4 The normative implications of human dignity

We should return to the distinct entitlements that Kant believes already inhere in the idea of innate right. Ripstein suggests that these have immediate appeal as entitlements: "The direct implications that Kant draws from the Universal Principle of Right – each person's right to be his or her own master, to be presumed innocent, and to speak in his or her own name – sit well enough with considered judgements" (Ripstein 2009, 7). They include the entitlement to bind and be bound by others provided this flows from equal sovereign status, not force. Moreover, natural juridical equality includes a permissive assumption that action should be permitted provided that it coheres with the freedom of others. This general link between natural status and liberties is accompanied by a specification of individuals' natural normative status, namely a kind of presumption of innocence, a natural absence of moral and legal guilt. The individual is only held publicly responsible for a class of duties for which she is properly the subject of public praise or blame.

Why does Kant feel entitled to unpack the (seemingly singular) innate right in this way and why, for Kant, are these normatively equivalent implications of a single idea? The normative force of these sub-principles of innate right could be expressed in two different ways, via the notion of the human person or via the notion of the right to have rights. However, in the light of the general account of innate right they amount to the same thing. Innate right encompasses what we articulated via the human person: a mixture of entitlements flowing from our natural equality but also our juridical equality; these ideas, like the components of innate right, make sense as the explication of our juridical standing, amongst other human persons, in the empirical social world. An argument for innate right also, I would argue, captures that normative-anthropological conjunction that is the common denominator of most contemporary philosophies of human dignity – that the natural individual is always and everywhere also a rights-bearer or has a 'right to have rights' – but does so with greater clarity on how such a conjunction is to be understood, namely through the drawing the implications of natural sovereign equality.

The importance of these derivations from innate right also lies in the fact that they are potentially constitutive of political and legal institutions and practices. They are neither direct norms (albeit they have some quite direct and familiar implications in the principles of contract and criminal law) nor are they a straightforward philosophical anthropology of the kind we might associate with general theories of human dignity. They are general commitments that we can bring to bear in encounters with others but they are also capable of forming much more complex institutional arrangements. The presumption of innocence constitutes criminal process; promising constitutes contract law. Kant has his own avenue for creating principles of private and public out of innate right, namely through the need (in the first instance) for private individuals to be able to secure property rightfully through the institutions first of private law then of public law (Kant 1996 [1797], 37–46). However, my own concern is closer to innate right itself and the core implications that it appears to contain.

Human dignity, as a status concept, can be treated as containing a cluster of 'status principles', principles concerning obligation, freedom, and change: obligation because human dignity concerns primordial obligations flowing from natural equality; freedom because this is our innate right, the natural state of rightfulness that exists in the absence of the contingencies of constituted authority; and change because the deriving of obligations from innate right is via principles, principles that will have different applications in different times and places. Innate right or natural sovereign equality concerns dynamic normative guidance mapping changes in our practices and our conditions.

What then are these principles? They are a sovereignty principle: a self-determination principle requiring human rights and human rights law. A permissive principle: a social-dynamic principle of freedom of contract, and role mobility premised on a public-private divide. And an obligation principle: a normative-dynamic principle, ensuring that our basic obligations, and the systems they are produced by, do not clash. This implies, by extension, limitation of law (moral limits to positive law), limitation of morality (the distinction between moral and criminal responsibility), and limitation of politics (the rule of law). How are these derived from Kant's conception of innate right?

The sovereignty principle is the core of any connection between human dignity and human rights. Being one's own master is not a form of self-ownership but freedom from the choices of another. Such freedom concerns the many, plural forms of human life; they may need positive support as well as negative prohibitions. The moral rights that we treat as human rights can be thought to have their origins in this principle: that we are naturally entitled to bind others, and in turn be bound by them. Accordingly, sovereignty does not imply an unchanging set of moral rights, nor only rights concerning activities in the public domain (i.e. civil and political rights). To the extent that human dignity is a foundation of human rights, it is a dynamic foundation, asserting our natural self-determination as sovereign individuals and, at the same time, the ability to form juridically enforceable relationships through the exercise of that will.

The permissive principle concerns the more general underpinnings of society and authority ('social systems') and the preservation of liberties in those social systems. It is, as the innate right to freedom itself implies, a principle guaranteeing freedoms. It suggests that there should be a presumption towards permissions, not direct command or prohibition, in the structuring of our societies and norms. Allied to that is the public-private divide. Any maintenance of a permissive principle must imply a clear division between those demands that can be made of us as part of our public and other-regarding obligations and conversely, the space, and the obligations, that are properly given over to self-constitution and immunised as far as possible from public scrutiny and intervention. It is indisputable that that divide, while broadly mapping a division of normative concern, is sometimes sociologically under-theorised (Luhmann 2008) and normatively problematic in many respects (Marx 1977; MacKinnon 1987). A broader sense of permission as the ability to move between social systems and social practices is the best normative expression of a permissive presumption that has sociological repercussions (see Chapter 6). Again, this is a principle of freedom but also of change and is intended to provide principled guidance that maps changes in our social structures. And note: this is a self-standing principle *prior* to the conceptualisation and implementation of human rights, rather than depending upon them. Thus, we are not simply seeking to protect individual autonomy and individual choices (as human rights laws do) but we are concerned with the conditions of that autonomy and the structural threats to that autonomy.

The obligation principle demands normative certainty across our structures of obligation (law, morality, and politics, i.e. our normative orders) such that there is coherence in the obligations placed upon individuals. There is, conversely, never any clash of normativities producing a clash of basic obligations or clash of basic values, at least so far as our innate natural status is concerned. This means that, at least from the point of view of our basic normative status, we should exclude the possibility that we *inevitably* face clashes between our moral, political, and legal obligations. Of course, in fact, there are inevitably tensions here of the form charted from the Greeks onwards where the law of the land (tragically and dramatically) clashes with an individual's sense of obligation. The obligation principle, in contrast, insists that our practices should strive to prevent such clashes. This requires, then, some clarity on the interaction of our normative orders. The obligations principle connects to Kant's presumption of innocence or natural rightfulness. This points in the first instance to the limits of morality vis-à-vis law: any moral blame that attaches to us should not necessarily be included within legal regulation. The limit of the political lies in the rule of law. The limit of law lies in the permissibility of some forms of rebellion. That latter principle requires more justification, not least because of its more radical departure from Kant's thought (for discussion, see Chapter 6).

Are these principles exhaustive of the normative implications of human dignity? While, like any principles, they require application to concrete problems and disputes, I believe they capture the core normative implications of human dignity. One potential rejoinder to this is the assumption that there is a free-standing '*right* to dignity' which represents a single moral, but enforceable, right encompassing the commitments outlined above. With such a right we could dispense with discussion of innate right in favour of a single master-right or human right that protects basic bodily and agentic needs. Recalling the idea of the idea of having a right to have rights, this should be rejected for two reasons. It is a kind of category error because we need principles to bolster our rights, not another right. And it is not defensible without a wider theory of human rights. Not only do we need an account of how such rights are determined and defended as a class, we need to explain how human dignity acts as a principle unifying this as a body of positive laws. A right to dignity would play no such unifying role; rather, it threatens to conflate the *status reflected* in our possession of rights with certain standards of treatment properly found within social and economic rights.

That criticism aside, do these principles properly synthesise the defensible elements of otherwise deficient discourses of human dignity (those anchored in values, philosophical anthropology, or the right to have rights)? Taken together, these dignitarian principles capture some of the fractured ethico-political demands often associated with human dignity while moving away from the obscurity of human dignity as a value. The danger of much value discourse (and some appeals to status) is that human dignity appears to be an inert property or condition: a *possession* with normative consequences, or a distinctive *position* above our normal commitments and above our normal practices. Status, in conjunction with principles, is a set of *starting positions for asserting obligations.* The generation of obligations from principles (as has been charted by the natural law tradition for centuries) may be through direct derivation of obligations or through adjudicative practices intended to apply the principles to different circumstances. There is not, then, always a simple relationship between principles and the precise norms they eventually yield (this is very clear when we consider the complex and fine-grained jurisprudence of human rights *law* which is nonetheless grounded in human dignity). But this is not a falsification of the idea of principles in general or in the context of human status. The point is precisely that they explicate our broad entitlements on the basis of a stable normative core but with the anticipation that the 'circumstances of justice' will change (see Chapter 3). Indeed, human dignity as it is explicated through these principles is – and must be – superior to any normative starting point that posits direct and simple commands and prohibitions. These principles appear to allow a certain kind of dynamism in linking the status of each individual to the structures they find themselves in. In contrast, claims about dignity as our special value tell us little about, for instance, resistance to unjust laws or the protection of the private sphere.

But what is to stop the principles becoming empty generalisations to be filled by sociologically contingent concerns? This challenge can come in two forms. Either an assertion that human dignity and the principles related to it are essentially products of a specific social constellation (a sociological reading of human dignity). Or, assuming human dignity must equate to certain social standards or capacities (a capabilities reading of human dignity). The first is reflected in classic Durkheimean sociology:

> what Durkheim often calls 'the cult of the individual' or 'cult of the human person' [. . .] demands unconditional respect for the dignity and autonomy of all individuals by virtue of their common humanity. In Durkheim's view, this is the only moral basis on which interaction between people can occur spontaneously, and with calculability, security, stability and mutual confidence, in complex modern societies. These societies are characterized by ever-increasing specialization of social roles and economic functions, so there are proliferating differences in citizens' life-styles, moral outlooks and social understandings. Moral individualism affirms what unites people – their basic, irreducible human worth – despite their being divided from each other in innumerable other ways. It provides an essential basis for interpersonal and inter-group communication, especially about rights and responsibilities; one that can link human beings together in bonds of mutual respect and human empathy, despite all social differences in conditions of great social complexity.
> (Cotterell 2011, 6; references removed)

Human dignity in this light is a remedial presumption generated by modernity. The *functional* role of human dignity is as a substitute for more organic bonds of social attachment; it amounts to a set of default assumptions concerning basic entitlements and basic sociability of those we encounter. The idea of status defended here no doubt has some similar functional implications. Nevertheless, this status has normative grounding in the implications of natural sovereign equality. And it avoids the genetic fallacy that the meaning of a concept like human dignity is exhausted by its complex sociological origins.

In contrast, cashing human dignity into static standards of human entitlement (see Nussbaum 2009), however universal they appear to be, faces a dual problem. First the reduction of human dignity to a few basic standards (standards of living, or basic standards of treatment) that tell us little about the organisation of social affairs more generally. Second, flowing from the first, there is a temptation to construe human status as always society-specific, conditioned by the hierarchies and material resources found, *de facto*, within a society. Status is thereby explicated via the structures and systems of existing societies with the only absolute normative necessity arising from human dignity being narrowly prohibitive obligations. If, conversely, we take status to be explicated via principles that structure our social and normative systems more generally, then we judge social systems *as a whole by whether they maintain human dignity*, not whether they can fulfil human dignity as an additional standard or composite of various capabilities. In essence, the movement towards principles has not only provided a move in the conceptual space within which human dignity can be conceptualised – the more dynamic space of principles as opposed to the ontological claims attached to value – but has also made a contribution towards clarifying the social and political aspects of human dignity. It does this not by making human dignity one additional norm or standard within our other standards. The dignitarian principles are prior even to our principles of social organisation, including that of justice (see Chapter 3).

It is also undoubtedly the case that what separates human dignity (as status) from the cult of humanity described in the sociology of modernity, from the capabilities approach, and (as we saw in Chapter 1) from the various virtue discourses that it is genealogically connected with, is human rights. These were earlier shown to be a non-accidental correlate of human dignity. They explain why human dignity should be connected to justice, not virtue. They capture that normative core of human dignity that cannot captured by 'respect'. So, with the broader human dignity principles in mind, it is timely to explicate this crucial relationship. Only then can we move on to applying the dignitarian principles to social governance generally (Chapter 3) and public law specifically (Chapters 4–6).

2.5 Human rights

An account of human rights – their nature, scope, and justification – must be provided by any account of human dignity centred on status. And any such account must take its place amongst a considerable volume of scholarship linking human dignity and human rights, albeit a body of scholarship demonstrating dramatic variation in the extent to which human dignity is given a justificatory or explanatory role (see Cruft et al 2015 for an overview). The notion of human dignity as foundation is common but its precise significance and function is often unclear.

Human dignity in the present account makes human rights arise from a dignitarian principle, the sovereignty principle. This means, in the first instance, human dignity acting as a foundation through being a principle, i.e. a broad commitment inviting and awaiting further specificity. This means that a number of other possible foundational relationships (see Waldron 2013 for the forms that this might take) are thereby side-lined. These include the idea, for instance, that a single set of necessary and sufficient conditions for identifying human rights can be found through interrogation of the *concept* of 'human dignity'. These would include, for instance, the idea that human dignity is a regulative idea, providing a kind of ideal state or condition that cannot be reached, only approximated, in our practices. Rather the sovereignty principle will provide necessary conditions and guidance in conjunction with other principles. The sovereignty principle, like human dignity as a whole, can be thought to arise from the idea of natural sovereign equality and it is there we should start.

Natural sovereign equality means the human person has equal basic power and potential within any social system or normative order. This is the seed of any coherent conceptualisation of, and coherence between, the competing obligations that can be placed upon us. As argued above, the notion of 'sovereignty' is useful for pointing to the special capacity to enter into relationships as equals, and it also stresses a certain kind of freedom from superior authority. But to build a link between innate right and an account of human rights as a whole requires using all those components.

Human rights as a class take their *function* from harmonising the action, freedom, and self-determination. Acting, including action free from the will of others and the capacity to freely enter into relationships with others, must be cashed out in the first instance as the 'generic requirements of agency'. That is, our freedom and our relationships presuppose the physical and bodily aspects of agency but also the absence of certain kinds of barriers to the exercising of the will. Whatever empirical assumptions we might bring to bear in understanding the human condition, the physical presuppositions of agency and the barriers that can prevent us achieving the objects of our will are the horizon within which any normative discourse must take its bearings (Gewirth 1981a). Any agent will have, once those generic conditions are in place, the capacity for choosing their own ends, including the wider projects they will pursue. Human rights are the functionalising of the many positive and negative norms necessary to make such self-determination possible.

Human rights as a class therefore find their *substance* in protecting the material conditions necessary for agency, protecting against vulnerabilities, protecting choice, and protecting equality. These are heterogeneous if they are assumed to be united by *interests.* Any attempt to combine them under the idea of interests would have to make the concept of interest so thin as to be all but meaningless, or it would require rationalising human rights to include only those entitlements that it is always, clearly, in everyone interest to exercise (rendering all but the most basic prohibitions questionable as human rights). Rather, what unites them is their arising from natural sovereign equality which is not tied to interest but rather to a status protecting the human person both in their basic bodily integrity but also in their juridical equality. The 'indivisibility' of rights (Nickel 2008) has been hard to defend in terms of the objects of rights given that they relate variously to goods, acts, interests, acts as individuals, acts as members of groups, and others. Moreover, the function they typically display of protecting the private against the public is also misleading if we want to make it the core of an account of *indivisibility.* We have to appeal to the principles that underpin them, not their typical functions (citizens' claims against their state); such a function is not normatively necessary in the light of their justification and material scope. The indivisibility of rights and their coherence as a group relates rather to their origin in innate right or basic human status.

The value of this account can be further outlined through two quick responses to common problems raised regarding human rights *per se*, namely a defence of their non-positive status and understanding their practical implementation in 'non-ideal' circumstances. First, we are not appealing to 'natural' (rights) in the sense that such rights could be found as a property in an individual irrespective of their social context. In other words, there would be no sense in ascribing human rights to a Robinson Crusoe or to those 'Gods or madmen' who live outside any polity (Aristotle 1998). The function of 'natural' in the present account is only to include, as is always necessary in any practical theorising, the embodiment of the individual and to exclude 'posited' foundations for these entitlements. Human rights as generic rights have no need for a special metaphysics of rights. Their status as *moral* rights, however, is given further consideration below.

Second, it has become common to assume that we must build into an account of human rights, from the outset, a special 'threshold' of importance that delineates the class. Griffin, for instance, treats human rights as rights protecting 'normative agency' and circumscribes the class of human rights through a two-pronged movement: treating human rights as encompassing all agency that is self-regarding or other-regarding, but to exclude from this class all rights that properly the domain of justice (constitutional and acquired rights) (Griffin 2008). The remainder is the special class of rights that can properly be said to flow from human dignity. He explores a number of ways to resist this 'programme of exclusion' and concedes that his own position, at times, is reducible to an all-things-considered judgement. For instance: "I cannot myself find any compelling reason, all things considered, to include claims to rectificatory justice, as such, in the class of rights. It is better – if for no other reason than so much clearer – to go on speaking of justice for deprived groups rather than of their having group rights" (Griffin 2008, 273). The demand for a threshold, as we can see, stops the scope of human rights intruding too much into settled practices and reflects an assumption (putatively intuitive) that human rights must include all and only those rights that we see of especial importance. No such assumption is built into the present account because the 'basic' and 'generic' elements appealed to are enough to connect human dignity with core or basic rights, without further contingent refinement in order to satisfy certain 'intuitions'. The work of fitting these rights into a wider social and political picture, including the demands of justice, is undertaken in the next chapter where a more careful, less crude connection between human dignity and justice is explored. But, suffice it for present purposes to say that no self-standing threshold of 'importance' or 'priority' is included within my conceptualisation of human rights, nor should it be. The place of human rights in our systems should be determined in concert with other dignitarian principles, not by extrinsic thresholds reflecting contingent concerns with existing practices.

The invocation of the idea of 'moral rights' in human rights discourse is now common, but its precise significance needs careful isolation. In more recent literature this is meant to mark a difference with 'political rights' being rights that have positive, constitutional sources, and which may carry significant political or ideological weight but are nonetheless positive rights. Moral rights by contrast claim an extra-positive source (see Feinberg 1992). This must, at the very least, be true of any account of human rights (as moral rights) that makes a qualitative separation between constitutional and human rights; in its absence, the class of human rights would be defined only by a special focus on human interests but without distinctive *justification* or distinctive scope in terms of *universal* entitlement. The idea of moral rights as I construe it insists upon any positive human rights law supervening on principles that provide precisely that distinctive justification and universal scope. Given the foregoing arguments concerning dignitarian principles, I assume that such principles are provided and, in that sense, the only problem to resolve regarding 'moral rights' is the precise meaning of *moral*. Again Griffin sounds a note of caution here, precisely because he feels human rights practices, and the discourse of moral rights, exist independently from one another: "Parts of the extension of the term 'human right' are widely agreed. The extensions of 'right', 'moral right', and 'human right' have developed in a fair degree of independence of one another" (Griffin 2008, 273). This leads to another rationalising move on Griffin's part:

> It seems to me that an account of general moral rights should be able to pass a redundancy test. The word 'rights' should not just provide another way of talking about what we can already talk about perfectly adequately. 'Rights' should mark off a special domain within morality, and there should be sufficient motivation to mark it off. The pass level for the redundancy test is, of course, fuzzy. It is obviously a matter of judgement when a motivation is 'sufficient'. But making the domain of rights coextensive, by definition, with the whole domain of moral obligation, for which we already have a perfectly adequate vocabulary, fails the test.
>
> (Griffin 2008, 272)

My response to this is two-fold. First, the independence of discourse of human rights and moral rights should not be taken for granted. For my purposes 'moral rights' should not be thought to relate to the moral duties produced by prevailing moral theories but rather the interstitial principles that flow from human dignity itself (for discussion of their 'interstitial' function see Chapter 3). Second is that we have, through rights theory, ways of ensuring that rights discourse does not colonise the entirety of our normative discourse (see below). But more to the point, if we take care in distinguishing the domains of human dignity and justice, the precise division between human rights and acquired rights becomes clearer (see Chapter 3). This should not be taken to mean, however, that we are concerned with a class of 'dignitarian rights' as opposed to 'human rights'. The temptation to make this a special class distinct even from human rights requires immediate attention.

Is it possible to talk of 'dignitarian rights' as a broad class of 'basic' rights that encompasses both human rights and constitutional rights? Theorists, in different ways, have assimilated ideas of human dignity and human rights with basic constitutional rights, be it with a Rawlsian underpinning (Shue 1996) or by simply focussing on any basic rights concerning bodily integrity and personhood (Daly 2012). I think we have to resist this, both as a matter of human rights theory (by definition we want all and only those rights that accrue to the individual *qua* human person) and as a matter of coherence within an account of human dignity. We are concerned with the normative implications of human dignity. The *sovereignty* implication gives us a defence of human rights as moral rights, enforceable by every individual on the basis of their status generally and their natural claim rights specifically. The permissive and obligations principles, by contrast, are concerned with the social ordering and normative ordering of social affairs more generally. It is there that constitutional rights have to be brought into harmony with human rights, not the one assimilated to the other. The idea of a broader class of 'dignitarian rights' is, in contrast, simply confused. There are human rights, and these protect bodily integrity and agency. And there are dignitarian principles that locate human status within wider social and normative structures. There is no class of rights sitting between the two, and it is part of the challenge of clear account of human dignity and law to dissolve the tendency (provoked by the language and theory of human dignity itself) to assume that human dignity simply denotes or supervenes upon a class of desirable rights ranging from bodily integrity to self-creation (see O'Mahony 2012).

This locates the present account within the prevailing debates concerning the nature of rights *per se*. I deny that interests alone can provide an adequate understanding of human rights and, by implication, defend a will theory centred on (what is sometimes helpfully called) the 'sovereignty of the individual' and their choice to enforce or waive a right. A positive defence of that position will follow, but the problems of the interest theory can be amplified. Under an interest theory, rights are defined by reflecting interests held by individuals, and human rights in particular clearly (even neatly) fall into a class of rights pre-eminently concerned with reflecting and enforcing human interests (see Raz 1986; Cruft 2010). Human rights theory, then, relies upon both the special justificatory force and the universal scope of certain basic interests (Tasioulas 2013). Aside from several perennial criticisms of such a position (we can possess rights that are not in our interests, and we can have certain limitations as an agent that mean we could never have such interests), the moral core of such a position is not clearly as justificatory of *rights* as we might hope. Certain protections might be afforded by more general legislative principles without saying anything about the specific bearers of interests. Interest theory treats the *particular* bearer of rights as their vehicle, not their justification. And, by extension, it allows the account of obligations to equivocate between rights and duties, with the interest-protecting capacity being easily expressed through the idea of 'directed duties' on the part of certain actors (Kamm 1992). In essence, no especial *status* is expressed through the ascription of rights when their function is equally accomplished through duties.

Under a will theory, by contrast, it is the particular status of the individual as holder of rights that is foremost. The special sovereignty of the rights-holder – to *exercise* rights, to enforce or waive rights, to stand in a special relationship of power with regard to the correlate duty-holder – has been conceptualised by various theorists as the distinctive respect or status that rights afford regardless of the interests that they may have as their object (Feinberg 1992; Nagel 1995). There are distinctive challenges in adopting this position. We ascribe rights to those who have no capacity to enforce or waive their rights; and we seem to have fewer resources to distinguish special rights from general rights (Hart 1955) when all rights seem to be ascribed to a special, uniquely empowered sovereign individual. Nevertheless, the deficiencies of the interest position are the concomitant gain of the will theory. We have a person-centred and status-centred position reflecting the moral rights and underlying principles associated with human rights; interest theory has no such connection with status. As Buchanan puts it:

> A moral agent is more than a being who has interests. To put the point somewhat paradoxically, a moral agent can *take an interest in his interests*, in the sense that he possesses the higher-order capacity to criticize, evaluate, and revise his interests. Moral agency, on this view, is that kind of practical rationality which enables a being with interests to distinguish himself from the interests that he happens to have at a particular time, or on the other hand, to identify with certain interests. To say that a being is a moral agent is to say that his behavior and even his attitudes and dispositions are subject to moral assessment because he is subject to moral requirements. Only a being who can stand in a critical relationship to his interests can be subject to moral requirements.
>
> (Buchanan 1984, 76; emphasis in original)

This link with responsibility is instructive and will be returned to below in light of the practical reasoning of the individual and in terms of their punishment (Chapter 6). But it also stands as a corrective to the assumption that a will-based theory of rights is either excessively individualistic or fundamentally 'atomistic' and theoretically, as well as practically, asocial. The ascription of rights to the human person is always ascription to a fully rounded juridical human being, one embedded within wider networks of social practices and normative orders, within society and politics. That they should have rights that maintains their sovereignty *within* those practices is no barrier to acquiring other rights and duties, nor is it incompatible with variation in the implementation of human rights subject to the demands of justice. That rights must be exercised within a community is no falsification of the idea that some basic rights reflect the special sovereignty, special status, of each individual. Reasonable variation between societies, communities and legal cultures is to be welcomed; the denial of basic rights reflecting the natural sovereign equality of human persons is universally wrongful.

Residual worries arise from will-based theories of human rights concerning correlativity, priorities between rights, and their being waivable. I shall address these immediately, beginning with the last, albeit some other aspects of these questions will be addressed elsewhere. That the ability to enforce or waive rights is central to the will theory seems to produce problems in terms of those agents ascribed rights who cannot meaningfully waive them, and in terms of the putative absurdity of individuals waiving their human rights if such rights are ascribed unconditionally by virtue of their status as humans. The possibility of waiving rights is important as a matter of individuals' choice. This has a number of elements as outlined by Buchanan:

> The ability to invoke or not invoke or to waive one's right is uniquely valuable because it (a) makes possible certain efficiencies which are not available

> in a pure obligation system; (b) allows rights to function as *non-paternalistic* protections of the individual's interests, and, indeed, allows rights to function as *nonpaternalistic protection against paternalism;* and (c) avoids a situation in which every instance of the nonperformance of an enforceable duty constitutes a *prima facie* case for complaints against the enforcement mechanism.
>
> (Buchanan 1984, 79; emphasis in original)

What was hitherto expressed purely in the language of sovereignty is here expressed in the language of (non)paternalism. The waiving of rights means that our interests are not definitive of our powers and not definitive of our relationships with others. Self-constitution through choice must be a plank of our normative conception of the human person and of human rights. That there may exist rights-holders (non-human animals, future generations, the disabled) who cannot waive rights ascribed to them *in the way that a human person typically can* is not a falsification of a will-based account of human rights. Human rights are in the first instance the rights of the human person, and the fact that there are *agents* who hold rights (like certain groups) means that we need a comprehensive account of agency rather than an interest-based theory of rights (see Chapter 4).

Note that these concerns with the nature of rights and their enjoyment by specific groups should not be confused with demands to tailor or condition human rights to 'non-ideal' circumstances. The scope and enjoyment of rights will be conditioned by social and economic contexts. That is, the identification of legal rights will always depend to some degree upon the social conditions and relationships in a given historical epoch (variation in their scope), and there is no contradiction in there being suspensions of rights on the basis of protecting other rights (there are always, in human rights law, grounds for variation in the 'enjoyment' of rights to reflect special general or self-imposed limitations on certain individuals exercising rights). They will nonetheless always face the charge of being too politically and economically demanding given the other, justice-based, demands made on states. These kinds of problems have been taken to be fatal to the assumption that human rights are moral rights and that they should be given priority in our practical reasoning. For the purposes of this chapter we can simply note that the present menu of international human rights is not perfect, nor would its drafters have expected it to be. The challenges facing the human person change over time and new threats emerge while, at the same time, certain kinds of expressions of the rights (and their qualifications) may well prove to be imperfect. But the foundations upon which they supervene remain the same, the sovereignty of the individual and the agentic (and social, and material) conditions upon which that status depends.

This supports the idea that rather than a having a single underpinning principle, human rights imply several underlying (dignitarian) principles. A univocal idea of human dignity, or a theory of rights on its own, will not be able to unify the field of human rights laws or exhaust their implications for legal or political practice. Certainly human rights law is, more than any other, a body of laws organised under principles. But it is problematic if this is assumed to mean human dignity is a singular notion with a singular formal set of implications. It is human dignity as a *cluster of principles* that is crucial to making human rights law morally necessary and non-positive. This also relates to what is ostensibly a quite different question, namely whether all human rights violations are human dignity violations. The dependence of human rights on human dignity to give them a principled unity seems to entail that all human rights violations violate human dignity, a claim which may appear too strong, especially where human rights 'violations' may include failures regarding the positive responsibilities of states. Such failures of positive responsibilities, while problematic in terms of individuals being able to claim their rights, do not obviously engage human dignity (not all human rights violations 'strike' at the inviolability of the body or the core of the personality). But here, in essence, we find the distinctive aspect of the account just given. When human dignity is detached from our expectations concerning egregious wrongs, protection of the body, and the claiming of a particular dignitarian right by an individual, we are better able to place human dignity discourse in its proper institutional framework. This allows us to say that violations of human rights laws are failures to fulfil demands traceable to the basic status of any and all individuals and their juridical entitlements. Any failings with regard to human rights engage human dignity concerns. But this is not to deny the independence of legal institutions to construct bodies of human rights jurisprudence are sensitive to their social context and social function are not, conversely, neatly contained within the concept of 'human dignity'.

2.6 Status and value

The claims about human dignity's normative core and normative implications made in this chapter have been necessarily general and schematic. Detailed work about their application in institutions and disputes await later chapters. It has been more important to grapple immediately with the philosophical problems that inevitably attend discussion of human dignity, finding the right starting point and drawing some general philosophical conclusions. Amongst those problematic starting points we have had frequent recourse to the problematic appeal to human dignity as a 'value', and for the remainder of this chapter I intend to clarify as far as possible the difference between value and status accounts of human dignity. This inevitably requires attention to the most common reference point regarding human dignity, namely the work of Immanuel Kant. I have relied in this chapter on his work in the 'Doctrine of Right' (half of the *Metaphysics of Morals*) rather than the more commonly used *Groundwork*. Explaining why that should be the case is an important contribution to distinguishing a status account, and it also allows us to situate such an account in our understanding of practical reasoning as a whole.

In the *Groundwork* (1965 [1785]) we find a now famous discussion of human worth or dignity which distinguished humans from components of the world that have variable or market *price*. Kant's remarks are glossed by Ambos:

> [T]hat which cannot be replaced has intrinsic worth or dignity. Accordingly, anything which is a mere means to satisfy wants has value; and that which constitutes the condition under which anything can be an end in itself has dignity. Thus, dignity is intrinsic, deontological and non-negotiable (replaceable), it is the basis of the individuality and the mutual recognition (inter-personal relationship) of the members of a society. Human dignity so understood is a self-sufficient, humanist concept which claims recognition and respect for and among human beings based on their status as persons with common peculiar characteristics (e.g. reason).
>
> (Ambos 2013, 305; references removed)

Ambos, we might note, makes a puzzling though common connection between unconditional value or worth and *possession* by human beings of certain 'characteristics'. It is better to connect the idea of our worth, rather, with the *creation of value*, not as possessors of peculiar characteristics. As Kant himself put it:

> *the law-making which determines all value* must [. . .] have a dignity – that is, an unconditional and incomparable worth – for the appreciation of which, as necessarily given by a rational being, the word 'reverence' is the only becoming expression. Autonomy is therefore the ground of the dignity of human nature and of every rational nature.
>
> (Kant 1965 [1785], 97; emphasis amended)

This is connected for Kant with the Moral Law and the Categorical Imperative. But, again, it is as *source of value* that dignity and the Categorical Imperative are connected:

> Undoubtedly for Kant, given our special worth, we have the status of 'ends in ourselves', i.e. we are never merely means, or elements within the calculation of ends, but are the basis or determinants of ends. Therefore, our status is that of sources of value. [Humans] are not just beings with value but also the sorts of beings that create or construct value to begin with. It is their capacity to give things value that implies they are, more precisely, 'above all value'.
>
> (Lagon and Arend 2014, 11)

It is certainly true that this is connected to Kant's conception of the Moral Law or Categorical Imperative where an individual is an 'end in themselves' or source of ends. As Korsgaard and others have argued (see Denis 2007, 252), value enters this picture as something conferred on the objects of our choice. We are sources of value, and in rational choice of our ends we are endorsing or endowing the objects of our choice with value. Thus the proper location of value in this account is in rational moral action and in the ends that are *chosen as part of rational moral action*. Value is not, conversely, that which inheres in humanity, be this through a species-based or cosmological claim or through there being a special standard 'humanity' that governs all of our other-regarding or self-regarding actions.

Ultimately, then, the Kantian picture of dignity taken from the *Groundwork* is a status one, but only if we attend carefully to primacy of the Moral Law, the capacity of the individual to act upon the Moral Law, and the ability of individuals to be sources of value. If we take dignity-as-a-value to be the core of Kant's claim, then we immediately face problems:

> Kant's thesis that rational agents have a dignity and not a price is often taken to be a thesis about a kind of incommensurability [. . .]. Some have interpreted Kant to be holding simply that respect for rational agents is of infinite value, or that it is to be lexically ordered over the value of anything else. Another thesis in the neighbourhood, however, would be somewhat weaker. It might be that a human life is 'above price' in the sense that killing one to save one is not an acceptable exchange, but that for some positive value of *n*, killing one to save *n* would be an acceptable exchange.
>
> (Shroeder 2017)

Either extreme here would be unacceptable in its own terms and incompatible with the coherence of Kant's work. Giving something 'infinite value' is a poor guide to action; giving 'lexical priority' to respect is far from ascribing unconditional dignity to individuals. Conversely, the idea that human value is merely a *pro tanto* claim that can be defeated in certain circumstances makes no sense of the Categorical Imperative or the remainder of Kant's practical philosophy.

What we gain, conversely, from an emphasis on the Doctrine of Right is precisely an account of basic entitlements in an empirical context where laws have to be made in order to harmonise the wills of individuals whose actions would otherwise clash. Kant did not disown the *Groundwork*. Rather, as I have argued, human dignity recurs in the guise of innate right: not a guide to the Moral Law, but an articulation of basic human status, the essentially juridical nature of the individual in an empirical context. What follows from this is a mixture of natural law and legal positivism. Kant produces a comprehensive account of both public and private law to the extent that both flow rationally from innate right and from the need to harmonise our willing. But he also leaves a great deal of discretion to the law-maker. He also makes the law of the land binding, not through the suspension of the Moral Law but rather because it demands that we leave the state of nature and enter into the civil condition where our, and others', freedom is possible (Kant 1996 [1797], 51–56).

Consequently, the account of human dignity offered in this chapter takes elements from across the Kantian *corpus*, but it clearly makes no attempt to engage in a sustained dialogue on matters of Kantian exegesis as such (for an overview of the relevant contemporary discussions regarding dignity see Sensen 2009).

I have instead used Kant positively in mining the rich discussions around innate right. But I have also intended to register concerns about the intelligibility of using Kant's *Groundwork* specifically, and value conceptions of human dignity more generally.

The work of Jeremy Waldron offers what might appear to be a much more promising *corpus* on which to ground a status conception of human dignity and law. Waldron has an explicitly status-based conception of human dignity at the heart of his work, and he has particular concern with the relationship between human dignity, legality, and the rule of law. Unlike Kant he is concerned with human rights and brings concrete sociological considerations to the theory and practice of human dignity. While I will endorse many aspects of his position (here and elsewhere) I also want to draw attention to an ambiguity that it is important to overcome. For Waldron (setting aside Waldron's genealogy of discourses of dignity, discussed above), human dignity has a distinctive function across our social practices: "Dignity, in my view, is a sort of status-concept: it has to do with the standing (perhaps the formal legal standing or perhaps, more informally, the moral presence) that a person has in a society and in her dealings with others" (2012, 201; footnote removed). Status describes here a correlation between individuals' social position and their participatory opportunities within that society. Regarding its function in law in particular, human dignity appears to have two roles – one interpretative and the other procedural – that maps onto these distinct elements of *social position* and *participatory opportunities.* Human dignity has a clear interpretive function with regard to human rights: "if human dignity is a status, then we should say that it comprises not just a set of human rights, but an underlying idea which explains both the importance of each of these rights in relation to our being human and the importance of their being packaged together in this regard" (2013, 27). This special interpretative role provides the unifying idea or unifying interpretative perspective on human rights, keeping its theory and practice consistent and reflective. But human dignity also has another function in justifying certain kinds of participatory possibilities for individuals within legal systems. This valorises those legal procedures that afford participation for ordinary citizens and enables them to be actors within law (not merely its object). In this sense, 'dignity' joins the other more flexible, non-formal components of law like 'equity' and 'reasonableness'. Human dignity allows the participation of individuals to keep law alert to 'pre-legal' ideas and perceptions that are difficult to systematise but preserve individual difference: "law [. . .] evinces faith in individuals' abilities to think about and proceed with the application of standards without any assurance that any two applications to similar circumstances will yield exactly the same result" (2012, 208). These two ideas entail that 'human dignity as status' has two slightly different complexions within Waldron's work. On the one hand, our status as rational individuals with certain irreducible interests in our own self-determination is operationalised as the entitlement to express our opinions and perspectives (to have standing) within legal proceedings. On the other hand, our status is the unifying idea behind human rights and stands in a dialectical relationship with them: we understand basic human status through consideration of what is protected by human rights, and we understand human rights on the presumption that these rights flow from the fundamental, basic status each individual possesses. The former (procedural) understanding of 'human dignity as status' might be implied by the latter (human rights) one. But the former – the dignity of standing and participation in our social practices – has a rich and relatively autonomous life in Waldron's work, allowing him to synthesise certain aspects of legal positivism and procedural natural law (2012). This means, importantly, that it is not reducible (or not wholly reducible) to human rights. Waldron's procedural naturalism concerns the dignitarian core of the rule of law, and would be expressible in the language of *constitutional* rights or *participatory* rights without any loss of meaning or normative force. It should be clear, then, that there is much to agree with in Waldron's work but that the two pre-eminent problems found in this area of study still have to be overcome: finding a clear distinction between what is constitutive and regulative in human dignity, and finding the proper role of human rights in making that distinction in theory and in practice. From that position I wish to conclude with some much more general comments about human dignity in practical philosophy and practical reason.

Human dignity and the principles it implies cut across the main fields of practical philosophy, normative ethics, and legal and political philosophy. And the isolation of a status concept, in opposition to a value concept, includes aspects of meta-ethics and with it axiology. To generate an account of human rights also requires a theory of agency and practical self-understanding such that freedoms naturally accruing to the individual, and their expression in innate right, can be translated into norms with suitable connection to (generic) agency, (embodied) agency, and (social) agency. While this is clearly far-reaching in terms of what it demands (and rejects) in practical philosophy, it is still not equivalent to the kind of 'unified theory' of practical reason that sometimes arises in connection with human dignity. One of the most recent and prominent examples of such a theory – Dworkin's *Justice for Hedgehogs* (2011) – takes human dignity to be the centrepiece of a comprehensive account of practical philosophy unified by the ongoing interpretive unfolding of human dignity within social practices. Human dignity, for Dworkin, points (in one direction) to the autonomous and authentic choices of individuals and (in the other direction) towards institutional design and rights. The breadth and unity of such an account is impressive. It is not architectonic in the sense of providing neatly scientific bodies of norms, but rather links, at its core, the emergence of an understanding of human dignity with practices respecting both individual needs and the collective good. What is difficult to fully endorse in Dworkin's position is the reducibility of core aspects of all practical reason, including individual virtue, to human dignity. Not only does this leave the precise status of justice unclear – one of the *desiderata* of linking law and human dignity – but I have already registered (in Chapter 1) my rejection of many of the virtue aspects of human dignity and argue we should limit appeal to its virtue components only so far as they speak to the virtues of governance and to respecting others' ability to exercise choice. We will, however, have cause to consider the combination of these two ideas when we consider (Chapter 6) the ways in which rational agency can be limited or bypassed by the state. My response there is not to posit additional dignitarian concerns about authenticity (as Dworkin and others might wish us to put it) but to draw better lines between legitimate governance and paternalism.

Dworkin's position can be compared with that of Neil MacCormick, who adopts a triadic division of principles for personal practical reasoning. These are intended to provide what he considers a "good and clear picture of how a person ought to live" (MacCormick 2008, 107). For present purposes it is striking that this division – obedience, freedom, and engagement – maps relatively neatly onto the division of principles I have associated with human dignity. Thus:

> [The first, obedience principle holds] that there are basic interpersonal duties (which have as their correlatives certain basic interpersonal rights, or fundamental common law rights, we might say) that we must observe. [. . .] [Second] we have freedom in the sense of normative liberty wherever no duty exists or applies. We are free to deliberate among whatever seem to us desirable courses of action, and in a large way we are morally free to construct and periodically revise our own plan of life, just so long as we do not plan to infringe the basic duties. [Third, our freedom] includes freedom to enter into all sorts of commitments with other people – promises, contracts, partnerships, marriages, trustee relationships and so on. [. . .] The principle of engagement delineates a way of exercising moral freedom, notwithstanding the specific limitations of freedom that follow from the undertaking of promissory or contractual obligations.
>
> (MacCormick 2008, 105–107)

While this does not map precisely onto the principles I have elucidated, there is a clear parallel in the movement from strict obligations to the employment and maintenance of freedom to the governance of obligations themselves (both those imposed and those freely chosen). MacCormick commends these to us as the core of practical reason in conjunction with Adam Smith's theory of moral sentiment (being a corrective to the formalistic problems he attributes to Kantian ethics). Be that as it may, the essence of personal practical reasoning is held to be a pattern of obligations similar to that here ascribed to human dignity. For my part, I argue that these principles produce means of reasoning about the legal and political governance of the public realm. Principles of practical reasoning for individuals require, in contrast, a clearer conception of how obligations (self and other, perfect and imperfect) are unified within the possibilities open to individuals in specific contexts.

Is there, then, an architectonic philosophy of human dignity that draws together every aspect of moral, political, and legal reasoning from international law to individual self-regarding duties and personal virtue? And is there a theory of personal practical reasoning underlying a general theory of human dignity, one that can guide action more precisely than the Categorical Imperative? I doubt these possibilities, both because of my rejection of the virtue aspects of human dignity and because of the need for *determinatio* (the translation of principles into judgments). For these reasons human dignity is not a guide to individual virtue, nor is it a theory of moral action intended to produce a Moral Law. Indeed, the idea of a status concept, as an anthropological concept, is meant to capture a dynamic phenomenon in dynamic social systems. If it were a value, then we might expect it to have a more singular meaning, and perhaps a clearer function as a personal virtue. But it is as a conception of status that human dignity should be understood and it must take its place amongst our social and moral ideas, not amongst our virtues.

References

Agamben, G. (2002) *Remnants of Auschwitz: The Witness and the Archive.* New York, Zone Books.

Alexy, R. (2010) *A Theory of Constitutional Rights.* Oxford, Oxford University Press.

Ambos, K. (2013) 'Punishment Without a Sovereign? The *Ius Puniendi* Issue of International Criminal Law' *Oxford Journal of Legal Studies*, 33(2), 293–315.

Arendt, H. (1958) *The Origins of Totalitarianism.* New York, Meridian Books.

Aristotle. (1998) *Politics.* Oxford, Oxford University Press.

Beyleveld, D. (2012) 'The Principle of Generic Consistency as the Supreme Principle of Human Rights' *Human Rights Review*, 13(1), 1–18.

Buchanan, A. (1984) p. 76, emphasis in the original.

Buchanan, A. (1984) 'What's So Special About Rights?' *Social Philosophy and Policy*, 2(1), 61–83.

Buchanan, A. (2010) 'The Egalitarianism of Human Rights' *Ethics*, 120(4), 679–710.

Ci, J. (2013) 'Agency and Other Stakes of Poverty' *Journal of Political Philosophy*, 21(2), 125–150.

Cotterrell, R. (2011) 'Justice, Dignity, Torture, Headscarves: Can Durkheim's Sociology Clarify Legal Values?' *Social and Legal Studies*, 20(1), 3–20.

Cruft, R. (2010) 'On the Non-Instrumental Value of Basic Rights' *Journal of Moral Philosophy*, 7(4), 441–461.

Cruft, R. et al. eds. (2015) *The Philosophical Foundations of Human Rights.* Oxford, Oxford University Press.

Daly, E. (2012) *Dignity Rights: Courts, Constitutions, and the Worth of the Human Person.* Philadelphia, University of Pennsylvania Press.

Darwall, S.L. (2006) *The Second-Person Standpoint: Morality, Respect, and Accountability.* Cambridge, MA, Harvard University Press.

Denis, L. (2007) 'Kant's Formula of the End in Itself: Some Recent Debates' *Philosophy Compass*, 2(2), 244–257.

Dworkin, R. (2011) *Justice for Hedgehogs.* Cambridge, MA, Harvard University Press.

Feinberg, J. (1992) 'The Social Importance of Moral Rights' *Philosophical Perspectives*, 6, 175–198.

Gewirth, A. (1981a) *Reason and Morality.* Chicago, University of Chicago Press.

Gewirth, A. (1981b) 'Are There Any Absolute Rights?' *Philosophical Quarterly*, 31(122), 1–16.

Griffin, J. (2008) *On Human Rights.* Oxford, Oxford University Press.

Hart, H.L.A. (1955) 'Are There any Natural Rights?' *The Philosophical Review*, 64(2), 175–191.

Hart, H.L.A. (1994) *The Concept of Law*, 2nd edition. Oxford, Oxford University Press.
Kamm, F.M. (1992) 'Non-Consequentialism, the Person as an End-in-Itself, and the Significance of Status' *Philosophy and Public Affairs*, 21(4), 354–389.
Kant, I. (1965 [1785]) *The Moral Law: Kant's Groundwork of the Metaphysic of Morals*. London, Hutchinson University Library.
Kant, I. (1996 [1797]) *The Metaphysics of Morals*, translated by M. Gregor. Cambridge, Cambridge University.
Kateb, G. (2011) *Human Dignity*. Cambridge, MA, Harvard University Press.
Lagon, M.P. and Arend, A.C. (2014) *Human Dignity and the Future of Global Institutions*. Washington, DC, Georgetown University Press.
Lebech, M. (2009) *On the Problem of Human Dignity: A Hermeneutical and Phenomenological Investigation*. Germany, Königshausen and Neumann.
Lee, P. and George, R.P. (2008) 'The Nature and Basis of Human Dignity' *Ratio Juris*, 21(2), 173–193.
Levi, P. (1987) *"If This Is a Man" and "The Truce"*. London, Abacus Books.
Locke, J. (1967 [1690]) *Two Treatises of Government*. Cambridge, Cambridge University Press.
Luhmann, N. (2008) *Law as a Social System*. Oxford, Oxford University Press.
MacCormick, N. (2008) *Practical Reason in Law and Morality*. Oxford, Oxford University Press.
MacKinnon, C. (1987) *Feminism Unmodified: Discourses on Life and Law*. Cambridge, MA, Harvard University Press.
Maine, H.S. (1939) *Ancient Law: Its Connection with the Early History of Society and Its Relation to Modern Ideas*. Oxford, Oxford University Press.
Margalit, A. (2011) 'Human Dignity Between Kitsch and Deification' in Cordner, C. and Gaita, R. eds., *Philosophy, Ethics and a Common Humanity: Essays in Honour of Raimond Gaita*. London, Routledge, 106–120.
Maritain, J. (1946) 'The Person and the Common Good' *The Review of Politics*, 8(4), 419–455.
Marx, K. (1977) *Critique of Hegel's Philosophy of Right*. Cambridge, Cambridge University Press.
Murphy, J.G. (1970) *Kant: The Philosophy of Right*. London, Palgrave Macmillan.
Nagel, T. (1995) 'Personal Rights and Public Space' *Philosophy and Public Affairs*, 24(2), 83–107.
Nickel, J.W. (2008) 'Rethinking Indivisibility: Towards a Theory of Supporting Relations Between Human Rights' *Human Rights Quarterly*, 30(4), 984–1001.
Nussbaum, M.C. (2009) *Frontiers of Justice: Disability, Nationality, Species Membership*. Cambridge, MA, Harvard University Press.
O'Mahony, C. (2012) 'There is No Such Thing as a Right to Dignity' *International Journal of Constitutional Law*, 10(2), 551–574.
Rawls, J. (2005) *Political Liberalism*. New York, Columbia University Press.
Raz, J. (1986) *The Morality of Freedom*. Oxford, Clarendon Press.
Ripstein, A. (2009) *Force and Freedom: Kant's Legal and Political Philosophy*. Cambridge, Cambridge University Press.
Rosen, M. (2012) *Dignity: Its History and Meaning*. Cambridge, MA, Harvard University Press.
Schroeder, M. (2017) 'Value Theory' in Zalta, E.N. ed., *The Stanford Encyclopedia of Philosophy* (Fall 2016 Edition), Available at: https://plato.stanford.edu/archives/fall2016/entries/value-theory/, accessed March 2017.

Sensen, O. (2009) 'Kant's Conception of Human Dignity' *Kant-studien*, 100(3), 309–331.

Shue, H. (1996) *Basic Rights: Subsistence, Affluence, and US Foreign Policy*. Princeton, Princeton University Press.

Statman, D. (2000) 'Humiliation, Dignity and Self-Respect' *Philosophical Psychology*, 13(4), 523–540.

Tasioulas, J. (2013) 'Human Dignity and the Foundations of Human Rights' in McCrudden, C. ed., *Understanding Human Dignity*. Oxford, Oxford University Press.

Tuck, R. (2001) *The Rights of War and Peace: Political Thought and the International Order From Grotius to Kant*. Oxford, Oxford University Press.

Waldron, J. (2007) 'Dignity and Rank' *European Journal of Sociology*, 48(2), 201–237.

Waldron, J. (2012) 'How Law Protects Dignity' *The Cambridge Law Journal*, 71(1), 200–222.

Waldron, J. (2013) 'Is Dignity the Foundation of Human Rights?' January 3, 2013. NYU School of Law, Public Law Research Paper No. 12–73, Available at: https://ssrn.com/abstract=2196074, accessed March 2017.

Weinrib, J. (2014) 'Permissive Laws and the Dynamism of Kantian Justice' *Law and Philosophy*, 33(1), 105–136.

Weinrib, J. (2016) *Dimensions of Dignity: The Theory and Practice of Modern Constitutional Law*. Cambridge, Cambridge University Press.

3 Human dignity, justice, and institutions

1 The principle of equality before the law requires that what are equal are to be treated equally and what are different are to be treated differently. The question arises: what is equal and what is different.
2 All human beings, notwithstanding the differences in their appearance and other minor points, are equal in their dignity as persons. Accordingly, from the point of view of human rights and fundamental freedoms, they must be treated equally.
3 The principle of equality does not mean absolute equality, but recognizes relative equality, namely different treatment proportionate to concrete individual circumstances. Different treatment must not be given arbitrarily; it requires reasonableness, or must be in conformity with justice [. . .].

—(*South-West Africa Cases* [1966] Judge Tanaka Dissent)

Introduction

The idea that justice is related to, but normatively distinct from, human dignity can be found expressed in three different but related propositions: that human dignity needs law but law does not need human dignity; that law is not a sufficient condition of human dignity; and that law is a necessary condition of human dignity. The first expresses concern (anticipated in Chapter 1) that although there is an important relationship between positive law and human dignity, human dignity itself suffers from regulative redundancy. There are, in other words, plenty of good reasons why 'human dignity' should not form part of the fabric of positive law. The other two propositions indicate more formally the idea that we need law to accomplish human dignity, but that the existence of law does not exhaust the demands of human dignity. This chapter seeks to clarify these propositions with sustained analysis of justice, law, and the institutional implications of human dignity.

The social and institutional implications of human dignity take three forms. First, as a justification for moral cosmopolitanism, human dignity concerns preserving the conditions of human agency, human plurality, and the juridical entitlements of all individuals. We have to understand how these individual-focussed and universal claims interact with the institutional forces of conventional state-based law and politics.

Second, as the grounding of a morality of governance, human dignity should be constitutive of our social systems and normative orders such that they are governed in a way consistent with human status. We have to understand how the very general dignitarian principles interact with the existing architectures of our political and legal systems.

Third, as a defence of maintaining the human condition itself, human dignity should be thought to contain substantive demands concerning the continued survival of humanity, protection of plurality within humanity, and protection of an open future for humanity. We have to understand how far these assumptions cohere with the connections already assumed by contemporary political philosophy to exist between human dignity and justice.

These ideas are linked to certain positions in the natural law and natural rights traditions, and it is also important to begin to draw a more precise, and critical, set of links between human dignity and this tradition. First, we need to contrast conventional justice with the ideas of natural right and natural justice. Second, we need to make use of the *lex permissiva*, i.e. the creation, via the prohibitions and commands of natural law, of a large space of permitted positive law. This is an important, but not uncontested, aspect of traditional natural law discourse; it is important to consider to what extent the natural law position itself distinguished human dignity from justice and whether a strict dividing line can and should be drawn. Third, it is useful to consider the idea of the 'human condition', which is distinguished here from appeal to either 'human nature' or the 'circumstances of justice'. The latter is a certain set of presumptions about human sociality and material constraints used for theoretical purposes within the contractarian tradition. We need to seek far greater clarity on how the individual, the collective, and the environment interact to link individuals to institutions while avoiding some of the persistent problems arising from the contractarian tradition. Fourth, while invocation of the idea of cosmopolitanism is inevitable in the context of a status-based account of human dignity, very different kinds of cosmopolitanism have arisen from different parts of the natural law tradition. Our concern here will simply be to begin to delineate how human dignity and cosmopolitanism should be connected. Cosmopolitanism, where it has specific critical implications for international law, is discussed in Chapter 4.

Chapter 3 moves from the idea of justice to the human condition, then from democratic institutions to a concern with the future. It concludes with a more general summary of human dignity's cosmopolitan and governmental implications. The logic of the chapter is to move from an over-arching concern with the conceptual difference between human dignity and justice, to a more specific account of what human dignity means for 'humanity' taken as a whole (the human condition). Only then will we be in a position to consider the justification of, and limits on, democratic institutions and the conditions of their sustainability.

First, however, we must return to the dignitarian principles to begin to flesh out how it is that human dignity already has social and institutional implications. In the previous chapter we treated these principles as the core *normative implications* of human dignity; here they are put into practice to determine what can be called the *institutional implications* of human dignity.

3.1 The institutional implications of human dignity

Dignitarian principles, as interstitial principles, speak to the connections between, and harmonisation of, our obligations. They concern the practices that are necessary for us to meet those obligations individually and collectively. This is not to say that human dignity provides comprehensive guidance on institutional design. It invites us to identify (negatively) how individuals might have been excluded or obscured within our practices. These principles demand (positively) a notion of how our practices, institutions, and the *human condition* interact. Human dignity should provide basic normative guidance on any and all human practices and institutions – labour, work in the public and private spheres, political action – attending to these not as rigid social conditions but as dynamic forces that sustain but also threaten individual lives. Before we reach those conclusions, however, it is necessary to return to the principles that flow from innate right or natural sovereign equality.

The 'obligations principle' concerns the interaction of our normative orders (broadly, the legal, the moral, and the political). These are not discrete and neatly distinguishable sources of obligation. Nor are they indistinct. We can for the most part distinguish the aspects of politics focussed on the public good from the more individuating obligations of law and morality. Law has a mediating function, synthesising individual and collective interests within institutions which are partially (but not wholly) insulated from the moral and the political. Morality ranges from other-regarding to self-regarding obligations; the latter should not be the concern of law, but other-regarding obligations inevitably form part of our political and legal obligations (and vice versa). These are, then, different normative orders within which different forms of practical reasoning are necessary. They are, nonetheless, all species of practical reasoning, they are all (at points) unified by our discourses of 'justice', and they never function in complete isolation from one another.

What then does human dignity bring to their ordering? Like justice, human dignity connects them and allows them to be mutually critical. However, human dignity is *not* a demand for justice insofar as justice encompasses demanding individual virtues, demanding remedies for wrongs, or demanding egalitarian distribution of goods. These discourses of justice are generated by other kinds of moral, legal, and political thinking. What is more characteristic of discourses of human dignity is the proper governance of these normative orders such that individuals are protected *regardless* of the moral, political, or legal obligations they are placed under or have placed themselves under. Where human dignity is treated as a broad principle of governance, it concerns human status regardless of the specific obligations generated by our different normative orders.

If the obligations principle concerns the ways we need to integrate our normative orders, the 'permissive principle' concerns the way we govern our social systems. The permissive principle could be thought to include at least three aspects concerning what might be termed natural, social, and moral liberties: the preservation of natural liberties, those permissions that arise from a shared planet containing unowned natural resources; the preservation of social liberties, those permissions that come from the silence of law, which seek to minimise the burden of the law, and which resist the 'colonisation of the human life-world' (see Chapter 6); and the preservation of moral liberty, those permissions that come from the public-private divide, strong permissions legally limiting the power of the state and public actors. The permissive principle therefore entails, *inter alia*, resisting the erosion of natural liberties through environmental degradation, not eroding social liberties by excessive technocratic governance or privatisation, and not eroding moral liberties through technological intrusion into the private sphere. We could explicate and defend these ideas through the conventional discourses of liberty, freedom, and democracy, but in positing a more primordial relationship between the human condition and permission (or reclaiming a relationship identified by the natural law tradition), we will be less beholden to the traditions of political philosophy in the consequences that we draw.

The 'sovereignty principle' concerns the juridical entitlements, self-constitution, and self-understanding of the human person. The natural sovereign equality (or innate right) of the human person implies both juridical equality and physical vulnerability. Human rights turn these generic ideas into claim rights holding between individuals and between individuals and the state. Their scope is limited by their relating to the human person and therefore core physical and juridical aspects of humanity. They do not distribute substantive entitlements. These are nonetheless dynamic claims, responsive to threats to the human person whether it be through loss of legal personality (migration, displacement) or through novel challenges to juridical equality within technologically sophisticated societies (surveillance, online retention, and exposure of private data). So, the sovereignty principle entails human rights laws which are dynamic and institutionally distinctive expressions of our core entitlements as individuals. But they are never 'merely' legal rights. They are moral rights *and* they have political implications.

3.2 The limits of justice

With these more distinctive functions for human dignity in our normative orders outlined (and awaiting further application in the chapters that follow), we can return again to why and how human dignity is distinguishable from justice. On the one hand, to the extent that our normative orders are inevitably conjoined, justice is the language with which we normally express such connections. On the other hand, justice is associated with the *dislocation* of our normative orders such that political and legal systems and institutions can maintain a usefully antagonistic relationship with one another. To the extent that justice is the 'first virtue of social institutions' (Rawls 1999, 3) it implies a certain unity in the underlying justification of our institutions, but it does not mean a simple unity of purpose *amongst* our many institutions.

'Justice', I will stipulate for present purposes, denotes procedures, transactions, and judgements that maintain equality and that provide redress or desert. My question is, How can this be understood in contradistinction to human dignity? Specifically, How might it be that these are procedures, transactions, and judgements *required by, but normatively distinct from*, human dignity? This requires us to take into account a number of distinct but overlapping ideas. First, that while there cannot be human dignity without justice, human dignity does not provide the *substantive* content of justice, i.e. it does not give us a single property or good that should be the object of redress or desert. Second, to the extent that human dignity implies entitlements related to rights and equality, some kinds of legal redress or legal correction on the basis of human dignity is intelligible, but more importantly it demands *processes* built upon our basic juridical entitlements. Third, human dignity, even as we find it imperfectly realised in the jurisprudence of the late twentieth century, reflects an effort to articulate the legitimate limits of positive law and political power, meaning human dignity has come to entail negation of the kinds of injustice characteristic of the abuse of state power. It is that common anti-consequentialist, or anti-utilitarian, function of human dignity which will provide our starting point.

A typical reconstruction of human rights law would point to limits of the state's power vis-à-vis the individual. Human rights protect the individual from states whose actions, while justified by the common good, are contrary to individuals' rights. Individuals' basic status is held to be unconditioned by the needs of the state and the common good, albeit the entitlements which flow from this are typically divided into two classes: unconditioned entitlements (usually rights against egregious abuse) and conditioned entitlements. The latter are where the state can condition the enjoyment of an entitlement provided that such conditioning serves defensible democratic ends and is done in such a way as to be lawful and proportionate (Tsakyrakis 2009). This way of articulating the legal-moral relationship between state and individual gives rise to a common understanding of human dignity, expressed most systematically by Griffin (2008), that human dignity and the rights that flow from it are a class of special rights that are nonetheless subject to normal standards and procedures of legal justice. They are, to be sure, generally anti-consequentialist in their implication and protective of individuals' normative agency (vital forms of agency related to self-constitution and basic other-regarding duties). They are, nevertheless, circumscribed by being embedded in a legal system with its institutionalised patterns of reasoning. Human dignity is certainly anti-utilitarian on this model, but within the limits of *law's own anti-utilitarianism*, that is, law's special responsibility to *synthesise* the demands of individual and collective.

This conceptualisation of the relationship between human dignity and anti-utilitarianism via legal morality is found with different inflections in Dworkin (1985, 1986) and Waldron's (2011, 2012) work. For Waldron,

> Dignity is the status of a person predicated on the fact that she is recognised as having the ability to control and regulate her actions in accordance with

> her own apprehension of norms and reasons that apply to her; it assumes she is capable of giving and entitled to give an account of herself (and of the way in which she is regulating her actions and organising her life), an account that others are to pay attention to; and it means finally that she has the wherewithal to demand that her agency and her presence among us as a human being be taken seriously and accommodated in the lives of others, in others' attitudes and actions towards her, and in social life generally.
>
> (Waldron 2012, 202)

The rule of law itself is understood by Waldron (2011) as demanding these participatory possibilities. In these ways individuals are not instrumentalised or objectified within our processes; they are respected by the processes. And there is connection between egregious wrong-doing and human dignity that calls for absolute limits of the powers of the state (Waldron 2012). But we thereby reassert the importance of law and legal institutions as a block on the dangers of the political. We are missing, therefore, a clearly worked-out account of the source of the anti-consequentialism associated with human dignity and missing an account of if and how that might have institutional consequences beyond our common and prevalent defences of the rule of law and the separation of powers (important though these might be).

The anti-consequentialism flowing from human dignity is neither merely resistance to gross instrumentalisation of individuals nor is it a simple block on the activities of the state. It should be associated with rational or natural limits on power. There are at least three ways in which human dignity might draw limits to the application of consequentialism. First, human dignity, and the status principles it implies, do not simply trump a certain class of actions but rather demands re-orientating or re-founding our conception of obligation on the core juridical entitlements of the individual. Those entitlements are not inconsistent with the use of consequentialism; rather, they inhabit a different and prior area of the concern, namely each individual, as a human person, and the juridical necessity that this implies. Second, human rights law is indeed a system of laws, unified by the sovereignty principle, which sits apart from other aspects of a legal system and in that position tends to be the area of law most likely to concern limitations on the state on the basis of individual entitlements. The evolution of coherent bodies of human rights jurisprudence amounts to a systematic but unfinished account of how the power of the state must be constrained. The ongoing evolution of human rights law has, for example, expanded 'horizontally' to relationships between individuals and to the positive responsibilities of the state (Pattinson and Beyleveld 2002). These are principled extensions of human rights law, but they cannot be explained merely by insisting that human dignity is simply opposed to consequentialism or the untrammelled power of the state. Third, and finally, it is true that human dignity itself is explicitly engaged in legal systems relatively rarely. But the reason for this often misleading. It is not because human dignity is attached to core rights that are only rarely engaged because of their egregious nature, but rather because in the normal functioning of a legal system, the demands implied by human dignity are articulable in other terms. It is only in crises – the denial of human rights law altogether, the denial of basic civil liberties, the creation of subordinate groups – that human dignity and the interstitial principles it implies find their proper place in our reasoning. Griffin and others wish to explain this in terms of human dignity being engaged when a certain threshold of violation has been reached. I, in contrast, want to suggest that it is under *qualitatively* distinct circumstances that human dignity is properly engaged. Griffin's assimilation of human dignity to legal justice glosses over the qualitative difference that exists between human dignity as giving rise to *rational* or *natural* principles flowing from the status of the individual and (in contrast) the *formal* and *institutional* but not necessarily rational content of legal justice.

This distinction between the rational demands of human dignity and the formal demands of law point to a crucial distinction. From the perspective of human dignity, as I have outlined it, justice is rightly understood as 'artificial' rather than 'natural'. Justice arises from our practices, not from the immediate dictates of reason, and thus (Hume (1978 [1739]) can be expressed as artificial, not natural, obligation. Such artifice relates to an admissible variation in the content of our entitlements. In contrast, and on the basis of the reconstruction of the previous chapter, human dignity must be prior to justice at least in the sense of governing social practices and normative orders so that they sustain human dignity, and governing the production of norms within those practices and orders so that they do not compromise human dignity in their interaction. Justice, too, governs social practices and normative orders, and it governs the production of norms. But these are social and political norms reflective of their historical and social origins, and they are governed by formal and institutional reasoning, not the determination of judgments from general principles.

The 'artificial' virtue of justice also signals that '*corrective* justice' cannot be isolated in a pure, general, and pre-political form and is always determined by its social and political context. The entitlements flowing from corrective justice rely upon conventional decisions about which wrongs will be the concern of the courts and which types of contracts will be enforced. To be sure, the capacity to enter into contracts is implied by human dignity, and the moral background of a contract is the presumption of an equal entitlement to enter into contract. Moreover, that background presumes equal susceptibility to wrongs by others – not merely the basic wrongs of violation of our individual sovereignty through violation of human rights, but the entitlement to claim remedy against *any wrong that others also have a right to a claim against*. But this is not the same as arguing for the direct application of human dignity within corrective justice or private law as it stands in contemporary legal systems. The implications of this lie in our conception of contract, property, and wrongs, and more will be said about them below.

'*Natural* justice' is markedly different in this respect. Especially where this is conceptualised as a cluster of core natural rights (as in Hobbes 1991 [1651]) the discourse of natural justice is precisely an assertion of the inalienable juridical entitlements of the individual. While it would be easy to overstate the connections between Hobbes's short list of natural rights and Kant's concern with innate right, there is nevertheless (even within the collectivising implications of Hobbes's political vision) a preservation of those rights naturally possessed by individuals. Justice *in general* is, for Hobbes, defined by the conventions – the enforcement of socially determined obligations – established by the sovereign, and we should endorse this division between conventional justice and natural justice. Nevertheless, specificity is needed to divide natural justice as a formal demand (for instance, 'no-one being a judge in their own case'), from substantive demands relating to natural liberties, from (in turn) individual rights and remedies concerning basic wrongs. Each has a claim to be related to human dignity, but each (in my terms) sits under a different dignitarian principle (the obligations, permissive, and sovereignty principles respectively).

The definition of justice by way of contrast with human dignity means treating justice as not only artificial but as a system of *permissible* laws relative to human dignity itself. Thus, a system of laws can and should contain a range of rules with the normal deontic forces we would expect: some command, some prohibit, and some permit. But those rules as a whole take their meaning from the constitutive commitment to human dignity which *demands the existence of law but also implies permissible variation between systems.* The idea of a *lex permissiva* – that set of rules which are demanded but whose contents are variable – is arguably one of the key components of the natural law tradition. For Tierney (2014) the natural tradition was defined more by the space of permissible in variation in positive law it created than the commands and prohibitions that are usually associated with natural law. This usefully characterises much of the early modern tradition, and indeed for Tierney there is much in Aquinas's work that makes an effort to carve out that area of competence for states that admits of variation and contestation (2014, 69f). Kant's work also makes use of the *lex permissiva* idea (see Flikshuh 2000; Weinrib 2014). It must be read in the context of the structure of the 'Doctrine of Right'. Kant himself said this:

> An action that is neither commanded nor prohibited is merely permitted, since there is no law limiting one's freedom (one's authorization) with regard to it and so too no duty. Such an action is called morally indifferent [. . .]. The question can be raised whether there are such actions and, if there are, whether there must be permissive laws (lex permissiva), in addition to laws that command and prohibit [. . .], in order to account for someone's being free to do or not to do something as he pleases. If so, the authorization would not always [. . .] have to do with an indifferent action [. . .]; for, considering the action in terms of moral laws, no special law would be required for it.
>
> (Kant 1996 [1797], 16)

A formal distinction is drawn here between what we now call weak and strong permissions: weak permissions being the absence of law concerning a particular action, and a strong permission being explicit permission in law (see Raz 1979).

But what emerges from Kant's doctrine is a more fulsome defence of permissions (freedom to act, freedom to create private property) and also a defence of legal positivism, i.e. a defence of the discretion of law makers to generate norms, under the general aegis of the *lex permissiva* but not directly determined by rational or natural laws. This does not, note, amount to legal positivism: "One can therefore conceive of external lawgiving which would contain only positive laws; but then a natural law would still have to precede it, which would establish the authority of the lawgiver" (Kant 1996 [1797], 17). Taking this natural conception of *lex permissiva* as the proper foundation for understanding legal justice means, then, that human dignity inhabits a similar position to justice as a first virtue of social institutions; there is no doubt that these are both normative ideas at the foundation of our social and institutional practices. Nevertheless, it is within the general boundaries of *lex permissiva* that justice functions. And this placing justice within the wide, reasonably variable practices of societies and forms of government is supported by the fact that 'justice' is now seen as a kind of common denominator or family resemblance concept but without any absolute and definable essence. (The lack of absolute or invariable meaning to 'justice' is already anticipated in Aristotle's analysis of justice; see Heyman 1991). Human dignity, in contrast, is not part of the *lex permissiva.* It is in the governance of social systems and normative orders that human dignity takes its meaning.

This begins to articulate a crucial division between constitutive and regulative meanings. Realising human dignity in a *constitutive* form in social systems and normative orders requires governing them in a permissive and obligation-harmonising way, consistent with the status of individuals. This diverges significantly from the prevalent understanding of human dignity and justice where human dignity is conditioned by the normative structures, and institutional independence, of law. In contrast, I consider the scope, and focal application of, human dignity to be found in problems that transcend even the scope of human rights law, namely collective interstitial problems requiring interstitial principles. Given, then, that our concerns necessarily insist on a conception of obligation prior to the separation of our political, moral, and legal practices, we need to consider how human dignity and justice should work together in practice but without assuming (in the first instance) that this is a question of political morality, separated institutional powers, or the division of distributive and corrective obligations found in the modern state. We turn, then, to a different perspective on the linkage between social being, human dignity, and justice.

3.3 The human condition

Concern with the human condition serves a number of functions. Its preservation is amongst the primary institutional implications of human dignity. It serves to provide a conception of the political elements of justice, displacing the cruder theoretical assumptions that sometimes are articulated as the 'circumstances of justice'. It provides an approach to the wider debates in political philosophy within which human dignity may be claimed. And it also offers reasons why democratic institutions may be necessary to maintain human dignity. In the final analysis, I will use the human condition to fill out the broad categories of law, morality, and politics that we have until now used relatively loosely.

Conventionally, the need for justice arises from social existence and the distributions and corrections necessary to maintain the benefits and burdens of social existence. This Aristotelian vision connects justice with the entitlements owed to political equals within a *polis* (Aristotle 1998). The precise determinations of justice will vary between polities. Those various determinations depend upon decisions made by a populace but also the physical and environmental context in which the polity exists. This is a wider set of concerns than those associated with the 'circumstances of justice', those circumstances being formal assumptions about human nature, human sociability (and its limits), and about the physical environment (Hume 1978 [1739]; Rawls 2005). For Rawls, "the circumstances of justice may be described as the normal conditions under which human cooperation is both possible and necessary" (Rawls 1999, 22). They are (subjective) limitations of compassion, imagination, and intellect. They are (objective) limitations of scarcity, interaction, and luck.

Reclaiming certain aspects of the Aristotelian tradition, Arendt's exploration of the human condition is a way of articulating certain primordial assumptions about human coexistence – our physical, agentic, and environmental 'being' – without resort to fictions about the state of nature or thin theoretical assumptions like the circumstances of justice (Arendt 1958). Justice takes its force and meaning not from simple theoretical assumptions about humanity and its natural context, but the individual, physical, temporal aspects of human activity. This encompasses the perpetual need for labour; division between the public and private realms; and temporal constraints on human action understood as combining human will (the decision to change the future) and natality (the possibility of new beginnings). The human condition, then, can be thought to encompass several ideas not captured in the contractarian tradition and which usefully problematise the idea that justice, alone, is the 'first virtue' of social institutions. It concerns plurality amongst humans as an end in itself, environmental concerns, a public-private divide, and the proper dynamics of the public sphere.

A first important element concerns action and plurality. Human action and agency are conditioned by specific temporal conditions. No action can change the past, and no promise can wholly guarantee an occurrence in the future. But we can punish, forgive, and make promises, all of which are actions by which humans can (morally, legally, and politically) change the past and future through making commitments and changing shared meanings. Action is also individuating. 'Action' (unlike work and labour) allows us to be revealed as individuals; 'action' is not a dormant set of agentic capacities but rather individuals' distinctive interventions in the public sphere. Thus action is inseparably connected to equality and plurality:

> If men were not equal, they could neither understand each other and those who came before them nor plan for the future and foresee the needs of

> those who will come after them. If men were not distinct, each human being distinguished from any other who is, was, or will ever be, they would need neither speech nor action to make themselves understood. Signs and sounds to communicate immediate, identical needs and wants would be enough.
>
> (Arendt 1958, 175–176)

The connection between human plurality and a basic aspect of the human condition – as basic as survival itself – has implications for Arendt's conception of politics. This is not politics as levelling or unifying, but as preserving innate equality and sustaining plurality. Put starkly, the dividing line between human and inhuman politics lies in whether or not it sustains human plurality and (by extension) whether it sustains a strong public sphere where human speech and therefore human plurality can be realised. This puts a certain kind of pressure not only on clearly immoral political or totalitarian systems but on liberal political models that have been charged with negating difference and plurality. One response to this would be to think in terms of whether a social system supports the interstitial concerns we have associated with human dignity. Can individuals move between public and private, between different social spheres, and have harmonised obligations under different normative orders? It is those systems, systems capable of maintaining the social and normative mobility or plurality, that we should be concerned with defending if we adopt human dignity as a core normative orientation. And, in most instances, liberal political philosophies will be better at articulating and protecting that plurality (and, as such, should not be censured from an Arendtian perspective, although they might face other kinds of Arendtian criticism; see Benhabib 2013).

Secondly, while the idiosyncrasy of Arendt's understanding of action has faced criticism as too focussed on action in the public sphere (see Pitkin 1972) she rightly places emphasis on the relationship between agency and politics and the possibility of choice, change, and deliberation in politics. Politics is not an organic phenomenon, nor architectural or utopian planning, nor spearheaded by world-historical figures, but it is fundamentally characterised by the capacity to make new beginnings ('natality'). Constitutions have an important role to play in this respect as forward-looking commitments to future generations and a promise to shape the future in a particular way (an idea we will return to in the context of sustainability): "The remedy for unpredictability, for the chaotic uncertainty of the future, is contained in the faculty to make and keep promises. [This, again, depends upon plurality, for] no one can feel bound by a promise made only to himself" (Arendt 1958, 237). I would argue this has a very distinctive significance in the context of human dignity where human dignity has typically symbolised a backwards-looking rejection of the past by previously criminal states. Abusive states adopt new constitutions, and with it new commitment to human dignity, as part of the pursuit of a 'new beginning'. Such new beginning, for Arendt, is a distinctive display of genuine politics. But societies cannot be defined by what they are opposed to, and Arendt encourages us to reject the backwards-looking 'never again' in favour of constructive future-orientated politics.

Third, the human condition and the politics that flows from it must involve a public-private divide. Such a divide is not incidental to our conception of society (arguably a legacy, in Western societies, of separation of church and state) but essential for agency.

> In order to understand the danger to human existence from the elimination of the private realm, for which the intimate is not a very reliable substitute, it may be best to consider those non-privative traits of privacy which are older than, and independent of, the discovery of intimacy. [First] our private possessions, which we use and consume daily, are much more urgently needed than any part of the common world. [The second] is that the four walls of one's private property offer the only reliable hiding place from the common public world, not only from everything that goes on in it but also from its very publicity, from being seen and being heard. A life spent entirely in public, in the presence of others, becomes, as we would say, shallow.
>
> (Arendt 1958, 70–71)

While the public-private divide can be understood dialectically – the one has to be understood as privation of the other – there is an essential relationship between the private realm and the self-constitution of the individual. While conceding the dangers of insulating the private sphere from public scrutiny in some cases, the existence of a private sphere is rightly defended as essential to human identity and not a historical accident nor something to be superseded in a future, more just, society with a non-antagonistic public sphere (see Chapter 6).

Fourth and finally, the human condition is also concerned with the human relationship with the environment and what is potentially irreversible in our relationship with it. The 'circumstances of justice' (theoretical, empirical, make-weights in theorising) have demanded assumption of 'moderate scarcity' and therewith competition for resources and concern with the relative merits of public or private governance of resources (for a critical overview, see Tasioulas 2002). Arendt's work on the human condition marks the beginning of environmental philosophy with a concern that the earth itself which, from the twentieth century onwards, has become irreversibly influenced by human activity and human science. Arendt anticipates our own concern with the Anthropocene as the era in which human activity is single most important determinant of the planet's climate. In comparison, the assumption of 'relative scarcity' and a moderately hostile environment have been shown to be dangerously short-sighted and reckless given the fragility of the environment. This relates to each of the themes already outlined. Climate change renders groups unsupportable and 'surplus' or mobile and 'unwanted' (Open Democracy 2016a, 2016b). Climate change negates the possibility of new beginnings and locks in certain kinds of futures. And technological change along with certain kinds of environmental change are challenging the balance between public and private such that a private sphere cannot be properly sustained any longer. That is, the economics of climate is connected to social and political trends deleterious to the public-private divide: the privatisation of profit and movement of risk into the public sphere. A concern with the human condition should shift our conception of the lived and natural environment away from resources and towards a dialectical understanding of how the structure of human affairs influences the natural world and vice versa.

Human dignity takes its function and place within these agentic, plural, and environmental conditions. In dignitarian scholarship there have been attempts to interrogate and move beyond the artificial assumptions of the circumstances of justice. This has involved materialism (in the leftist tradition), attention to human vulnerability (in the liberal tradition), or the absence of barriers to individual action (in libertarian positions). The normative implications of human dignity as I have outlined them represent principles sitting between, and making coherent, any moral, legal, or political arrangements that arise within a particular group. But they also mean protecting human status through maintaining the stability and sustainability of the human condition itself. This means maintaining the conditions of agency, plurality, and the environment. These are not, from the point of view of the human condition, different ideas but rather inseparable aspects of the same condition of humanity. Without protecting choice and agency there can be no plurality; preservation of plurality conserves the conditions of agency for diverse groups; environmental sustainability preserves both.

Focus on Arendt's work also supports a critical position towards the understandings of justice found in the various political philosophies making a claim to a dignitarian focus. Crudely, the libertarian position has given especial attention to corrective justice (i.e. justice being driven by individual claims against other individuals particularly regarding rightful possession) while the Marxist tradition has given especial attention to distributive justice. In the latter case, human dignity has been associated with a narrow set of basic material goods – food, shelter, and clothing – as sufficient conditions of human dignity (see Buchanan 2010, 690–691, for analytical comparison of autonomy-based and material-based readings of human dignity). The problem, however, is the now familiar collapse of human dignity's critical potential. These demands are direct and, where such goods are being denied, morally forceful. But the constitutive is absent here, unless human dignity is, rather more ambitiously, equated with a *telos* for a just society. This can be it through a (Marxist) vision of justice (Bloch 1987). Or through understanding liberalism's core commitment to be perpetual resistance to and overcoming of the many forms of degradation and vulnerability (Shklar 1964). Regarding the latter, the idea of human vulnerability has taken on a priority of its own in certain kinds of liberal political theory, and some scholarship (indeed, explicitly dignitarian scholarship) makes human limitations and human vulnerabilities part of the core of their theories of obligation (e.g. Fineman 2008). Arendt encourages us to reject these positions, not because they are reformist or liberal, but because they are too little cognisant of the importance of human plurality (e.g. Bloch) and too concerned with the backwards-looking commitment to avoiding injustice and thus too little concerned with human action as constructive future-orientated action (e.g. Shklar).

By this route, through the work of Arendt, we find ourselves with a broad defence of liberal institutions (including the public-private divide) and democracy. We have a substantive commitment to plurality as an end in itself and an essential gauge of legitimacy. We are encouraged to adopt a productive, not reactive, conception of human dignity. And we are presented with a (broadly anthropocentric) defence of sustainability (see Grear 2011 for a kindred position). However, we reach that point having avoided reliance on generalisation about human nature, reliance on simplifying assumptions about the circumstances of justice, or assumption *a priori* of the moral defensibility of liberal political philosophy. Equally, we should reject the assumption that the actual and theoretical models of liberal democracy found in the twentieth century are automatically defensible, not least because they are not sustainable. They have systematically failed to consider the wider physical (climatic and resource) context that should constitute the horizon of our theorising (Mulgan 2011).

Aside from the specific *desiderata* that Arendt provides us with for theorising about justice, her work provides an opportunity to reflect on the broad categories that I have until now been using quite loosely. Our normative orders of 'law', 'morality', and 'politics' are sufficiently distinct in our language, and in practical philosophy, to serve as rough categories. But more precision is needed because of their importance in distinguishing justice and human dignity and because the dignitarian principles link these categories in a variety of ways.

The most important place to start, for Arendt, is the *political* in its distinctive relationship with the human condition. Action requires a public space in which participation is possible and collective judgments can be made. The latter points to the central importance of free expression. This is traditionally, and rightly, protected by human rights law subject to certain conditions compatible with the preservation of other rights. Arendt's position lends itself to defending the right and its partial qualification because harm is done to judgement when propaganda or oppression close down the possibilities for public expression (Arendt 1967, 470–471) and because the preservation of the marketplace of ideas is consistent with individuals protecting their reputation or being protected from hate. As importantly, Arendt's concerns with action, plurality, and the shaping of the polity in public political practices cuts across the divide between liberals and communitarians that has shaped political theory in the past few decades. While a grounding in Aristotle (and by extension sympathy with certain communitarian themes) is evident in her emphasis on the protections afforded to individuals by states and small social units, a defence of moral rights and plurality is a more clearly liberal theme. For our purposes, the notion of the political is, in Arendt, rightly aligned (in practice) with democratic participation and (in terms of its primary responsibility) with plurality. The principles of governance that I defend, via the interstitial dignitarian principles, are consistent with this distinctive responsibility for politics to exclude private interest, to be accountable, but also to have a distinctive moral orientation. Arendt would also emphasise the potential and permissibility of radical change through the exercise of power (though not necessarily of violence) (Arendt 1970). This takes its meaning, however, against a complex backdrop of concerns with the proper scope of public interests and, conversely, the dangers of private interest and fanaticism intruding into the public sphere.

The *moral* is a more complex phenomenon to capture in Arendt's work. On the one hand, a robust defence of the private sphere suggests the relegation of morality to 'private conscience' and by extension that which is (merely) excluded from public concern. On the other, conduct within, and the governance of, the public realm are irreducibly moral phenomena subject to moral judgement. How, then, to define the moral in its own terms without reduction to, or negation of, public reason? Curthoys argues that Arendt's wider ethical thinking is Aristotelian or casuistical, but has a specific focus on individuals capable of resisting the ideology and blind instrumentality characteristic of the public sphere in the twentieth century:

> Arendt's post-war ethics is deeply invested in expounding a heterodox ethical subject, the robust, defiant, wilful 'personality' who 'strikes roots' through remembrance, principled volition, and discursive thought. As Arendt puts it, an individual's 'personal quality' is 'precisely his "moral" quality'. [. . .] For Arendt, personality or character is a second birth formed both through the rigorous will that is bound to principled maxims and the discursive will that insists on a constant two-in-one dialogue of the self with the self. Arendt theorizes personality as ethically reliable precisely because it refuses logical consistency, instead calibrating its response to the world with the humanizing faculties of taste, judgement, and the Ciceronian desire for good intellectual company even if it be at the expense of abstract truths.
>
> (Curthoys 2011, 37)

Whether or not this is a faithful reconstruction of Arendt's own dynamic thought on judgement and action, it reminds us again of the centrality of plurality in her philosophy of the human condition. It is also a reflection of the fact that the moral is not reducible to private conscience (a reduction that would flow from a strict division between moral, legal, and political). Rather, the sphere of moral action encompasses self- and other-regarding duties, and imperfect and perfect duties. Arendt's concern is how these can be allowed to exist without being distorted by heteronomous forces (external constraints on our autonomy) and how they require the existence of an open society and open public sphere in which judgement can be freely shaped and formed. Between the thin idea of a morality of autonomous action and an obscure idea of individual authenticity, Arendt's demand for maintaining a separation of private and public (and maintaining freedom within both) should be seen as the core of her moral position because it is such a division that makes both justice and virtue possible.

Regarding *law*, the previous chapters have broadly assumed that 'law' is a practice and a product (something we do and something we create) and that, in light of the traditional schools of jurisprudence, it is the older natural law tradition that should be our focus if we are concerned with human dignity. Arendt herself had important general insights about our changing conception of law, with the Greek conception of law as a *work* (an artificial product instrumentally necessary to bind a polis together) replaced by a Roman conception of law as *action* (a practice wherein individuals could excel and forge change in society) (1958, 194–195). My own concern in this chapter has been with law's synthetic character, its responsibility to bridge the claims of individual and collective and combine them in a way bounded by human dignity but accomplished, on a day-to-day basis, through a concern with justice. In the next section we encounter two slightly different synthetic claims of this kind; first, Waldron's idea that law synthesises the products of a legislature with the participatory and procedural possibilities of adjudication, both being necessary for law's special claim to protect dignity; and second, Dworkin's idea that a distinctive synthetic role can be found in judicial practice in hard cases where the temporal and policy demands of a state are reconciled in a way that accomplishes integrity. This difference will have further consequences when we come to consider the importance of judicial review. Suffice it to say, while Arendt had no wish to create a theory or philosophy of law, her extended reflections on the prosecution of Eichmann (Arendt 1963) produced two important insights. The first is that we cannot use law and legal procedure alone to create new foundations for our polities. The effort to use a trial to create a narrative of emancipation and justification collapsed through law's distinctive openness to *evidence*, evidence that cannot be harnessed to wider narratives of self-vindication. (In that sense we might sound a note of caution about Dworkin's emphasis on the potential of legal judgement to reveal deep truths about our state and its underlying integrity.) The second insight is that ultimate judgement about an act, individual, or epoch is never solely a legal, moral, or political judgement. It is always more complex, but also less conditioned than these different fields of norms permit. Her judgement on Eichmann – that he did not deserve to live after his assault on the very plurality that is so central to the human condition – does not follow neatly from evidence, from positive law, or indeed from his own motives and *mens rea*. These laws and these forensic tools broke down in the face of the banality of evil. The judgement that was delivered was, then, not just. But finding Eichmann guilty was consistent with our understanding of human dignity. And in that sense, Arendt reminds us that we are sometimes right to insist on the divergence of the artificial demands of justice and the judgement demanded by human dignity and that obligation and judgement cannot be confined to isolated fields of practice.

3.4 Democratic institutions

With these broad categories in mind, we should consider the relationship between the dignitarian principles and democratic institutions. In part, that means the kinds of articulated institutions associated with democracy, namely separated judicial, executive, and legislative institutions. In part, it must also mean the specific foundations and functions of democratic institutions, both representation and accountability. The question of human dignity's relationship with liberal institutions has already been touched upon in terms of human dignity's anti-utilitarian function and with regard to the inadequacies of reliance on the 'circumstances of justice' as theoretical substitutes for principled concern with the human condition. We turn now more directly to the demands of good governance and democracy.

Human dignity has been associated with the exercise of certain virtues as necessary conditions of stable democratic states (see Ober 2012, 828f); it has also been associated with voting, representation, and direct democracy (Waldron 1999). My concern, in contrast, is democracy's connection with a certain kind of constitutionalism and a 'morality of governance'. Dupré, I think, is close to expressing this when she aligns self-determination, collective will, and human dignity:

> democracy [is] the 'organisational consequence of human dignity'. As a result, a new type of democracy, with respect for human dignity at its heart, is arguably beginning to emerge, challenging and developing a purely procedural, i.e. majoritarian democracy. From this analytical perspective, the concept of human dignity is much more than the individual (intuitive and elusive) sense of self-respect and respect of others, it positions human beings at the heart of democracy, determining thus the exercise of political power.
>
> (Dupré 2012, 264; footnotes removed)

Democracy as an 'organisational consequence of human dignity' sits closer to the dignitarian principles discussed so far and it signifies a justificatory task that faces us, namely to think beyond the mere stipulation that human dignity entails democracy. We have to give specificity to what this means in terms of the organisation and justification of democratic institutions.

Positively, and in terms of the *substance* of democratic practices and institutions, we would expect democratic institutions, and the norms that flow from them, to be organised around preservation of human rights, natural liberties, and the sustainability of both. This means supplementing the rule of law, and the separation of powers, with entrenched constitutional commitments to human rights and the conditions of their realisation (see Chapter 5). Put another way, we would expect democracies to be the best systems for the preservation of these kinds of institutional arrangements and substantive commitments. While it is possible for majoritarianism to undermine good institutional arrangements, parliamentary democracy is unlikely to dissolve its own foundations and, on the basis of democratic accountability, it is likely to provide the best political foundations for continued commitment to human rights.

Human dignity, via the permissive principle, also concerns the special *authority* of democratic institutions, an authority that can be understood only through the contrast between public authority and private interests. As Harel (2014) demonstrates, it is crucial to maintain the link between the authority of the state and coercive actions taken against individuals in line with the Kantian argument (see preceding chapter) that only public authority can turn illegitimate force into legitimate coercion. Legitimation of coercion requires a direct normative link of common consent, and not merely a functional or instrumental link with public power. We will return to this below as essential to a morality of governance. But again, and inverting the order of justification, only democracy can claim an implied consensual exercise of force over citizens because executive and legislative power is conditioned by the practices and procedures of accountability. If the essence of justified state authority is that the state's monopoly on the use of force is a *de jure,* not merely *de facto,* monopoly, this is not simply for the functional reason that the state exercises force more effectively and systematically but because it is conditioned authority constituted by citizens.

However, human dignity also clearly supports limits to democratic legitimacy and to the permissible products of democratic practices. This will be considered more fully elsewhere in terms of the entrenching of certain constitutional commitments because of the demands of sustainability; it also prohibits the democratic dissolution of democracy itself. Nevertheless, the limiting of the powers of democratic bodies, even by judicial review, requires careful justification. The 'dignity' of legislative practices (where representatives create law through 'head-counting' procedures) has been defended by Waldron (1999). For Waldron, legislation and governance by representative bodies are not merely tolerable compromises necessary to encompass conflictual groups within a polity in the absence of better, more rational, decision-making practices. They are forms of recognition of the status of individuals, through their representatives, and enmesh these representatives within rational discursive practices (i.e. within our legislatures). The human right to democratic participation exists because of the potential for political processes to support our general permissions and to provide accountability in the name of the public itself.

Conversely, the limits of such a position are captured in Dworkin's 'checkerboard' question (1986, 178f). If we could parcel states into checkerboards with each square offering different choices for individuals – particularly choices when it comes to divisive or controversial topics – we would fulfil the demands of majoritarianism (the largest group will always have the possibility to exercise their choice, albeit without imposing its will on everyone) and the rules would be clear (there are clearly promulgated, if different, options permitted in different areas). Thus, despite the combining the merits of rule utilitarianism, majoritarianism, and the coordination model of law, Dworkin seeks to elicit an intuitive unease with this compromise, namely with regard to the 'integrity' of the state under such circumstances. The responsibility of the state is to legislate and govern in a coherent way, to govern in a way that pursues moral unity and is not simply driven by the dictates of the majority or being rule-governed to a fault. In essence, to lack integrity is to be unprincipled: "The state lacks integrity because it must endorse principles to justify part of what it has done that it must reject to justify the rest" (1986, 184). The analogy between individual and collective integrity is important to Dworkin's work as a whole, and similarly the idea of a certain kind of morality of governance based on principles which is reducible to neither general will nor the rule of law (or governance of rules) will be important in what follows.

If Dworkin's defence of integrity, then, offers a *prima facie* better connection with dignitarian principles than Waldron's defence of the dignity of legislation, much then turns on how we construe the power of the judiciary to limit legislative will and in some instances exchange it for 'judge-made' law. I am concerned with two aspects of judicial power and authority, both of which engage the obligations principle. The first is the institutional and counter-democratic power of judicial review, which has been treated as an issue engaging basic or fundamental rights (Waldron 2006). The second is in terms of the special role of the judiciary in hard cases and the importance such cases have in bridging the legal and political (Dworkin 1986). The basic tensions, however, with democratic legislative power include consent and good order:

> The problem with a judgment of a court is that it does not allow members of a community in general to be able to predict how others will act, and it is purely reactive to disagreements that emerge. For this reason, court judgments cannot *preempt* disagreement and instead can only be reactive to the particular dispute. Enacted legal norms, however, are a form of general collective willing that establish zones in which each member of a community can have freedom to act. This is how it is possible to preempt disagreement and establish the conditions by which coordination and cooperation can occur.
> (Rivers and Capps 2010, 239; emphasis in original)

This is usually collapsed in the problem of the 'counter-majoritarian' power of the judiciary (Waldron 2006; Harel 2014). The critique of judicial review is important but depends upon potentially incommensurable comparison of the value of democratically produced legislation versus the proper means by which rights are recognised and upheld. Harel's arguments depend upon the defence of rights requiring non-instrumental recognition through judicial processes that are not qualified by the instrumental concerns of the other organs of government. In other words, only the judiciary can uphold rights *qua* rights rather than as interests within a shifting set of policy projects and objectives.

Human dignity is likely to be explicit in our legal decisions only in certain crucial cases where the human condition itself (plurality, sustainability, and the preservation of public and private spheres) is at issue. But a distinction needs to be made between those cases and what are more commonly understood to be 'hard cases'. The decision-making of the courts in hard cases – where cases will have far-reaching constitutional importance, encompass political matters, and face a clash of rights or of principles – are often taken to be crucial for understanding the special place of the judiciary in the state. They are clearly much closer to constitutional, not merely regulative, issues of law. But need this imply a special interpretive role for human dignity in those contexts? In Brugger's 'anthropological cross' (2009) – a model of decision-making in hard cases – a 'good and human' legal system respects all of the aspects of the 'decisional' or anthropological cross: higher and lower needs, past and future being "the basic facts of human existence" (2009, 44). There is an important sense in which Brugger (like Dworkin) privileges the hard case because of a parallel between individual and collective decision-making. Self-legislation, self-constitution, basic needs, and higher goods jostle together in both personal and judicial deliberation. In such a model, law's coercive power is justified not by prudence but by the justice of legal decisions being in harmony with the (real or underlying) nature of the human being and their need for a kind of coercive self-control over themselves. While the 'integrity' that Brugger and Dworkin defend in the name of human dignity has attractions, there is a danger of both distorting the demands of practical reasoning in law (derived from justice and formal equality) and of the proper function of human dignity as constitutive (which is principled and interstitial). We await further discussion of the rule of law and the legitimate scope of state powers to explicate those functions (Chapter 6). But it remains to complete the present survey of the organs of government by turning to executive power.

Executive power, as the power least easily constrained by institutions, is the aspect of governance most threatening to human dignity. Democratic governments function normally under the separation of powers and reduce the executive to promoting law and refining policy. However, the executive is also the locus of ultimate power under conditions of emergency and, arguably, with the extension or normalisation of the notion of 'emergency', the executive monopolises the potentially untrammelled and violent aspects of power normally hidden from view. Emergency powers can include suspension of the law, including constitutional and human rights. Thus, I am concerned with the limits of executive power, particularly where these threaten the basic rights of individuals and where such powers are held to be superior to the constraints and procedures achieved in concert with other institutional bodies.

While under normal circumstances the power of the executive is automatically limited by the other organs of the state, the contemporary manifestations of executive power betray more than merely being the ultimate arbiter of disputes and executor of policy. The use of extra-judicial powers of execution, detention, and the passing of emergency legislation, mean that executive power not only retains but exercises the violence that the state monopolises. The normalisation of emergency need not take the form of executions. Forms of 'rendition' use extra-territorial spaces to allow coercive interrogation to take place through third parties at some administrative and territorial remove from the state. Moreover, where terror suspects are concerned we have seen legal 'derogation' from core components of human rights treaties and obligations (Ferejohn and Pasquino 2004). Altering the normal conditions of detention and trial, derogation from treaties means expansion of power over the detained individual without the normal safeguards and procedures, and the loss of judicial scrutiny of evidence and form of detention. While the right to life cannot be derogated from other human rights, it can be legally suspended upon the assumption of certain kinds of emergency or pressing exigency (ICCPR (1966) Article 4). The consequences are subjecting individuals to forms and quantities of detention, without full and open judicial scrutiny, and with evidence flowing from (and often confined to) private channels between the executive and the intelligence services. While it could be assumed that this is problematic for human rights *law* given that there is explicit provision for the suspension of rights in certain legally defined circumstances, the spirit of the law is defined by human dignity and, by virtue of the obligations principles, insists that individuals cannot have core rights taken away by the political acting independently of the legal. Does this mean that legal derogation principles are illegitimate or inconsistent with human dignity? To the extent that derogation provisions pursue a defensible end – namely the partial suspension of liability for violation of human rights, by the state, under conditions of extreme or pressing emergency – then those principles are legitimate and governed by justice. They reflect a special exigency that can be invoked in good faith, and whose use in good faith should be overseen by courts to ensure its proper use. However, the use in good faith by military regimes and heavy-handed security-focussed states can be doubted, and the normalisation of human-rights-violating processes in the absence of existential war or imminent threat seems a matter of injustice that also reflects a violation of human dignity.

These reflections on democratic institutions take us to important boundaries in social and political thought. They are needed to think through the underlying conditions that humanity finds itself in, and to think through the claim that the democratic tradition has on giving support to individual status within human affairs. Together these are meant to enrich the more formal, and more variable, forms of justice that a state might seek to deliver through its institutions. However, the human and climatic future is sometimes taken for granted. We assume that the future will hold more of the same or that the future will play out the trajectory on which existing political and social plans are already set (Mulgan 2011). Along with the discrediting, or at least denigration, of philosophies of history where these involve the positing of laws of progress, discussion of the future has been kept under scientific and conceptual constraints. The environmental threat has changed this, requiring more serious reflection on future environmental conditions and future generations, and the organisation of national and international affairs to prevent irreversible damage to the climate (alongside more specific but also international concerns with ecosystems, species conservation, and pollution). This demands a different conception of justice, with intergenerational justice taking on a significant meaning as a driver of constitutional and policy design (Riley 2016). With no aspect of the environment untouched by human action (and indeed by a blurring of work, labour, and action through automation and human interventions in the food chain). The sum of these concerns lies in (ir)reversibility and how we might keep the future 'open'.

'Keeping the future open' has environmental and historical-normative meanings. In the first case we want a future where something like 'Locke's proviso' is applicable: that we take from the world its natural resources provided we leave as much and as good for future generations (1967 [1690]). The historical-normative meaning takes its meaning from a philosophy of history that, counter to many trends in nineteenth- and twentieth-century philosophies of history, insists that the future is unknowable and must stay that way. That is to say, we can irreversibly determine the future through deep environmental damage that limits the choices of future generations to the point of making their right to life uncertain. These assumptions are certainly a bulwark against the 'presentism' that characterises contemporary human rights law. The law looks to past and contemporary violations of individuals' rights without concern for future changes and threats.

Dupré offers us a further possibility, that keeping the future open is in part an epistemological claim, and one that has particular reference to human dignity itself:

> In most constitutions, dignity's key role in this respect is to keep the future of the constitution (and that of democracy) open. [. . .] In this sense, an open future contrasts with a 'utopian' future, and promotes a future that is gradually constructed, one step at a time, by a range of actors and following a range of processes, including human rights adjudication. Seen from this perspective, judges have a crucial role to play in the step-by-step construction of the future, and the transparency and publicity of judicial reasoning, together with the possibilities of dissent and appeal form an integral and essential part of dignity's construction. Therefore, allowing people to choose and build their own future as they imagine or wish it [. . .] is arguably a crucial part of dignity's definition.
>
> (Dupré 2012, 277)

There is, then, a double 'openness' being defended here in the understanding of the concept of human dignity itself, and in the open development of a constitution.

This relates to the democratically problematic question of 'entrenching' constitutional provisions such that normal democratic practices or democratic majorities cannot alter those provisions. The extent to which this is found in existing constitutions varies, as will the relative difficulty of amending provisions (simple majorities, supermajorities, or unrevisable) (Gosseries 2014). The normative significance of such provisions is conflicted. On that one hand, we commit ourselves to values or ends that will require the continued support of many generations. On the other, there is something potentially disempowering (or even 'criminal', as Kant asserts (Gosseries 2014, 528)) in reducing a future generation's choices. To put it more acutely, we can ask: "What should we fear more: the non-rigidity of a fair constitution, or the unfairness of a rigid constitution?" (Gosseries 2014, 533). Such entrenchment could be an instance of intergenerational injustice if it left future generations worse off in terms of their responsiveness to problems they face, but there seems to be a *prima facie* case for making certain fundamental or particularly urgent problems part of the unchangeable fabric of our laws. In terms of the continued existence of an international society threatened by climate change, and in terms of respect for individual rights, constitutional rigidity or entrenching law seems an unavoidable means of better orientating towards the future, even at the cost of limiting future democratic possibilities. There is no contradiction in human dignity being used to justify those limitations on democratic power, albeit we should be concerned about the potential incoherence of making laws for future generations whose precise needs must remain (empirically or logically) inaccessible to us. Entrenchment of transnational partnership on climate change seems a better candidate for a perpetual commitment than any specific target or side-constraint.

These reflections, on both democratic institutions and the future horizon against which we must consider their design and defensibility, have implicitly touched upon two central aspects of human dignity in its most 'political' guises and forms – that is, in connection with cosmopolitanism as an institution and moral commitment, and with the governance of polities with human dignity as a fundamental commitment. What properly connects these political positions with our discourses of human dignity is, I argue, the dignitarian principles that bridge the entitlements of the individual and the structure of our normative orders and social systems. We turn therefore to a clearer realisation of these principles in political practice.

3.5 The morality of governance

To say that human dignity implies a kind of 'morality of governance' is to argue that the principles derived from human dignity partially determine the ends, and the limits, of the political. A morality of governance is not focussed (as Fuller's 'morality of law' might be thought to be focussed) on legislators; rather it concerns putting the political in a proper relationship between law and morality to ensure human status. What I take to be the dignitarian principles flowing from human dignity here intersect with familiar themes in political morality and normative jurisprudence. We are concerned with how individuals' obligations are harmonised (how, amongst other things, human dignity interacts with *fairness*); how permissions are to be maintained (how human dignity interacts with *liberty*); and how individual rights are maintained (more familiarly, how the entitlements and *security* of individuals are protected). The fact that these can be translated into the language and core values of modern constitutional democracy is not to side-line human dignity. It is human dignity that draws them into a coherent whole, theoretically, through an understanding of the juridical entitlements of the human person, and practically, in producing certain constitutional and regulative dignitarian obligations. Thus a dignitarian morality of governance stands in a coherent, but complex, relationship with justice. While fairness and justice can be maintained through formal equality, we cannot place contradictory normative demands on an individual. Such contradictions are most commonly found in interstitial problems for which interstitial principles are the solution.

One clear and important example of this is the provision of the bare administrative necessities and entitlements necessary for individuals to function as either (public) citizens or (private) actors with social bonds. The denial, for whatever reason, of the ability to register as a resident, to have sufficient documentation to open a bank account, or to have clear rights of residency renders individuals' public status equivocal or perilous (Open Democracy 2016b). These denials have an impact, in turn, on the capacity of those individuals to form or maintain personal or familial bonds (Open Society Foundation 2011). Depending upon the reason for such a status (be it migration or poverty), individuals' entitlements sit between divergent political, legal, and moral imperatives. The law might be ambiguous, political will absent, and the moral reduced to a humanitarian minimum. In those instances, the most appropriate discourse is human dignity. This is the case not because we are considering basic material entitlements (though this forms part of it) but because we are concerned with both material and basic juridical entitlements to personhood. A morality of governance would pick out precisely this kind of problem, and these kinds of individuals, as priority cases with the concomitant obligation to re-calibrate the legal and political to prevent the creation of individuals in this situation. A morality of governance can, then, be contrasted with short-term governance that focusses on the actual or potential will of an electorate. Human dignity, in contrast, focusses on the entitlements of those rendered marginal by our normative orders.

In what way would a morality of governance differ from 'mere' governance? Our normative orders, our social systems, and the application of interstitial principles to their governance can be illustrated if we consider some of the more complex issues arising from 'social engineering' and a tendency towards technocratic forms of governance. The forms of governmental intervention in our lives are varied and include certain kinds of social change programs – of varying degrees of subtlety or directness – seeking to change behaviour. All but the most libertarian is likely to allow some welfarist element to government, from benign campaigns to paternalism to full-blown social engineering. How do we make qualitative and quantitative distinctions here? Each intrudes upon, or undermines, our autonomy in some way or another. Thus a moral defence of autonomy faces a difficult task of distinguishing legitimate or illegitimate intrusions upon our autonomy. This means distinguishing, perhaps, where not only autonomy but 'authenticity' is compromised, i.e. some deeper or more systematic aspect of self-determination.

The most interesting cases of the interaction of paternalism and autonomy relate to 'nudging': the altering or engineering of (welfare or consumer) choices to optimise the interests of both public and private actors (see Alemanno and Spina 2014). Bypassing rational agency through nudging is amongst the least invasive or disrespectful forms of intruding upon our autonomy. Yet it remains tempting to express what is potentially problematic here through the language of human dignity (McCrudden and King 2016). The possibility that rational choice is being short-circuited is not always obvious when we are dealing with certain kinds of 'choice architecture' that sets defaults (e.g. in opt-in or opt-out possibilities) such that socially beneficial outcomes are favoured. Simply framing choice in a particular way is unobjectionable (except where commercial gain is at issue and nudging serves ends that are non-socially beneficial). Where lifestyle choices are 'nudged' by the state, it is perhaps the form and not the content of the influence that is at issue. In other words, government intervention in our lives should be explicit and seek to be directly persuasive. Where it is, on the contrary, sub-conscious and bypasses the rationality of the agency deploying certain typical tendencies and short-cuts in decision-making capacity, the state has chosen means that directly pose a threat to individual agency and human status. It is at the permissive principle that this strikes home. The state's responsibility is to maximise permissions and keep contingency within our social practices. After all, the state cannot prevent all wrongs, nor should it strive to, given the dangers this would pose to our liberty. Thus, the bypassing of agency is arguably inimical to natural sovereignty, but it is potentially difficult to make such an argument normatively persuasive without a much more complex philosophy of action and authenticity. It is much clearer to treat it as problematic in light of the permissive aspect of human dignity. What human dignity gives us is not simple opposition to paternalism. It gives us, via the permissive principle, concern with the *exclusion of contingency from human affairs*. And it means, via the obligations principle, harmonising the legal, moral, and political such that we have a coherent collection position (one with 'integrity') on the situations where social engineering is defensible. Unthinking acceptance of technocratic rationality will give us ever more elaborate (and ever more privatised) governance of our 'choices'. Dignitarian thinking demands setting limits such that our status as sovereign individuals capable of self-determination is bolstered by a principle favouring permission.

The essence of this example is to show that human dignity implies a morality of governance in the sense of capturing an overall approach to governance – principled, rights-protecting, and sustainable – but one wherein human dignity remains interstitial in an important sense. The precise structure of states and governance cannot be dictated directly by 'human dignity' as a unitary value. Where human dignity is rightly invoked is in interstitial issues where law, morality, and politics need to be brought into harmonisation and where the tools usually supplied by the language of justice are inadequate, either because of the novelty of the problem or (more precisely) because law, morality, and politics yield different and competing answers.

3.6 Moral cosmopolitanism

What is left of human dignity's institutional implications after a morality of governance? One important theme would be the rights of individuals transcending the state. The responsibilities captured by a morality of governance would sit within, and be largely confined to, the discharge of responsibilities within and by a state. But human dignity has long been assumed to identify obligations that necessarily transcend the boundaries of states. Given that here and elsewhere (see Chapter 6) I also defend the existence of the state as such, we face a dual task of showing how human dignity implies cosmopolitanism, going beyond the boundaries of the governance of the state, but also encompasses the existence of the state.

The essence of any moral cosmopolitanism is making claims that are universal in scope, which defend the moral importance of individuals, and which reduce many, if not all, claims based on collective authority and obligation to the protection of individual rights. This broad definition generates three questions which require addressing. First, universalisation might be thought to also entail the displacement of duties of benevolence with stricter claim rights or, alternatively, the displacement of all our moral discourse with rights discourse. Second, the moral importance of individuals might be thought to entail the moral indefensibility of states and other authorities. Third, the reducibility of collective claims to individual rights might neglect the intrinsic value of both groups and certain practices and institutions in themselves. Understanding the moral cosmopolitanism that follows from human dignity must be articulated in relation to these claims.

First, can and should we distinguish obligations of right and of benevolence? Does human dignity unify our political, moral, and legal thinking such that all issues of global justice can be resolved? If so, are the claims of human dignity and human rights so strong that they leave no room for what are recognisably acts of benevolence? The contribution of human dignity to discourses of global rights seems to encompass familiar cosmopolitan themes concerning the irrelevance of distance in articulating our obligations and the parity of 'economic, social, and cultural rights' with other human rights. These are commitments which structure our conception of global justice as a whole: rights claims are universal and not confined to the delivery of entitlements in states, our obligations are therefore global not local, and the structuring of those obligations should take place through considering rights, not benevolence or supererogation (for versions of these claims, see Caney 2005 and Fine 2007). The fact that these are highly demanding claims has been, famously, addressed by Singer:

> Given the present conditions in many parts of the world [. . .] we ought, morally, to be working full time to relieve great suffering of the sort that occurs as a result of famine or other disasters. Of course, mitigating circumstances can be adduced-for instance, that if we wear ourselves out through overwork, we shall be less effective than we would otherwise have been. Nevertheless, when all considerations of this sort have been taken into account, the conclusion remains: we ought to be preventing as much suffering as we can without sacrificing something else of comparable moral importance. This conclusion is one which we may be reluctant to face. I cannot see, though, why it should be regarded as a criticism of the position for which I have argued, rather than a criticism of our ordinary standards of behavior.
>
> (Singer 1972, 238)

But the question not of practicability but of intelligibility remains equally pressing. Is it defensible to express our global duties in the language of human dignity and human rights? There are three reasons for thinking this is the correct approach. The first relates to the ability of human rights to provide practical and justiciable standards than can be monitored by international bodies. While the precise content of the right to health or education is contested, the expression of these as *rights* at the international level prevents trade-offs with other goods and collective political pressures. The second, and related, point is that we are able to produce hierarchies of responsibilities using rights without thereby succumbing to 'trade-offs' between equally obligatory responsibilities. We can prioritise the basic entitlements and agency of individuals as vulnerable humans, while also demanding those entitlements that accrue to individuals as self-determining persons. Third, we are forced through rights to think in terms of sustainable obligations, not those obligations presuming moderately conflictual individuals or moderately scarce resources. There are, put bluntly, threats to survival of the species which change the regulatory demands made on, not only states, but on the institutional arrangements of humanity as a whole.

In this way, human dignity and human rights do indeed displace supererogation, i.e. the choice of what global concerns to invest our resources in. Rather, there is a global obligation to protect human rights. This does entail, in one respect, the colonisation of our obligations by human dignity and rights. But it is significant that global *justice* is, unlike justice within states, a form of justice that cannot be characterised by 'reasonable variation'. There can only be one global justice (as opposed to isolated contributions by states *to* global justice) and this requires unified principles. Further analysis of international and global obligations await analysis in the next two chapters, but it should come as no surprise that the boundaries between state and international arena do not condition or attenuate our obligations from the point of view of human dignity.

What of the defensibility of states in the light of cosmopolitan human dignity? This, too, awaits further exploration (Chapter 6), but for present purposes we should note that there are both functional and intrinsic aspects to a defence of the state that are compatible, or are presumed by, the foregoing analysis. To the extent that the state is a useful form of organisation for realising corrective and distributive justice it has functional value. Moreover, certain kinds of coercive powers exercised over any individual require justification through being effected by a body of actors and institutions (the state) that are intended to harmonise the will of free individuals, and to do that to the exclusion of private interest. Moreover, from the point of view of cosmopolitan ends and principles, it is significant to note that, without a state, we can have neither welfare states nor a right of exit from an oppressive state if there are no other states to enter. The federation of states in international law harmonises the wills of states, as actors, under principles designed to protect human dignity. As a consequence there is no dignitarian justification for the abolition of the state.

One further functional justification of the state lies in its protection of groups and minorities. Assuming that we are not valorising the *nation*-state as an organically constituted, homogenous people, the state is a means by which groups and minorities can have their distinctive demands harmonised with the interests of others. Where this difficult task fails, international law through its various institutions and conventions seeks to impose minimum standards, and afford minimum protection, to groups as such. The moral cosmopolitanism implied by human dignity both supports and limits the scope of those protections. On the one hand, it is very clear that certain groups and their interests are interstitial; groups do not 'fit' within prevailing rights narratives, and it is the function of the discourse of human dignity to stress the centrality of plurality in our thinking about politics and the morality of governance. Moreover, human dignity is rightly associated with international criminal justice where crimes by groups against groups are prosecuted. These are 'cosmopolitan trials' not merely because they are international but because they assert obligations transcending the state. And the specific function of human dignity in those contexts is to stress the value of plurality and to unify law and morality by negating the validity of national laws which authorise abuse of groups (see Chapter 4). On the other hand, group demands can amount to insular claims, potentially oppressive in themselves, and the construction of groups (through self-determined standards of inclusion and exclusion) undoubtedly challenge prevailing understandings of the division between public and private. Accordingly, deployment of the permissive principle would insist that while group rights are defensible and indeed intelligible as human rights in some instances, this is conditioned by the sovereignty of the individual (as the unifying principle of human rights law) and by the permissive principle, which stresses liberal criteria for entering and leaving membership of groups. Defence of group rights is part of a defence of plurality, but group rights cannot be justified to pervert the underlying principles associated with human dignity.

The implications of human dignity, as they have been articulated here, are intended to claim a large portion of both moral and institutional cosmopolitanism as implications of human dignity. Given that uses of cosmopolitanism are particularly prone to distortion, the nature of this claim and its implications require reiteration. Note, first, that this moral cosmopolitanism sits alongside the other, principled, systemic implication of human dignity (a morality of governance) which speaks to the political and institutional practise of state governance. Cosmopolitanism speaks, in contrast to governance, to the moral and legal at a transnational level. Nevertheless, these are conjoined ideas and it is held that human dignity, on the reconstruction offered here, is precisely a concept intended to draw these kinds of ideas together such that social practices and normative systems are organised around individuals' status.

As the examples used here imply, interstitial principles yield interstitial applications. Even with a moral cosmopolitanism which trades on universal rights and entitlements, we do not and should not need to invoke its underlying dignitarian justification in the normal course of events. We can use the language of justice, fairness, distribution, and so on to deal with a great number of national and international questions about the entitlements that sit between us as individuals and as members of groups. But where there is continuing contestation between political reality and moral obligation, or positive law and political will, the solution will not be to retreat to the underlying principles of those normative orders: the legal does not simply 'beat' the political, and the 'moral' does not simply 'trump' both. We stand in need of principled resolutions when these kinds of tensions arise between different normative paradigms. This explains the long antagonisms that can arise on complex issues where they are expressed in the language of justice. Justice admits of reasonable variation. Human dignity governs the legitimate forms that a just answer can take.

How, then, should we move towards specific institutional implications for human dignity? After all, these reflections are intended not merely to produce general abstract principles but to have application in systems of governance. That they fundamentally entwine the legal, moral, and political means that they are applicable to constitutional states with separations of powers. This broadly takes us to the sphere of public law and the governance of public authorities and publicly distributed power. But why 'public law'? How do we define public law, and why is it of particular importance in our understanding of human dignity?

Public law is jurisdiction – the ability to speak law – over a large social and political entity (sometimes, but not necessarily, a nation) which displaces other authorities and has no superior within that domain. Thus public international law is the ability to speak the law internationally with no higher source of law. National public law does the same within the state. Transnational law sits awkwardly between these two ideas; because certain actors and practices fall within neither the international or the national jurisdiction, there is no neat basis of jurisdiction for them, no-one to 'speak law' to them. Nonetheless, as governance and regulation takes place at this intermediate level, and because there is no superior agency able to impose law superior to the transnational law that (self-) regulates them, we have something approaching a form of public law. The idea of superiority and jurisdiction are, then, helpful for understanding public law. But certain practices are of public concern, use public law principles and some public law institutions, and as such fall partly, but not neatly, within the concerns of public law.

What I think is more useful for understanding the three types of public law discussed here is their relationship with *time* and *territory*. It is these two ideas that form the fabric of public law and within which we need to embed dignitarian principles. Territory concerns the state's (functional) claim to better accomplish justice (distribute goods or govern resources) through control of space and the exclusion of others. This functional claim can be bolstered by other, more nationalistic concerns with nation and land, but the functional argument is defensible as a basic assumption. Human dignity, however, means that functional claims cannot exhaust the internal moral responsibilities of the state and that they have extra-territorial responsibilities. Accordingly, public law as a concern with space draws together the strands of the state's responsibility, the boundaries of justice, and the countervailing interstitial demands made by human dignity.

Time, as we have seen, is also a crucial aspect of our institutions and of the governance of states. Constitutions bind past and future generations; superior court decision draw upon the past to determine the future. And, it has been argued, it is partly the role of human dignity to keep a 'human' timescale alive within our constitutional thinking even when technocratic forces compel an ever-accelerating approach to social and economic governance.

With time and space we identify the basic coordinates of public law and connect it with the human condition as outlined above. Thus, as we turn to the forms of public law and their different challenges, we will nonetheless have recourse to time and territory to define their functions and their scope. It has been my intention in this chapter to prepare us for the introduction of certain dignitarian principles into the fabric of those systems of governance, and to find, in the process, the core constitutive elements of these systems, not merely to find a place for human dignity as a regulation.

References

Alemanno, A. and Spina, A. (2014) 'Nudging Legally: On the Checks and Balances of Behavioral Regulation' *International Journal of Constitutional Law*, 12(2), 429–456.

Arendt, H. (1958) *The Human Condition*. Chicago, The University of Chicago Press.

Arendt, H. (1963) *Eichmann in Jerusalem: A Report on the Banality of Evil*. Harmondsworth, Penguin Books.

Arendt, H. (1967) *The Origins of Totalitarianism*, 3rd edition. Boston, Houghton Mifflin Harcourt.

Arendt, H. (1970) *On Violence*. Boston, Houghton Mifflin Harcourt.

Aristotle. (1998) *Politics*. Oxford, Oxford University Press.

Benhabib, S. (2013) 'The Legitimacy of Human Rights' *Daedalus*, 137(3), 94–104.

Bloch, E. (1987) *Natural Law and Human Dignity*. Cambridge, MA, The MIT Press.

Brugger, W. (2009) 'Dignity, Rights, and Legal Philosophy within the Anthropological Cross of Decision-Making' in Brugger, W. and Kirste, S. eds., *Human Dignity as a Foundation of Law*. Germany, Franz Steiner Verlag, 41–62.

Buchanan, A. (2010) 'The Egalitarianism of Human Rights' *Ethics*, 120(4), 679–710.

Caney, S. (2005) *Justice Beyond Borders: A Global Political Theory*. Oxford, Oxford University Press.

Curthoys, N. (2011) 'Ernst Cassirer, Hannah Arendt, and the Twentieth Century Revival of Philosophical Anthropology' *Journal of Genocide Research*, 13(1), 23–46.

Dupré, C. (2012) 'Dignity, Democracy, Civilisation' *Liverpool Law Review*, 33(3), 263–280.

Dworkin, R. (1985) *A Matter of Principle*. Oxford, Oxford University Press.

Dworkin, R. (1986) *Law's Empire*. Cambridge, MA, Harvard University Press.

Ferejohn, J. and Pasquino, P. (2004) 'The Law of Exception: A Typology of Emergency Powers' *International Journal of Constitutional Law*, 2(2), 210–239.

Fine, R. (2007) *Cosmopolitanism*. London, Routledge.

Fineman, M. (2008) 'The Vulnerable Subject: Anchoring Equality in the Human Condition' *Yale Journal of Law and Feminism*, 20(1), 10–22.

Flikschuh, K. (2000) *Kant and Modern Political Philosophy*. Cambridge, Cambridge University Press.

Gosseries, A.P. (2014) 'The Intergenerational Case for Constitutional Rigidity' *Ratio Juris*, 27(4), 528–539.

Grear, A. (2011) 'The Vulnerable Living Order: Human Rights and the Environment in a Critical and Philosophical Perspective' *Journal of Human Rights and the Environment*, 2(1), 23–44.

Griffin, J. (2008) *On Human Rights*. Oxford, Oxford University Press.

Harel, A. (2014) *Why Law Matters*. Oxford, Oxford University Press.

Heyman, S.J. (1991) 'Aristotle on Political Justice' *Iowa Law Review*, 77, 851–863.

Hobbes, T. (1991 [1651]) *Leviathan*. Oxford, Oxford University Press.

Hume, D. (1978 [1739]) *A Treatise of Human Nature*. Oxford, Clarendon Press.

ICCPR. (1966) International Covenant on Civil and Political Rights, GA res. 2200A (XXI), 21 UN GAOR Supp. (No. 16) at 52.

Kant, I. (1996 [1797]) *The Metaphysics of Morals*, translated by M. Gregor. Cambridge, Cambridge University Press.

Locke, J. (1967 [1690]) *Two Treatises of Government*. Cambridge, Cambridge University Press.

McCrudden, C. and King, J. (2016) 'The Dark Side of Nudging: The Ethics, Political Economy, and Law of Libertarian Paternalism' in Kemmerer, A., Möllers, C., Steinbeis, M. and Wagner, G. eds., *Choice Architecture in Democracies*. Baden-Baden, Nomos, 75–140.

Mulgan, T. (2011) *Ethics for Broken World: Imagining Philosophy After Catastrophe*. Canada, McGill-Queen's Press.

Ober, J. (2012) 'Democracy's Dignity' *American Political Science Review*, 106(4), 827–846.

Open Democracy. (2016a) 'Climate Change and Migration', Available at: www.opendemocracy.net/sarah-louise-nash/moving-targets-moving-people-climate-change-and-migration, accessed March 2017.

Open Democracy. (2016b) 'Statelessness as Forced Migration', Available at: www.opendemocracy.net/openglobalrights/kristy-belton/statelessness-as-forced-displacement, accessed March 2017.

Open Society Foundation. (2011) 'Statelessness', Available at: www.opensocietyfoundations.org/voices/statelessness-what-it-and-why-it-matters, accessed March 2017.

Pattinson, S.D. and Beyleveld, D. (2002) 'Horizontal Applicability and Horizontal Effect' *Law Quarterly Review*, 118, 623–646.

Pitkin, H.F. (1972) *Wittgenstein and Justice: On the Significance of Ludwig Wittgenstein for Social and Political Thought*. CA, University of California Press.

Rawls, J. (1999) *A Theory of Justice*, Revised edition. Oxford, Oxford University Press.

Rawls, J. (2005) *Political Liberalism*. New York, Columbia University Press.

Raz, J. (1979) *The Authority of Law: Essays on Law and Morality*. Oxford, Oxford University Press.

Riley, S. (2016) 'Architectures of Intergenerational Justice: Human Dignity, International Law, and Duties to Future Generations' *Journal of Human Rights*, 15(2), 272–290.

Rivers, J. and Capps, P. (2010) 'Kant's Concept of International Law' *Legal Theory*, 16(4), 229–257.

Shklar, J.N. (1964) *Legalism: Law, Morals, and Political Trials*. Cambridge, MA, Harvard University Press.

Singer, P. (1972) 'Famine, Affluence, and Morality' *Philosophy and Public Affairs*, 1(3), 229–243.

South-West Africa Cases. (1966) '(Ethiopia v. South Africa; Liberia v. South Africa); Second Phase, International Court of Justice (ICJ)', July 18, 1966, Available at: www.refworld.org/cases,ICJ,4023a9414.html, accessed April 2017.

Tasioulas, J. (2002) 'International Law and the Limits of Fairness' *European Journal of International Law*, 13(4), 993–1023.

Tierney, B. (2014) *Liberty and Law: The Idea of Permissive Natural Law 1100–1800*. Washington, DC, Catholic University of America Press.

Tsakyrakis, S. (2009) 'Proportionality: An Assault on Human Rights?' *International Journal of Constitutional Law*, 7(3), 468–493.
Waldron, J. (1999) *Law and Disagreement*. Oxford, Oxford University Press.
Waldron, J. (2006) 'The Core of the Case against Judicial Review' *The Yale Law Journal*, 115, 1346–1406.
Waldron, J. (2011) 'The Rule of Law and the Importance of Procedure' *Nomos*, 50, 3–31.
Waldron, J. (2012) 'How Law Protects Dignity' *The Cambridge Law Journal*, 71(1), 200–222.
Weinrib, J. (2014) 'Permissive Laws and the Dynamism of Kantian Justice' *Law and Philosophy*, 33(1), 105–136.

Part II

4 International law

> [T]he animating conception of any international law of human rights is, at its core, a humanistic world view: a conception of the human being as an end in himself and a legitimator of power and not as an instrument of a corporate society, deriving his right to existence from that society. This root conception of 'international concern' antedates the so-called 'modern law of nations' with its dogmatic emphasis upon state sovereignty, and goes back to the very origins of international law and sources of humanism. With the advent of the nation-state system, this conception was relegated to the position of a marginal exception.
>
> —(McDougal, Lasswell and Chen 1969, 269)

Introduction

The modern notion of human dignity is found in international law. It is found in the treaties and institutions of the post-war era and in the legal and political discourse of international courts and actors. This is, in large measure, where the 'universality' we associate with human rights and human dignity arises. The universality of human dignity linked to the universality of international law. And it is in the use and enforcement of human dignity that the 'international community' takes its principal meaning, i.e. as a group of states with explicit concern for global or humanitarian issues.

But international law is a complex and contested set of practices and norms that frequently fails to meet the aspirations we have for it. The minimum standards demanded by international law can often (though need not) mean minimal standards. The 'international community' (as opposed to the mere coexistence of states coordinated by law) exists primarily in response to crisis, not as a community that conceives of itself as a society with a shared common good.

The human dignity promulgated by international law is itself no less problematic, and international law and international legal theory have given us some of the most contradictory and contentious theorisations of human dignity. We will encounter, for example, a policy goal, a humanitarian norm, an 'affective' concept, a heuristic, and a place-holder. Finding a coherent place for human dignity in our thinking about international law must avoid, in particular, the extremes of empty generalisations in political rhetoric and narrow prohibitive rules in practice. A link with human rights partially secures that place. But understanding human dignity through international human rights *law* is, I will argue, an inadequate substitute for understanding human dignity through the status principles I have previously outlined.

Despite the idiosyncrasies of the international arena and its legal system, many of the tensions and contradictions outlined in this chapter will be relevant for all forms of public law, and in certain respects international law provides a large or amplified version of conceptualisations of human dignity found elsewhere in national public law. We will here, as elsewhere, have to consider what it might mean for human dignity to be associated with 'progress' in politics and law. We have to consider how we should evaluate the human rights discourse we have inherited with its contradictory 'generations' of rights and its claim to 'indivisibility'. And we must continue to articulate a clear relationship between human dignity and justice.

I argue that the most important roles that human dignity plays in relation to public international law are an obligation-determining role in relation to failed states and states at war, and a role in determining the permissibility of bypassing the rules of international law to permit use of force despite positive international law. Thus, the core role of human dignity in relation to international law lies at the limits of legality: where the rule of law has failed at a domestic level, and where the international rule of law has failed such that unilateral humanitarian action is morally permitted.

To get to those conclusions we must initially frame enquiry into international law with certain contradictions that have particular resonance with the idea of moral cosmopolitanism defended in the preceding chapter. The initial contradiction (and perhaps the one that is most obvious, so the one most easily overlooked) is between a system created for states but from which we demand a focus on individuals. This is accompanied by a more specific contradiction when we come to try to see international law as 'cosmopolitan'. On the one hand this can be construed as an orientation towards 'solidarity' between peoples and individuals globally; on the other it can be construed as a defence of 'pluralism': the plurality of groups, cultures, and nationalities. I argue here for the importance of a certain kind of qualified pluralism in the implications of human dignity, leaving solidarity as a concern better aligned with our discourses of global justice. The first half of the chapter focusses on these discussions.

The remainder of the chapter concerns warfare and its consequences. Warfare, and the breakdown of legality, require especial attention to how we reach judgements using human dignity. The moral and agentic complexity of warfare entails the necessity of 'all things considered' judgements about responsibility and reasons for action. This is found in the use of dignity in judgements about international criminal responsibility and humanitarian intervention. In both cases human dignity is used not only as a 'place-holder' where law is unclear, but as the principled core of an 'all things considered' judgement. The morality of governance in international law can be associated with drawing certain activities (voluntarily or through compulsion) within the jurisdiction of international courts and international judgement. But, as ever, the normative implication of human dignity is that judgements in those contexts will not be, and in this context cannot be, exhausted by application of positive law.

4.1 The contradictions of international law

My initial concern is to chart some of the contradictory manifestations of human dignity in international law. The point is not to impose an interpretation upon these uses of human dignity but rather to show that these betray certain underlying contradictions within international law itself.

A number of studies collate the explicit uses of human dignity in international law (for example, Schachter 1983; Joerden 2014). There are also theorisations of their relationship (for example, Capps 2009; Reisman 2013). For immediate purposes we can simply note the following. Human dignity appears in the UDHR's Preamble: "[R]ecognition of the inherent dignity and of the equal and inalienable rights of all members of the human family is the foundation of freedom, justice and peace in the world." It appears in the UDHR as a right: "Everyone who works has the right to just and favourable remuneration ensuring for himself and his family an existence worthy of human dignity, and supplemented, if necessary, by other means of social protection" (UDHR (1948) Article 23 (3)). And it appears in the International Covenant on Civil and Political Rights (ICCPR) (1966) Preamble as a property of the human person: "[T]hese rights derive from the inherent dignity of the human person." These references and others like them are frequently appealed to as the common reference point, or focal expression of, the modern, legal notion of human dignity. However, these represent (respectively) a foundation, a right, and a property. And, as we might expect, the presence of human dignity in the jurisprudence of international law is normatively inconsistent in the ways discussed in Chapter 1. Studies of the variations and inconsistencies in its positive legal uses can be found in a range of scholarly surveys (McCrudden 2008; Petersen 2012; Barak 2015) where normative imprecision, regulative redundancy, and constitutive incoherence are in evidence.

As previously discussed, variation in the legal use of human dignity is to be expected. What is unwanted is contradiction. And contradiction is particularly pronounced at the international level. We certainly *find* human dignity in international law, but if we were to isolate and focus on its *meanings and functions* in international law, we would find the full spectrum of (precise and vacuous, aspirational and empty) forms that 'human dignity' talk can take. This is, on the one hand, because of the ambiguity of the expression and function of human dignity in international instruments, ambiguity above all concerning how human dignity in international law should be thought to have *application* at a domestic level and in international courts. This is, on the other hand, because the foundations of international law itself – the contracting between states, and the source of law in the will of states – provide little by way of a *constitutional* framework within which human dignity could take a constitutional meaning, a point we will return to.

This is not to say that international law offers mere rhetoric with regard to human dignity. In its foundational relationship with international human rights law we are, admittedly, given an important component of its normative core, namely human status, including individual sovereignty and the possession of rights. Interestingly we also have, in a slightly confused form, a sense of the dignitarian principles more generally. That is to say, we have (under the UDHR 1948) a human right to an international order conducive to the realisation of all human rights demanding the rule of law and conditioning of the authority of the state: "Everyone is entitled to a social and international order in which the rights and freedoms set forth in this Declaration can be fully realized" (UDHR 1948, Article 28). To treat this entitlement as an individual *right* is not unintelligible but it is better expressed in terms of principles (obligation-governing principles) that in turn imply moral cosmopolitanism, a morality of governance, and preservation of the human condition (see Chapter 3). International human rights law, then, points to a defensible reading of human dignity, albeit one that needs fundamental reconstruction via status, not human rights as a set of international standards (see below and Chapter 2).

If we turn from international instruments to international legal practice, human dignity veers between a function that reduces it to the prohibition on degradation and atrocity on the one hand (Weinert 2015), to a new world order or *telos* for the international community on the other (Teitel 2011). There is a related tension between readings of human dignity as denoting 'humanity' and as denoting 'humanitarian' where, roughly, the first is generally aspirational and constructive and the second ameliorative, reactive, and concerned with human vulnerability. The assumption that these two concepts must nonetheless be coterminous (e.g. Tsagourias 2000; Teitel 2011) is under-theorised at best.

These tensions can be found not only between but within instances of scholarship on international law. Tsagourias, for example, seeks to place human dignity at the heart of international legal discourse and in the process put humanitarian intervention on a sound normative footing (Tsagourias 2000). For Tsagourias human dignity can be associated with various different, but ultimately purposive, conceptions of international law. International law is, variously, founded on natural law, driven by Benthamite utilitarianism (2000, 46), and has human dignity as a *telos* drawing the legal towards moral ends (2000, 44). Human dignity itself is an 'affective' concept which reveals the underlying value that we should find in international legal practice: our senses of humanity and solidarity (2000, 95) which also have components of well-being and *eudaimonia* (2000, 97). He places it within a 'discursive model' that accepts that there is no definitive statement of human dignity but encourages re-description of disputes and crises such that humanity can be centralised and moral obligations revealed (2000, 97). Human dignity is, functionally, a heuristic useful to draw out interests and needs beyond the state, ensuring that international law's conception of individuals is never purely beholden to states' interests. While there is undoubtedly the outline of a valid functional account of human dignity here – that human dignity imports, or insists upon, deontic concerns in a system that is more often consequentialist – the appeal to a 'heuristic' function is ambiguous, allowing Tsagourias (as it allows others) to render human dignity both aspirational and prohibitive. That is, there is a characteristic, and understandable, effort here to retain the *foundational* idea from human rights law and the *prohibitive* idea from humanitarian law (see below). But the price is a blurring of the constitutive and regulative as well as conceptual uncertainty, given that human dignity tracks any and all moral ideas (or at least morally individuating ideas) that can be deployed at the international level.

In a more critical way, Heath considers the tensions found specifically within international criminal fora and the ways in which human dignity sits uneasily in relation to the rule of law and good criminal procedure (Heath 2012). Human dignity's changeable and questionable contribution to international trials arises

> due to the multi-functional role of human dignity, in which it serves at once as a ground for all human rights, as a substantive right at issue in the particular case, and as a basis for legality. This may lead to the suggestion that legality concerns should fall in the face of overwhelming injuries to dignity. This kind of reasoning would be self-justifying; because international criminal tribunals are charged with prosecuting only the most serious crimes, the conduct at issue will almost always involve a grave threat to someone's conception of human dignity.
>
> (Heath 2012, 353; footnotes removed)

Moreover, because of human dignity's ability to bypass 'legality concerns' – it seems to apply regardless of existing positive law, regardless of existing procedure, and to provide morally justified legal decisions regardless of precedent – some judges in international courts are increasingly suspicious of its use. Heath's diagnosis is helpful:

> discomfort with operationalizing human dignity can be attributed to four features of the concept: specifically, human dignity is contested across domestic legal systems; it is indeterminate at the international level; it is malleable to serve a broad and unpredictable array of situations; and it may be adapted to an impressive array of functions, including specific rights, ground for all human rights, and an interpretive principle for existing provisions.
>
> (Heath 2012, 342; footnotes removed)

We will return to the specific demands of international criminal justice. There human dignity does, I think legitimately, allow us to deploy dignitarian principles in a relatively malleable way because of the limitations of the positive law in the area and because of the moral uncertainties arising from applying law to war. But Heath rightly draws attention to the challenge that human dignity appears to mount to legality itself in international law, functioning as an unpredictable norm unconditioned by normal legal reasoning. These problems are by now familiar problems of normative indeterminacy, regulative imprecision, and constitutive incoherence (Chapter 1).

But why is human dignity apparently *especially* indeterminate in international law? As I have maintained through earlier analyses, there is a confusion of the constitutive and the regulative which means that the *use* of human dignity in law veers dramatically between the general and the particular. But this takes on more specific meanings in the context of international law. What is crucial is the distance between the statism of the international legal system and the individualised and individualising implications of human dignity. With the interests of states as the prevailing constitutive assumptions, a constitutive commitment to human dignity appears to be a kind of category error: the international system concerns the coexistence of states not the interests of individuals directly.

Is the quest for a foundational commitment to human dignity a category error? There is certainly historical and conceptual sense in treating the foundations, and limits, of international law as Hobbesean, not dignitarian. The international legal system is effectively characterised as a set of prudential contracts made in the face of anarchy; as such, international law lacks purpose or real moral content beyond *pacta sunt sevanta* ('agreements must be kept'). From this perspective we can speak of the 'normative poverty' of the international system. That normative poverty reflects its construction under conditions resembling a prisoner's dilemma rather than an original position, i.e. where cooperation can be rewarded but where it is also prudent to be reactive and distrustful (Shaffer and Pollack 2012). Put another way, states have agency, interests, and virtues just like individuals. But practically, and strategically, these similarities can be rejected: "states choose, on the basis of prudential reason, to reject [this analogy]. This is because they claim that they are better off, prudentially, in a state of nature. Instead, a state can build up its capacity to coerce others so that it can achieve its purposes, and fashion international relations as a reflection of these interests" (Capps 2009, 231). By extension, there is a pronounced disjunction between actual public international and philosophical aspirations regarding international law. Cosmopolitanism and Enlightenment philosophies have assumed the rationality and purposiveness of international law, meaning certain kinds of federalism or even perpetual peace have been assumed to be the *telos* of international law (Kant 1991). In contrast, the classic theorists of international law built their bodies of jurisprudence in reaction to conditions of trade war and colonialism, conditions that made the state of nature – with its widespread fear and limited trust – never wholly eliminable (Tuck 2001).

It should not be assumed that the changes found in international law following the Second World War have fundamentally altered this picture. This is clear when we consider international law's *sources* as opposed to its potential foundations. Public international law is usually delineated by reference to its sources found in Article 38 of the Statute of the International Court of Justice, an Annex to the Charter of the United Nations (1945). Treaties, custom, general principles, and the writings of scholars are the recognised sources of international law. It is these sources that, alongside the equality of states, form the constitutional bedrock of international law. This emphasis on sources rather than foundations arises from the absence of a constitution as the substantive and procedural grounding of international law. And note that these sources exclude the precedent of international courts except as subsidiary grounds of interpretation. This means the system is not 'common' in the limited sense of evolving through precedent. Each source can be interpreted anew by each court and each generation.

The continued absence of a constitution, and the absence of precedent in international law's principal judicial organ, point us towards an understanding of international law's core relationship with time. International law does not accrete precedent and does not build a body of ideas that can be integrated into larger principled decisions about the nature of the law and the community it serves. Indeed, there is no international society that a constitution would serve to constitute (Allott 2001). International law is, then, a law without a society to constitute, an unconstituted polity with no past or founding moment to which it might show fidelity. Certainly, the establishment of the United Nations and the International Bill of Rights (i.e. the UDHR and the Twin Covenants) represent a new beginning after the failures of the League of Nations and the events of the Second World War. But this implies fleeing from horrors, not movement towards a conception of an international society and its values. Positive values could be identified by opposing these kinds of atrocities, but not enough to guide international law constructively into the future (see McDougal, Lasswell, and Chen (1969) for an attempt to do just this).

International law's relationship with space is equally important. The assumed origins of public international law in the Peace of Westphalia (1648) tied authority to territory. The territorial rights of states ground more specific rights and duties – rights to use resources, rights to exclude other states and some aliens, duties to avoid atrocity with regard to one's own populace – because of the state's exclusive territorial control. Jurisdiction, the power to speak law to a population, depends upon being recognised as having effective control over the territory to which the state lays claim (see Gross 1948). Control of territory is the precondition, but also the content, of the international legal rights of states. This Westphalian system has been changed and perhaps eroded by the emergence of transnational actors, systems, and norm entrepreneurs who have to, or choose to, bypass association with one space or territory and thereby avoid the jurisdiction of states. Such is the putative 'neo-medieval' world of contemporary transnational law (Bull 2012). Nevertheless, the *sine qua non* of conventional international law is territory. And many familiar questions of distributive justice, warfare, and individual rights have the territorial rights of states as their background conditions.

Returning to human dignity, then, we should I think be wary of two related temptations: to assume that international law has evolved in a dignitarian direction, and painting any and all positive developments in international law and international relations as contributions to human dignity. We can gesture broadly towards the work of the UN and its organs (along with the work of NGOs) and suggest that it is all evidence of the protection of human dignity (see, for instance, the wide, and heterogenous, range of international policies and activities covered in Lagon and Arend's 2014 volume). In response to this we have to note that human dignity thereby loses its descriptive and normative clarity: if anything novel in international law (or anything under the auspices of the UN) is a contribution to human dignity, then we lose any sense of what specific contribution human dignity might make to our thinking about international law. If the contribution human dignity makes is to be extracted from this network of activities, then it is tempting to identify human dignity with those more fundamental *humanitarian* activities and processes concerning the protection of basic needs, basic entitlements, and basic obligations (Rawls 1999; Weinert 2015). But this is not only to confuse discourses of humanity and the humanitarian (see below) but also threatens, once again, to identify the constitutive with the regulative.

More specifically, evolutionary or progressive accounts of international law and human dignity are subject to a specific kind of critique explored in Koskenniemi's work. Our understanding of international law tends to oscillate between state-focussed accounts which stress the state-based sources and functions of international law and competing positions which centralise humanity in giving international law purpose and justification. This is systematised in Koskenniemi's account of international law as perpetually shifting between 'apology' and 'utopia', i.e., legal arguments understood as apology for state action, and legal arguments construed as utopian (Koskenniemi 2006). Put in general terms, international law is characterised by an ineradicable argumentative dialectic between positive versus ideal sources of law:

> Either something is binding as an effect of a subject's will or command or it is binding independently of that will, because it is just that the standard should be so. Much of what international lawyers have to say about the sources of the law captures this dualism. But though the setting of the problem seems to demand a firm decision one way or another, neither seems fully able to trump its contrary. The 'justice' of an agnostic (liberal) society can only be what its members have 'consented' to – while why 'consent' should have such force, and where its limits lie ('you cannot consent to genocide'), must be received from some non-consensual principle of 'justice'.
>
> (Koskenniemi 2004, 237)

This grounds a distinctive opposition within international legal argument. International legal arguments attempt "to explain why the law it projects is both normative and concrete – that is, not vulnerable to the criticism of being apologetic or utopian" (Koskenniemi 2006, 158). It is not simply that international legal arguments are divisible into those that are utopian and those that are apologetic. Rather, each position represents a hazard from the perspective of the other position: we must valorise state consent lest we be considered utopian; stress moral justification lest we be mere apologists for state action. Nevertheless, one position cannot be understood without the other, there being no position outside these poles from which the 'right legal answer' becomes possible.

There are important threads here which, together, allow us to critically intertwine moral cosmopolitanism, a morality of governance, and international law. In making international legal arguments, we cannot escape from making our justifications ultimately rest upon the conventional sources of international law or the extrinsic justification they draw upon. Human dignity arguments, like any other arguments in international law, are judged by how well they distance themselves from being ultimately 'utopian' or 'apologetic'. Put more sharply, any explicit appeals to human dignity in international legal argument should not be taken to be evidence of the moral or legal maturity of the system: the force of any such argument can always be traced, with equal force, to its legal validity within positive law or the justificatory force of moral obligation outside positive law.

For example, humanitarianism in the name of human dignity is contradictory. On the one hand, we find arguments retrospectively apologising for state action and legally rationalising as the formation of customary law (rather than utopian defence of a moral end). On the other hand, humanitarianism is taken to represent the emergence of moral maturity in the international community (rather than a statist defence based on regional security or custom). The precise foundation and force of human dignity in this context can remain opaque (as per Tsagourias's analysis above) provided it contributes to rationalising these broadly defensible ends. And the presence of the discourse of human dignity in international law remains, therefore, ambivalent. It is not possible to divide those uses in international law that are 'mere' positive law or 'mere' rhetoric from those that have a 'progressive' meaning. No simple evaluation of that kind is possible within international legal discourse itself.

4.2 Global constitutional principles

The problem of finding the proper role for human dignity in international law can be deepened if we try to identify where and how its role should be constitutional. When we come to construct a critical perspective on international law, one with human dignity as a constitutive principle, we are presented with two ostensibly similar but quite different choices. The first is a kind of *internal* critical perspective on international law associated with the idea of 'humanity's law' which sees certain dignitarian trends and processes within international law itself. The second is an *external* cosmopolitan perspective that insists that law and legal institutions alone are incapable of re-constructing themselves in a morally defensible way. We have already encountered some reason to reject the former and endorse the latter position. I will amplify those arguments here.

The fact that international law now encompasses much more positive and constructive standards in the form of human rights has been taken as evidence of a shift in the normative centre of international law. Indeed, much has been made of the notion of progress towards human dignity or away from one precondition of its systematic violation, principally the sovereign inviolability of states (Peters 2009; Teitel 2011; Weinert 2015). Increased concern with humanity and the human in international law appears to reflect a deeper concern with the individual and not merely the state (Teitel 2011; Slaughter 2012). We have entered a period of emerging 'humanity's law' (a term coined by Teitel, but endorsed by Weinert, Slaughter, and others) which is combining certain fields of legal practice together under human dignity as a value (see, especially, Teitel 2011, 47–49). While the self-understanding of international lawyers and the international community may or may not have fundamentally altered, the internal dynamics and internal resources of international law are such that an orientation towards the individual is evident and irreversible.

My first concern with this narrative is precisely as a progressive narrative. Ruth Macklin (1977) has provided one of the most useful analyses of 'progress' for our purposes, because it maps usefully onto analysis of human dignity itself. Moral progress is a combination of two separate ideas.

> The principle of humaneness asserts that one culture, society, or historical era exhibits a higher degree of moral progress than another if the first shows more sensitivity to (less tolerance of) the pain and suffering of human beings than does the second, as expressed in the laws, customs, institutions, and practices of the respective societies or eras. The principle of humanity holds that one culture, society, or historical era exhibits a higher degree of moral progress than another if the first shows more recognition of the inherent dignity, the basic autonomy, or the intrinsic worth of human beings than does the second, as expressed in the laws, customs, institutions, and practices of the respective societies or eras.
>
> (Macklin 1977, 375)

And

> the concept of moral progress unpacks into two principles, and it is natural to wonder how these principles are related to each other so as to yield one univocal concept. The most plausible answer seems to be that satisfaction of either the principle of humaneness or the principle of humanity is sufficient to warrant a judgment that moral progress has taken place; if both principles are satisfied, there is a greater degree of moral progress than if only one principle is exemplified when a particular judgment is made about moral progress having occurred.
>
> (Macklin 1977, 375)

'Human dignity' in international law bifurcates along the lines indicated by Macklin, as does the discourse of 'humanity's law'. Sometimes we are indexing 'progress' and human dignity to the scale of international responses to atrocity and disaster. Sometimes we identify them with the ideals to which the system, however imperfectly, approximates. For defenders of 'progress', evidence of either is vindication.

This is tied to a more specific concern with progressive narratives, namely that there is no fundamental interrogation of the constitutional deficiencies of international law in discourses of humanity's law. There is no written constitution for the international legal system. Instead, there is a body of constitutional '*acquis*' – i.e. certain groups of principles and institutions are taken to be necessary presuppositions of the system. The UN Charter forms part of that, as does the agreement on the sources of law under the Statute of the International Court of Justice. However, there is no body of basic constitutional rules spelling out the nature of the community it serves or the basic institutional arrangements that constitute the polity. There are certain impermissible acts and obligations that cannot be contracted out of ('*jus cogens*' norms), but these do not preclude the rejection of legal norms by persistent objectors (Reisman 2013) or indeed the dissolution of the international legal system itself (Riley 2016). They also fuel the idea that much of international law is aspirational or 'soft' law, with only *jus cogens* norms having the combined moral and legal force to be considered law analogous to our 'normal' understanding of binding law (Weil 1983, 423). Structurally, public international law has no clear set of rules about precedent or rules providing mechanisms for law reform (the workings of the International Law Commission are advisory and tortuously slow). International law has, it could be said, the equivalent of a 'minimum content of natural law' (Hart 1994, 193f), being the basic prohibitions on harm and egregious wrongdoing that are necessary for international society's survival. And, to the extent that it has rules against use of force and rules on the conduct of warfare, there is semblance of the kinds of constitutive commitments that would ensure the basic continuation of the subjects of the system. But, conversely, the WHO advisory ruling on the legality of the use of nuclear weapons (*WHO Advisory Opinion* [1986]) failed to render their use necessarily illegal. As such, we might question whether international law has genuine commitment to the conditions of humanity's survival. In such circumstances, the progressive narrative of humanity's law remains at best a description of the blurring of humanitarian and human rights law but not a constitutional vision based on human dignity. At worst, it obscures the fact that the international system is inhuman a fundamental sense: it serves the interests of states, not humans.

Does the cosmopolitan tradition fare any better in these respects? The first thing to note is that the cosmopolitan *tradition*, as it considered and conceptualised international law, has encompassed very different ideas from an individual and rights-focussed position (typically treated as 'moral' cosmopolitanism) to a concern with the international rule of law and institutions (typically 'institutional' cosmopolitanism). Fabre gives expression to the first with three principles:

> (a) individuals are the fundamental units of moral concern and ought to be regarded as one another's moral equals; (b) whatever rights and privileges states have, they have them *only* in so far as they thereby serve individuals' fundamental interests; (c) states are not under a greater obligation to respect their own individual members' fundamental rights than to respect the fundamental rights of foreigners.
>
> (Fabre 2008, 964; emphasis in original)

David Held lists the conditions of a more institutional cosmopolitanism:

> 1. equal worth and dignity; 2. active agency; 3. personal responsibility and accountability; 4. consent; 5. reflexive deliberation and collective decision-making through voting procedures; 6. inclusiveness and subsidiarity; 7. avoidance of serious harm and the amelioration of urgent need.
>
> (Held 2002, 24)

Fabre's core concerns would be realised through the revision of our (international) norms such that states' rights are validated only by their being decomposable into human rights. Held's universal commitments would be realised through, *inter alia*, strengthening the existing United Nations system, enhanced democratic practices and participation, better integration between national and international law, and greater accountability for governmental and economic practices. What we find shared between the two (and put negatively) is the absence of a demand for cultural cosmopolitanism (that differences between cultures should be levelled) or a demand for world government (a demand that most theorists, following Kant, consider to be a pathway to tyranny).

What, positively, is the underlying force of cosmopolitanism? Two answers are possible. A *solidarity* amongst humans that transcends the accidents of statehood and geography, or a commitment to *plurality* that protects individuals and groups regardless of any deeper solidarity. In the former case, rights are always individually held and are typically protections against states and groups; in the latter case, rights could accrue to groups as such. These represent positions on a spectrum, identified by Bull (2012) and described by Caney (2005, 12f) between international 'pluralists' and 'solidarists'. Pluralism embraces difference in international society as an end in itself and the defence of states as means to that end. Solidarism emphasises the shared values and the possibility of general shared international practices. This is, nonetheless, a spectrum "at one end of which is the pluralist extreme which admits no common aims, and at the other end of which is a solidarist extreme which emphasises a considerable number of shared objectives" (Caney 2005, 12–13). The constitutional commitments that we might hope to find in international law continue to be frustrated not only by state practice but also by an equivocation between these two conceptions of cosmopolitan obligation.

Is it possible to transcend these oppositions, and with it find a reading of human dignity and moral cosmopolitanism that provides a morality of governance for international law? Patrick Capps has stressed a definitive moral significance for human dignity, embedding this in the practical (self-)understanding of the international system. At first blush his position appears to be a demand for adoption of a particular value: "International law, like all forms of law, is a normative practice which is value-orientated towards the respect and protection of certain rights associated with human dignity. The rights of states are, in a moral sense, corollaries of this fundamental value-orientation" (Capps 2009, 272). But a value-orientation need not mean explicit championing of a single cluster of obligations. It can be, rather, a practical orientation, linking practical reason with human dignity:

> The rational aim of any action is to bring about a state of affairs which is consistent with the dignity of all human beings: that is, to bring the social relations which comprise our communities closer to the kingdom of ends. From the perspective of our own communities, actions can be said to be practically reasonable to the extent that they are consistent with recipients' human dignity. Our systems of public governance and our other organised activities are reasonable for the same reason. As much is true for normative practices such as law or international law and is the basis upon which they should be conceptualised.
>
> (Capps 2009, 125)

Any defensible reasoning in international law includes principles, or 'solidarist values', which order legal and political reasoning towards the status of the individual.

At this point, certain kinds of characteristic tensions recur in our understanding of international law. It may well be the case that underlying the explicit doctrinal *sources* of international law are certain *principles or values* that orientate it properly to sound social and moral ends. But this still maintains the state as a kind of fiduciary intermediate between legal system and individual and at liberty to decide how best to determine the rights and interests of individuals. We also find, by extension, an ambiguity in the role of rights in the overall normative justification of cosmopolitanism. Capps's own solution will be to link rights with human rights *qua* the generic entitlements arising from agency (as defended in Gewirth's work (e.g. Gewirth 1981)). But, given that in Gewirth's position any defensible normative claims are ultimately reducible to individual human rights, it faces a double challenge from both solidarist and pluralist positions: it does not seem to be a defence of solidarity as such but nor does it support the group rights necessary for plurality.

What I defend, in contrast, is a form of 'qualified pluralism' both because of the problems of the solidarity position and because of the importance of plurality (defended in Chapter 3 and elsewhere in this chapter). Even if it could be successfully combined with a theory of international human rights, the demand for solidarity has links with the assumption that, prior to the existence of any polity and prior to any defensible constitutional arrangement, there must be an organic agreement between people (or peoples) such that their constituent power can legitimate the institutions that are formed, and acts decided, under the constitution. This Rousseauean position should be rejected in favour of a form of qualified pluralism. By qualified pluralism I mean a defence of natural groupings as such (national, religious, ethnic, linguistic groups, etc.) as already constituted and legitimate sources of authority. This entails rejecting the idea that there must be any further solidarity – any further agreement, pact, or conscious transferal of authority – between those groupings or the individuals who make them up to justify national or international obligations. Put negatively, justified cosmopolitan commitments do not require every individual transcending their group identities and asserting an international solidarity. Nor does it mean, by extension, that the existence of general or universal obligations must mean the negation of group identities. It means that we should be allowing groups, up to and including nations, to exist and have their own rights to the extent that these rights are conditioned by the demands of human dignity: i.e. groups should be expected to respect human rights and the dignitarian principles that bolster them. This does not mean the dissolution of groups, but it may mean that the membership conditions, and identity, of groups is challenged if they fail to respect the rights and liberties of their members. Qualified pluralism is, then, the key to reconciling moral cosmopolitanism and the continued existence of the state, at least to the extent that states protect human rights, contribute to protecting groups, and insist that those groups respect human rights. What, then, are those rights and why should we accept the articulation of them that we find in international law?

4.3 International human rights law

In addressing international human rights law we face a three-fold but conjoined task: to find a proper conception of the meaning, and the underlying unity, of this group of human rights; to relate them to constitutional concerns in international law; and to relate them to human dignity reconstructed as status.

We should begin with a familiar regulative understanding of international human rights laws. Conventionally divided into generations, human rights laws form three classes: civil and political rights, social and economic rights, and third-generation group rights. These are supplemented by a number of instruments outlining the specific entitlements of women, children, and the disabled. They reassert and rearticulate existing rights on the basis of the special disadvantages these groups face in realising the objects of human rights.

These human rights laws are universal standards in two senses. First, we expect the objects of human rights – be they civil and political, or social and economic goods – to be delivered without discrimination. Second, to the extent that many (if not all) of these rights have a claim to being customary international law, they bind states regardless of whether the state has explicitly signed a relevant treaty or not. Conversely, 'universal' does not mean unchanging and absolute standards; any legal regime admits some variation on the basis of the principle of '*ought* implies *can*'. International human rights are, therefore, legally universal, but the determination of human rights obligations requires a 'margin of appreciation' allowing variation in interpretation, and permits 'progressive realisation' allowing situation-specific variation in thresholds of achievement (Green 2001). Nevertheless, international human rights laws are universal regulations requiring implementation by states in good faith. Monitoring takes place through 'universal periodic review', which, through a peer review process amongst states and overseen by the UN, demands systematic assessments of states' observance of international human rights law (OHCHR 2017a). 'General Comments' have been used to explicate international human rights norms in the absence of an international human rights court capable of advancing their jurisprudence through case law (OHCHR 2017b). And various regional courts have given positive effect to regional instruments, instruments enforcing a proportion of the UDHR rights tailored to maximise ratification and enforcement in that region.

These laws could be considered constitutive in the sense of their having a more general function to re-orientate national and international regulations towards individual rather than collective interests. As such, Article 28 of the UDHR – "Everyone is entitled to a social and international order in which the rights and freedoms set forth in this Declaration can be fully realized" – is a regulative expression of a constitutive commitment already latent in international human rights norms. Human rights imply stable and general international legal structures. Conversely, they cannot be of only immediate concern, or local concern, or of merely moral concern. And they are found linked, in the discourse of the UN, with 'rule of law' indicators (UN Rule of Law Indicators 2011) whereby the UN actively uses international human rights laws as standards within a wider model of assessment of states and their commitment to the rule of law. Thus international human rights laws form part of a wider concern with international law 'assessing' domestic law even as it admits variation in the domestic enforcement of individual human rights norms just as it admits variation in approximation to the rule of law.

Nevertheless, such talk of 'assessment' and 'standards' leaves us with two different possible readings of international human rights law as a body of norms. Either these are direct standards that should be applied in domestic legal systems or, conversely, they are minimal *aspirational* standards that we do not expect to be enforced *per se* and represent, in the main, 'manifesto' rights. Both extremes should be rejected. The interaction of domestic and international law is inevitably more complex than the imposition of norms downwards from the international to the national; there is neither practical nor legal sense in seeing the international system 'imposing' a comprehensive set of positive laws on each of the states of the world. Conversely, the manifesto model (with variations on this theme found in McGinnis 2003; Raz 2007; and Beitz 2013) cannot make sense of the resilience and continuing legal importance of international human rights law. It neglects the ideological power that human rights have in international affairs; and it neglects the fact that these norms are widely codified by states within their own domestic law (however imperfectly they are enforced).

International human rights laws are laws which are intended to be applied – i.e. brought to bear in different ways – to various situations across the world. Using human dignity as their core, they can be norms that can be violated but also standards used in (all things considered) judgements about the governance of a state. In that sense international human rights laws are connected to *both* human dignity *and* justice. Their principled core in basic human status holds good universally. They are applied (i.e. they are operationalised in legal and political discourse) with concern for justice: reasonably variable between states and equality within states. The international legal system does not function to impose uniformity on states but strives to articulate the international community's common – legal, moral, and political – denominators through international human rights law. This means that there are limits to what is 'reasonable' in the functioning of states. It means that international law constitutes the international community, using human rights, through defence of rights that are not positive legal rights and can, through those rights, articulate the limits of positive law.

From that perspective we can engage with some of the more challenging or idiosyncratic aspects of international human rights laws. These include understanding human rights' various 'generations', the status of group rights, and the possibility of generating new rights (for an overview of each, see Nickel 1987, 2008). Regarding the last, persistent concerns about 'rights inflation' reflects legal and philosophical anxiety: the anxiety, in part, of cheapening the argumentative effectiveness of human rights in practice; and the anxiety, in part, of introducing a form of normative relativity where some sets of norms appear to be 'more legal' than others (Weil 1983). Here the concerns are fundamentally doctrinal and they reflect Koskenniemi's analysis. The international practitioners of human rights are understandably eager to remain close to the letter and scope of the UDHR as a primary expression of international law on the matter because the UDHR has (at least in part) customary status and force. That is, respect for *states' will* entails doctrinal fidelity to the letter of positive international law. Conversely, the principles underlying the UDHR demand dynamic, principled interpretation and cannot be limited by the will of states; international human rights argument must be *utopian*. In that sense the question of the expansion of international human rights law cannot be conducted within international legal discourse without producing an antinomy. The ultimate, principled, answer will lie outside the system of positive legal norms.

The problem of 'generations' of rights is dissolved in a different way. Solidarity rights (or third-generation rights) to development, peace, environment, and humanitarian assistance are a complex of concerns which need application of the basic dignitarian principles rather than human rights law (see Rao 2011). Humanitarianism and peace have to be treated separately and are considered below; these 'rights' must be converted into dignitarian obligations that can be deployed in international argument but cannot be codified. After all, we expect to hold states to account for failing to maintain peace, but we do not expect to possess an individual right to peace. Development is a concern with justice and the identification of just distributions, not human dignity *per se*. The protection of groups does, however, require further attention.

Concern for the interests, agency, and autonomy of groups is of especial importance in international law. The international system, defending both solidarity and plurality, seeks to uphold the rights of groups, including minorities and other non-dominant or subaltern groups. The group rights in international law have been divided into three main types: "those stemming from the right to self-determination, those required for the protection of non-majority group members, and others predicated on the collectivisation of certain individual rights" (Bantekas and Oette 2013, 411). Each presents moral and political challenges. The first concerns the right of peoples to secede from a larger state and is politically, as well as legally, controversial. The second attaches to specific religious, ethnic, racial, or other groups and their interests (as a group) within a larger administrative or national group (a state or nation-state) which are problematic regarding the protection of rights for those within the groups (including the rights of those wishing to exit the group). The third (aggregating the rights of many individuals) might be thought to include "the right to peace, the right to a healthy environment or the right to be free from corruption" (Bantekas and Oette 2013, 412), although (as above regarding peace) it is challenging to defend these as rights claims at all.

Historically, group rights have their origins in both the human rights and the decolonisation movements (Bantekas and Oette 2013, 413f). These place different inflections on the rights. The protection of minority groups, to the extent that they are formed of vulnerable individuals, is certainly a human rights concern; the right to self-determination is, conversely, a product of decolonisation. Collectivised rights might be thought to rest at different times on both, but also on more recent concerns with global or distributive justice as it confronts the disproportionate burdens that are often borne by minorities or less developed countries (i.e. experiencing a disproportionate burden of the consequences of climate change). Nevertheless, the more nebulous rights, like that of the right to development or solidarity (see the UN (Draft) Declaration on Human Rights International Solidarity (2016)), are more clearly issues of justice than of human dignity given that the burdens and entitlements that they encompass are likely to be conceptualised and resolved through global distributive practices as opposed to reorientation towards the status of the individual (though the line is not entirely sharp).

As *human* rights this class of rights could be justified like any other more specific human rights instrument (e.g. for the disabled or for women) in terms of their compensatory or restitutive function. That is, they are premised on the existing (first two) generations of (individual) human rights. However, to the extent that certain groups have been and will be prevented *through social practices* from the full realisation of (normal/generic) human rights, there must be additional legal measures in place both to serve the expressive function of asserting these groups' equality. Third-generation rights restructure governance and social practices to achieve the preconditions of the other rights. This broadly 'compensatory' explanation of group rights does seem to reflect the post-colonial and the restitutive duties flowing from colonisation.

Note, however, that (in distinction to the more specific instruments tailored towards women, children, or the disabled) group rights in international human rights law are not explicitly intended to be reassertions or articulations of pre-existing rights. Groups are entitled to rights *qua* particular groups, i.e. 'the human rights of religious group *x*', or 'the human rights of linguistic minorities' rather than collections of individuals possessing rights *qua* humans but in distinctive groupings. Moreover, the problem of ascribing the human rights to a group is not only their questionable status as human rights but their potential to be claimed in bad faith or in pursuit of illiberal ends (Bennett 2009). Thus, ascribing any rights to groups could be assumed to be a threat to individuals' rights. The alternative would be to argue that these rights do indeed supervene on the rights of individuals within the groups. As such we reach the most obvious point of tension in thinking of groups and human rights: the individualising thrust of human rights, and the aggregating and consequentialist calculating of group welfare. A reading of the law reducing group rights to the entitlements of individuals within the group is preferable to maintain a normative connection with human dignity. However, this does not resolve all the possible problems.

The idea that groups might possess certain moral rights seems relatively unproblematic; to the extent that a group can be ascribed agency or interests it should also be able to possess rights (see, e.g., Buchanan 1997). Why then should these not be human rights? On an interest theory, groups have rights because they have collective interests to protect; on a will theory, groups can exercise or waive those rights as a reflection of their self-determination. At the same time, a claim might be made for the existence of a moral right *and* the existence of the relevant interest, but the international community might not countenance the exercise of such a right; the interest of some religious groups (along with theocratic states) to have international defamation laws to protect the beliefs of religious groups might be such a right that should not be recognised (Bennett 2009). The interests of the group might well be advanced by such laws, although the self-determination of groups yields rather more ambiguous implications (groups will undoubtedly seek laws that protect their beliefs and standing within a wider state, but such laws can also oppress out-groups). We should, in contrast, broadly endorse a compensatory view of group rights which supports their status as human rights only to the extent that this can be disaggregated into individual rights. This in turn points to more complex issues about the entrance into and exit from groups, i.e. whether and how groups allow membership and thereby share benefits and burdens within that group and to what extent this is democratic and equitable. To the extent that groups can be exclusionary and, for their own members, limiters of human rights, it is difficult to valorise 'groups' and their rights in a general sense.

The essential tension here, as regards the implications of human dignity, is between the importance of groups as a contribution to human plurality and the threat that such groups may compromise individual rights. We should defend the former while being alert to the latter. International law rightly protects groups as such even while at root the normative core of the status claim concerns individuals' juridical entitlements. This, then, is the basis of a commitment to 'qualified pluralism' that I think we should see as the basic point of interaction between human dignity and international law. Pluralism must be defended to the extent that it, in turn, is a contribution to the sovereignty of the individual: the potential for individuals to be free from authority and exercise self-determination. This does not give freedom to cultural or religious groups to oppress, but it does mean that such groups should be allowed to exist without being dissolved into larger nations or societies. This is a particularly important role for international law, i.e. managing the proper defence of, and controls on, groups. It is for states to do the more specific work of defending individual rights. Thus, the initial contradiction we encountered (that the system is not ultimately tailored for individuals but for states) must be overcome by international law's defence of ***human rights law*** as something that can be harmonised at the international level, and ***group rights*** defending plurality.

International human rights law has, then, not provided a perfect hinge between the constitutive and regulative demands that human dignity might make of international law. On the one hand we require better orientation, in the practice and the products of international law, towards human status. On the other hand we need to avoid equivocation between human dignity as a prohibitive norm and as a unifying set of principles. In the latter sense, international human rights law offers a disordered and unclear contribution to human dignity: principles are treated as rights, rights as aspirations, and their various 'generations' betray a contradiction with the 'indivisibility' we expect of human rights law. The problems usually associated with this area of law ('rights inflation', 'manifesto rights') should be rejected for being a misapprehension both of the relevant laws and the principled unity that underlies positive law. It is also assumed that, via human dignity, international human rights law can be connected with the laws of war, producing a unified body of law protecting, in particular, civilians caught up in warfare. We turn to these ideas in order to problematise them.

4.4 Warfare

Here we consider the application of human dignity in judgement. One unifying theme will be finding ways to apply dignitarian principles to conduct at the limits of moral, legal, and political justifiability. I consider more specific questions of humanitarian intervention and international criminal justice, but first I consider the general interaction of warfare, human dignity, and human rights.

What is international law's fundamental relationship with force and armed conflict? First and foremost international law is perceived, and perceives itself (Allott 2001), as a Hobbesean order formed without social purpose other than the avoidance of the misery of universal war. The publicists of international law (Grotius, Pufendorf, and others) made the right of war the centrepiece of their theories as a whole; for these theorists, as Tuck puts it, "self-preservation was a paramount principle, and the basis for whatever universal morality there was – for, they believed, no society could be found or imagined in which people were denied the moral right to preserve themselves" (Tuck 2001, 5). The defensive rights of states (in some instances pre-emptive rights of self-defence) were, according to Tuck, the core natural rights around which grew the philosophies and practical applications of the theories of early modern natural law. Be that as it may, our concern is with similar underlying principles, but also with more recent structural transformations of the international sphere, changes in the notion of the authority necessary to justify warfare. These speak, in turn, to the important but sometimes distorted role human rights play in the international arena, as well as back to the normative deficiencies of international law itself.

Legally, the UN Charter does allow for the use of force by states in self-defence and authorises the Security Council to deploy force for the purposes of regional security (UN Charter 1945, Chapter VII). However, the era of interstatal warfare where large, professionalised military forces engaged one another in a theatre of battle diminished over the twentieth century. The traditional dynamics of warfare – annexation of territory and the use of force to repel aggressive forces – were replaced by the Cold War with its smaller proxy wars and nuclear deterrence. After the Cold War three themes emerge: the stultification of the Security Council as an international policing force because of the veto of its permanent members; the use of 'humanitarian' discourse both as a positive development of conscience in the international community and as a fig-leaf for land and resource annexation; and finally, asymmetric warfare between states and terrorists. These characteristics of modern warfare sit quite uneasily with the rules of war (both of justifying armed force and the conduct of wars) found in existing international law. And,

> whereas violations of the prohibition on the use of force which occurred during the Cold War at least triggered significant legal debates in State practice, recent developments may suggest a disregard for international law which is systematically more relevant [. . .]. Unilateral interventions and unilateral interpretations of UN Security Council resolutions in the cases of Kosovo, Iraq and Libya may have contributed to undermining the credibility not only of the intervening States, but may even have called into question the Charter system as a whole.
>
> (Kreiger and Nolte 2016, 11)

We will return in the next section to the question of whether unilateral action is necessarily harmful to the international rule of law, but this 'disregard for international law' is certainly a recognisable and important phenomenon.

These developments are not without their own dignitarian aspects (Lagon and Arend 2014; Weinert 2015). Most significantly, the legitimation of the use of force outside the Chapter VII powers found in the UN Charter are often justified using the language and rhetoric of human dignity (see, e.g., ICISS Report 2001). This connection between force and human dignity is also drawn, philosophically, quite directly (Tsagourias 2000), or more often through the idea of enforcing certain human rights (Rawls 1999). This has recently been conducted within a period of renewed interest in 'just war' theory, the discourse of the Right to Protect ('R2P'), and the defence of 'cosmopolitan' grounds for war (Fabre 2012). Each of these has some consideration in what follows, but my initial concern is with the more general interaction of human dignity, use of force, and international legal human rights law.

A systematic cosmopolitan position on warfare has recently been produced by Fabre (2012, 2016). Fabre argues that warfare, if it can be justified, must be justified in a way that is normatively reducible to the protection of individual rights. The United Nations rules regarding self-defence, for instance, can be reconstructed on cosmopolitan lines as defences of the interests of individuals, as can the governance of warfare through humanitarian law. Moreover, military action taken outside that framework can be justified (as has frequently been done) under a wider set of 'just war' considerations (Walzer 2015). But these Thomist just war criteria stand in need of refinement such that they can be properly reducible to individual rights. Thus, a just cause requirement for waging justified war can take its meaning from individual rights and should not be read through other (typically Thomist) lenses. For Fabre we can, despite focus on the justificatory centrality of human rights, salvage much of the just war tradition. But where the rights of individuals, not states, are the normative driver, we must accept both expansion in the grounds for waging legitimate war and a greater amount of self-restraint in the conduct of war (Fabre 2012).

Lest we think that international armed conflict admits simple determinations of obligations or simple attributions of responsibility, Fabre insists on the importance of an 'all things considered' standard. Justice in this context faces considerable obstacles: "epistemic constraints, resource constraints [. . .], and agents' unwillingness to accept just terms" (Fabre 2016, 19). The possibility of distinguishing 'a just peace' from 'a just peace *all things considered*' provides the analytical tool necessary to distinguish principled but unconditioned moral claims from principled but *conditioned, given the context of warfare*, claims. The device is important for giving normative weight to the context in which decisions are being made, namely where the parties may have been morally compromised by their own conduct and ideal outcomes are impossible given tragic losses on both sides. It allows us to say a just peace (all things considered) would include "a state of affairs where individuals do not enjoy all of their non-basic rights as a result [of certain common post-war obstacles] but where they nevertheless enjoy their basic rights" (Fabre 2016, 20). Fabre thereby shows us a way to combine the 'normal' components of moral theory and human rights theory with the 'abnormal' aspects of warfare.

Does Fabre's overall position cohere with the dignitarian one defended here? It has not been an article of faith in these reflections on international law (or elsewhere) that we should be able to trace the justification of all practices, principles, and institutions to individual human rights. Thus Fabre's reshaping of the laws of war to conform to a normative basis in individual rights is attractive but not the *sine qua non* of a defensible position. Note, in a different vein, that the distinction made herein between the implications of human dignity and of justice means that we should draw a distinction between the 'reasonable' and an 'all things considered' standard. Fabre rightly eschews a special reasonableness standard for the assessment of conduct in this area in favour of a standard related to basic rights. To that extent her position is correct; any attempt to make the 'reasonable' the core of judging actions in warfare is likely to lapse into incoherence. However, even then it should be noted that appeal to 'basic rights' as normative bedrock will always be an incomplete justification without supplemental *principles.* Accordingly, if we attempted to justify the use of force through human rights alone, we would end up, like Fabre, relying upon a neat and decisive line between basic and non-basic rights (2016, 20) where a certain threshold of violations of basic rights will justify force. Rather, when we come to think of the justification of armed conflict and warfare, particularly when it is much more obviously moral rather than legal justification, we must consider the protection of individuals that such action will accomplish. But we need not assume there is a single threshold of violations of basic rights, nor (by extension) must the use of force have its grounding in appeals to certain human rights laws.

Turning from the justification of warfare to the conduct of warfare, the most striking legal feature of the area is the nominal suspension of human rights law in favour of the more basic principles of humanitarianism. Humanitarian law is intended to humanise, as far as possible, the brutality of war by distinguishing treatment of combatants and non-combatants and by attempting to minimise the inevitable impact of conflict on the latter. Two elements of this are of especial importance: first, the putative 'suspension' of human rights laws in this context; second, the distinctive ways in which 'dignity' and 'humanitarian(ism)' have become linked sometimes in ways at odds with the prevailing functions of human dignity associated with international human rights law.

The suspension of human rights law (or, more properly, the inability to make a claim concerning its violation) in times of war is not only philosophically problematic but legally unclear. In legal terms, it has long been argued (*WHO Advisory Opinion* [1986]) that the *lex generalis* of human rights is replaced by the *lex specialis* of international humanitarian law. This means that conformity to (and making claims on the basis of) human rights is suspended (for the parties to, and citizens caught up in, a conflict) in favour of the body of norms better suited to the situation. Asserted by the International Court of Justice in their 1986 Advisory Opinion, this rejected the argument that the human right to health could be used to deny the legality of nuclear weapons. But it defended the more general proposition that a specialised field of law, given its better purchase on the kind of situation at issue, should be the determinant of rights and obligations. In warfare, it says, we must look through the lens of international humanitarian law, not human rights law. In practice, however, international and regional courts have been increasingly willing to consider the human rights entitlements of civilians and soldiers during armed conflict, and while it remains lawful (all things being equal) to take another combatant's life during conflict, the state has positive responsibilities under human rights law to investigate wrongful killing of civilians and combatants (*Al-Skeini* [2011]).

In practice the primacy of humanitarian norms is essential to guide the conduct of warfare and limit its excesses. International humanitarian law represents the laws of war, encompassing the Geneva Conventions (which speak directly to soldiers about the conduct of warfare) and a number of treaties and principles governing specific and potential forms of weaponry. This field of law, moderating and ameliorating but not outlawing warfare, allows the killing of innocent individuals, amongst other human rights violations, in favour of prioritising principles like proportionality (avoiding force in excess of that needed for military advantage) and discrimination (between civilians and combatants).

The pragmatic value of this focus is difficult to dispute. During warfare we need a form of law in place that better fits with a state of nature and that ameliorates the worst possible excesses of war for civilians and combatants. This means that all sides can use force, within certain limits that both would accept, and it also means adopting a simpler body of laws that soldiers themselves carry onto the battlefield and apply to their own conduct during conflict. Thus the Geneva Conventions and their additional protocols are addressed to states, but they should be intelligible to the individual soldiers that need to apply them in the theatre of war. As Henry Shue puts it, the laws of war enforce certain minimum humanitarian ideas "in order that the breaches in [our normal moral] standards are not torn more widely than the persistence of international conflict makes necessary" (Shue 2010, 511). He argues that this creates remedial, not ideal, standards: "Rather than condemning the violations inherent in violent conflict, the laws of war have concentrated on preventing the exceptions from swallowing the rules. This has involved insisting upon limits where ordinary law and morality maintain complete prohibitions: limitation, mostly without endorsement of what is not condemned" (Shue 2010, 511).

This provides important background to the putative meeting point between *jus in bello* (law in war) and human dignity, namely the Geneva Conventions' Common Article 3 prohibiting 'outrages on personal dignity' (see, generally, Petersen 2012). The specific provision is as follows:

> Persons taking no active part in the hostilities, including members of armed forces who have laid down their arms and those placed 'hors de combat' by sickness, wounds, detention, or any other cause, shall in all circumstances be treated humanely, without any adverse distinction founded on race, colour, religion or faith, sex, birth or wealth, or any other similar criteria. [. . .] To this end, the following acts are and shall remain prohibited at any time and in any place whatsoever with respect to the above-mentioned persons: (a) violence to life and person, in particular murder of all kinds, mutilation, cruel treatment and torture; (b) taking of hostages; (c) *outrages upon personal dignity, in particular humiliating and degrading treatment* [. . .].
>
> (Geneva Conventions Common Article 3 [1949], paragraph 1; emphasis added)

The background and function of Common Article 3 is explained in the case of *Alekovski* [1999]:

> A reading of paragraph (1) of common Article 3 reveals that its purpose is to uphold and protect the inherent human dignity of the individual. It prescribes humane treatment without discrimination based on 'race, color, religion or faith, sex, birth, or wealth, or any other similar criteria.' Instead of defining the humane treatment which is guaranteed, the States parties chose to proscribe particularly odious forms of mistreatment that are without question incompatible with humane treatment. The [drafters] sought

> to adopt wording that allowed for flexibility, but, at the same time, was sufficiently precise without going into too much detail. For 'the more specific and complete a list tries to be, the more restrictive it becomes.' Hence, while there are four subparagraphs which specify the absolutely prohibited forms of inhuman treatment from which there can be no derogation, the general guarantee of humane treatment is not elaborated, except for the guiding principle underlying the Convention, that its object is the humanitarian one of protecting the individual qua human being and, therefore, it must safeguard the entitlements which flow therefrom.
>
> (*Alekovski Case* [1999], paragraph 218)

This shows Common Article 3 mapping out a humanitarian core of basic protections, expressed in the language of dignity, drawing the basic boundaries of what is permitted in war. The prohibition on outrages on personal dignity is amongst the clearest examples of dignity being used in a narrowly prohibitive way but also being assumed to carry enormous symbolic importance and form a link with human rights law. Indeed, the 'outrages' at issue would overlap with the prohibition on 'torture, inhuman and degrading treatment' found elsewhere in international human rights law. Clearly both areas of law were created (human rights law) or codified (humanitarian law) in the immediate post-war period. Moreover, there is no doubt that at some level both areas of law represent a turn in international law towards the human. Nonetheless, the link between the two areas is easy to overstate, and it is not clear that it is helpful to identify personal dignity with human dignity. If the latter is a status concept, the former is intended to be a norm, addressed to frontline soldiers, prohibiting cruelty and humiliation of opponents in the theatre of war. More to the point, the legal and practical functions being aimed at here are distinct: to speak to soldiers about the conduct of military operations and to speak to the international community about universal obligations.

Are moral norms and moral reasoning altogether out of place in this context? In the theatre of war we have a suspension of the justiciability of human rights but not of moral obligations altogether. As has been argued, the language of 'reasonableness' would be out of place in governing the brutality of warfare. But certain aspects of the laws of war have a similarly open texture (for instance, Common Article 3), allowing the law to expand to cover new eventualities and to ensure that cruelty does not escape liability. This can be found clearly in reasoning related to the 'Martens Clause', a broad principle of international humanitarian law insisting that not everything explicitly prohibited by positive law is permissible:

> The Martens clause supports the claim that IHL [International Humanitarian Law] more closely resembles a moral system than a legal system in several ways. First, in terms of IHL's content, the Martens clause declares that principles of humanity and the dictates of public conscience are essential parts of IHL. That is, a morality of chivalry and humanism is integral to IHL. Second, the Martens clause emphasizes the resemblance between IHL

> and moral systems in terms of structure. [. . .] The Martens Clause [applies] when the agents are required to fill the gaps using 'the principles of humanity and the dictates of public conscience'.
>
> (Khen 2016, 34)

Assuming this is correct, what role, if any, is there for human dignity specifically within legal reasoning?

One of the most striking operationalisations of human dignity in international humanitarian law is found in *Furundzija* [1998], which concerned the question of whether penile penetration of the mouth constituted rape under Additional Protocol II (Article 4(2)(e)). This question had never before been considered in an international court, and rather than appeal to emerging consensus on the issue amongst domestic systems the Court struck a principled stance appealing to the unifying principle of human dignity in human rights and humanitarian law.

> The general principle of respect for human dignity is the basic underpinning and indeed the very *raison d'être* of international humanitarian law and human rights law; indeed in modern times it has become of such paramount importance as to permeate the whole body of international law. This principle is intended to shield human beings from outrages upon their personal dignity, whether such outrages are carried out by unlawfully attacking the body or by humiliation and debasing the honour, the self-respect or the mental well being of a person. *It is consonant with this principle that such an extremely serious sexual outrage as forced oral penetration should be classified as rape.*
>
> (*Prosecutor v. Furundzija* [1998], paragraph 183; emphasis added)

This passage, linking the two areas of law as a means of securing a conviction, has value. As a piece of reasoning it is not convincing. Undoubtedly human dignity here contributes to a just conviction and a valuable clarification of the law. Nevertheless, it is easier to see why the human dignity of human rights law can give rise to a prohibition on egregious mistreatment than the converse argument that we can understand human rights via a narrow prohibition.

This overview of the interaction of warfare and human dignity is intended to expose both new and familiar themes. A certain kind of blurring of regulative and constitutive is to be expected. But it is a distinctive aspect of this area that we face extreme difficulty linking our principles to the lived reality of warfare. Fabre's cosmopolitan approach has distinctive merits, but I want to turn to a wider concern with human dignity and the international rule of law. The precise challenges of linking our principles with individuals' conduct in armed conflict will receive specific treatment in our discussion below of international criminal justice.

4.5 Humanitarian intervention

These general reflections on the connections between war, human dignity, and human rights reflect the complex and legally uncertain place that warfare has even in contemporary international law. While the ICC Statute (2002) forbids the crime of aggression, and the UN Charter permits defensive use of force only in response to aggression, precise judgements about the permissibility of any particular use of force remain difficult to draw. This, as we will see, is because of the political contestation of how 'aggression' is to be characterised in any particular case (a recent example would be the possibility of aggression through cyber-attacks). But it is also because our conceptualisation of the making of war has always set the legal against the moral. So, while legality has presumed the setting aside (or consensual pooling) of the right to use force, the moral discourse of just war seeks to form realistic criteria for legitimising recourse to violence. Fabre glosses the traditional 'just war' criteria as follows: "At the bar of *jus ad bellum* [the legality of waging war] traditionally understood, a war is just if, and only if, the harms it causes are outweighed by the goods it brings about, and if it is waged for a just cause, to just ends and by a legitimate authority" (Fabre 2008, 963). And, despite the relatively unequivocal position of the UN Charter in this response, the publicists of international law have always been more subtle and concerned with the public and private grounds, and the public and private authority, to wage war:

> Grotius is quite clear in *The rights of war and peace* that a private man may wage war against his own state if no legal recourse is available, as well as against a sovereign other than his own. [. . .] [O]n principle, individuals may sometimes go to war, without permission from the sovereign, in defence of their fundamental interests in life and property.
>
> (Fabre 2008, 970; references removed)

We will turn below to the particular features of modern warfare. But it is humanitarian intervention that forms the focus of my concerns here.

Humanitarian intervention is of primary importance here because of the primacy of moral principles over positive law in the international arena. The intervention by NATO in Kosovo was roundly held to be morally justified but legally unjustified (Zolo 2010, 555). In part this concerns the general framework provided by the UN Charter which presumes that self-defence (conceived in a traditional sense concerned with territorial integrity) will be the starting point of any justified use of force. More specifically it is a question of authority, particularly the residual 'moral' authority of a state or states, to engage in warfare for reasons other than immediate self-defence. It is generally agreed (amongst the classic publicists of international law and contemporary commentators) that punishment of a state would not be a legitimate ground. Conversely, a more general appeal to 'justice' or 'protection of civilians' may be. However, such justifications are ambiguous in terms of their legality. These grounds are not permissible grounds under positive international law. The question is whether they would be (morally and legally) analogous to civil disobedience where bad law is displaced by defensible moral grounds for action. Buchanan demonstrates that this, too, would be ambiguous:

> The chief justification [of humanitarian intervention] presents the illegal action as a necessary exception to law-abidingness in the name of justice, without in anyway implying that the system as a whole, or even the particular rule that is violated, is in need of improvement. Employing this justification is fully consistent with believing that the existing rule that requires Security Council authorization for humanitarian intervention is a good rule, even that it is the best rule possible.
>
> (Buchanan 2001, 675)

Here Buchanan distinguishes such intervention from civil disobedience proper, which would be an example of breaking a rule in pursuit both of good ends and of *communicating the indefensibility of the rule itself*:

> The second justification is quite different: it justifies the illegal intervention as an act directed toward reforming the system. Its implication is that the existing rule requiring Security Council authorization is not optimal, and that a new norm of humanitarian intervention, according to which Security Council authorization is not needed, is morally preferable.
>
> (Buchanan 2001, 675)

On this basis, the parallel with civil disobedience holds. The question then is: for a dignitarian defence of humanitarian intervention must one or other of these justifications be clearly fulfilled? In other words, is the connection between human dignity and humanitarian intervention one of reacting to atrocities (reacting to a certain threshold of human rights violations), or, rather, does the relation lie in a reform of the law itself and reformation of the prevailing UN Chapter VII powers?

We are, I would argue (in line with Buchanan's second argument), confronting legality at its limits when we consider humanitarian intervention. It is not simply the case that the UN systems offers an idealisation that cannot be applied to reality (namely, only use of force in self-defence). Rather, humanitarian intervention properly understood must inhabit the same place in our thinking as civil disobedience. It concerns the conditioning of law by morality (the obligations principle) and the presumption that permissions exist where the law is silent (the permissive principle). It is, then, broadly justified on dignitarian grounds to use force in legally uncertain circumstances.

It is, however, for an independent international court in possession of the facts to decide whether a state has acted in *good faith* in that use of force. That is, not whether it was justified under existing law – we are concerned with cases not clearly authorised by the law, and the ICC rules on 'aggression' are not yet fully developed – but whether it was justified, all things considered. It is for the

ICC to determine, on principled grounds, the distinction between legitimate and illegitimate force. Thus, the question for an international court is whether a state acted in good faith, and whether the spirit of the international rule of law (if not the letter) has been respected. Again, Buchanan rightly prises the legal and moral apart:

> Approximation of the ideal of the rule of law is a necessary, not a sufficient, condition for our being obligated to comply with legal norms, even if a deep commitment to the ideal of the rule of law is assumed. A system might do a reasonably good job of exemplifying the elements of the rule of law and still be seriously defective from the standpoint of substantive principles of justice. [. . .] And if justice is to enjoy the kind of moral priority that is widely thought to be essential to the very notion of justice, then one cannot assume that illegal acts directed toward eliminating grave injustice in the system are always ruled out by fidelity to the ideal of the rule of law. Since many, indeed perhaps most, extant theories of justice include more than the requirements of the rule of law, it would be very misleading to assume that any illegal action for the sake of reforming the international legal system by making it more just must be the imposition of the reformer's subjective view of morality or merely personal views.
>
> (Buchanan 2001, 685)

My only hesitation with Buchanan's expression of this position is that it encourages us to take justice (however wide theories of justice may be) to exhaust the extra-positive discourse justifying humanitarian intervention. Human dignity allows us to do that, albeit not by creating thresholds (i.e. moral thresholds expressed in the language of justice) but by insisting upon the limits of legality.

Where does this leave recent attempts to clarify the legal position under 'the Right to Protect'? These 'R2P' principles have connected human security with human dignity:

> [The] international community has a responsibility to act decisively when states are unwilling or unable to fulfil these basic responsibilities. The Commission has sought to give clear articulation to this consensus, and calls on all members of the community of nations, together with non-governmental actors and citizens of states, to embrace the idea of the responsibility to protect as a basic element in the code of global citizenship, for states and peoples, in the 21st century. [. . .] Meeting this challenge is more than a matter of aspiration. It is a vital necessity. Nothing has done more harm to our shared ideal that we are all equal in worth and dignity, and that the earth is our common home, than the inability of the community of states to prevent genocide, massacre and ethnic cleansing. If we believe that all human beings are equally entitled to be protected from acts that shock the conscience of us all, then we must match rhetoric with reality, principle with practice. We

> cannot be content with reports and declarations. We must be prepared to act. We won't be able to live with ourselves if we do not.
>
> (ICISS Report 2001, 75)

This is an attempt to codify, at least through the guidance of soft law, those circumstances when intervention is required. Relying upon 'just cause' criteria, it links legitimate intervention with the major ICC crimes (genocide, crimes against humanity) and not, we should note, international human rights. Just cause exists where there is

> large scale loss of life, actual or apprehended, with genocidal intent or not, which is the product either of deliberate state action, or state neglect or inability to act, or a failed state situation; or large scale 'ethnic cleansing', actual or apprehended, whether carried out by killing, forced expulsion, acts of terror or rape.
>
> (ICISS Report 2001, 32)

We should agree with this broad commitment and reiterate (as above) a connection with the International Criminal Court. The criminal acts themselves, along with military responses to them, fall within the jurisdictional purview of the Court. Prevention is certainly better than prosecution after the fact. But intervention plus answering to the jurisdiction of the Court is the best outcome under present conditions.

The Right to Protect nonetheless retains the contradictions already found in just war and humanitarian intervention. Just as there can be no law justifying the breaking of law, these principles can never become codified other than through reiteration of the validity of the UN Charter and the ICC Statute. The attempt to put them outside 'hard law' in 'principled' form masks the impossibility of ever properly integrating them into positive law. R2P, if litigated, would inevitably face the kinds of stultifying equivocations identified by Koskenniemi. These principles would, if litigated, invite competing arguments stressing either resistance to 'utopianism' or resistance to the reducibility of moral obligations to state will. The humanitarian impulse that underpins these ideas is laudable. The system they would operate within would not permit them to succeed.

At the limits of legality, humanitarian intervention cannot be properly conceptualised through the positive law of international law but nor can the additional 'moral' or 'political' concerns be captured purely through human rights. Human rights law is not merely a set of norms whose abuse is capable of triggering intervention (see Tasioulas 2009). And human dignity itself is not a threshold concept of 'unacceptable atrocity' for similar political purposes. The 'solution' to humanitarian intervention is both further away from, and closer to, international law than these arguments suggest. We need interstitial principles for use in argument such that the moral, legal, and political can be harmonised. At the same time we need judicial bodies to make judgements using such principles. The solution to humanitarian intervention lies, then, in judgement and politics, not in the fabric of positive law.

4.6 International criminal justice

While there are various ways to characterise international criminal justice, my concern is with its claim to restore legal order after conflict (and what this means) and with the inclusion of human dignity within the processes themselves. This contrasts with other accounts which focus on the nature of the crimes at issue (see Heller 2016) and the human right to a fair trial as a standard with which to judge the processes (see Heath 2012; Hoyle and Ullrich 2014; Fabre 2016). Linking all these questions, however, is the way in which international criminal institutions and their procedure are required to negate the validity of positive law in order to assert the priority of 'principles of humanity'.

Prosecution is only one of a number of possible responses to armed conflict; amnesties, truth commissions, and foreign administration are all possible avenues open to states themselves or to the international community. Lawfully, however, where there is evidence of international crimes, criminal prosecutions (or the engagement of international criminal processes) are a legal necessity (ICC Statute 2002, Article 12). International responses to conflict are juridical, not political, but recent resistance to the jurisdiction of the International Criminal Court is evidence that two cannot be easily separated (ICC Forum 2017). After all, while commencement of prosecutions is necessary when there is a *prima facie* case of criminal wrongdoing, it is also within the power of the Security Council to suspend investigations, and within the power of international courts to be selective in those they prosecute 'in the interests of justice' (ICC Statute 2002, Article 52(1)(c)). So, while the charge of victors' justice is still routinely levelled at international prosecutions, it is too crude to capture the established positive law and the procedural safeguards that now characterise international prosecutions. But the utility of prosecutions is still in question, as is their ability to provide *international* justice when the choice of conflicts appears selective.

Responses to atrocity take a variety of forms, and this is an area frequently characterised by oppositions: trials versus amnesties, accountability versus truth commissions. The contemporary field of post-conflict or transitional justice evidences a range of processes and hybrids of these kinds of activities. Nevertheless, the international community's professed goal to 'end impunity' found in the Rome Statute of the International Criminal Court means that the international legal presumption is that widespread international crimes – genocide, crimes against humanity, and war crimes – will always be prosecuted (ICC Statute 2002, preamble). The forum in which they are prosecuted will vary depending upon whether relevant states are able and willing to pursue prosecutions. In cases where they are not, the Security Council can refer the situation to the Court (ICC 2002, Article 13(a)) or the ICC Prosecutor herself may begin an investigation (ICC 2002, Article 15). Contemporary international criminal justice is, therefore, no longer characterised by *ad hoc* tribunals for particular situations, and it does not rely on the defeat (partial or complete) of one party to a conflict to be engaged.

International justice nevertheless still bears many of the marks of its origins in Nuremberg and Tokyo and the prosecution of major Axis war criminals. The imposition of criminal procedural norms is principally on the activities of those with command responsibility. It is assumed that a trial will contribute to an authorised narrative of the period of conflict being a point of certainty to which formerly antagonistic parties can turn. And it is hoped that these prosecutions will prove deterrent despite this being incalculable and speculative. As with Nuremberg, however good the procedural norms are, they are never strong enough to dispel the suspicion that international justice is always imbalanced, with courts always looking at poorer or weaker states. These criticisms are important and my concern hereafter will be to explore these and a number of other specific problems in the light of human dignity.

First, a persistent criticism of international tribunals is that of the instrumentalisation of defendants. Globally, retribution is selective, and defendants can become means to wider political ends of regional security or general deterrence (Fabre 2016). There is selectivity with regard to the 'situations' of concern and with it (given that most recent situations have been in Africa) the charge of neocolonialism. Broadly, any retribution that is selective (or as selective as it appears to be at an international level) is morally questionable. Specifically, deterrence is meaningless for internationally prosecuted individuals (the conditions of further relevant criminality have passed) and only general deterrence is possible.

Second, existing international crimes (including genocide, crimes against humanity, war crimes, and the 'crime of aggression') reflect an era of conventional inter-statal war, not contemporary threats to the international common good. It is uncertain what scope there is to expand the material jurisdiction of the Court by courts themselves (see Appazov 2015). A conservative interpretation of existing crimes is stultifying. A progressive interpretation is potentially unprincipled if this violates *nulla crimen sine lege* (no crime without law). Moreover, international law has no coherent jurisprudence concerning the use of force where this is for putatively humanitarian purposes.

Third, given the incompleteness of international criminal law – both because of the slow accretion of jurisprudence and because of its application to a dynamic phenomenon like warfare – moral notions like human dignity are used to fill gaps in the law. The uses of human dignity are often intelligible but equivocal (Heath 2012). Human dignity is loosely 'heuristic' insofar as it supports progressive or purposive readings of positive law. At some points, human dignity is potentially reducible to conventional sources of international law (general principles of law recognised by civilised nations) and is therefore not as radical or fundamental as it might appear (it has a broad gap-filling function but no extra-positive force). Thus human dignity has neither constitutive nor regulative clarity in this area.

Fourth and finally, international criminal law must be superior to, and have the right to negate, national law. Criminal legislation and criminal military orders are stripped of sovereign immunity along with heads of state. However, it is unclear with whose authority this takes place (Ambos 2013; Megret 2015), and the trials themselves simply invoke 'the prosecutor' as the authority who stands versus a defendant. The statutes or reasoning of international courts never directly acknowledge the legal and moral superiority of international law over criminal national laws. Anti-positivist principles, like the negation of egregious national laws as laws, are articulated through the defences available to a defendant, i.e. there being no defence of superior orders (ICC 2002, Article 33). Jurisdictional superiority over prosecution of the crimes is not the same as explicit, natural law–based negation of national laws as laws.

Given this range of problems and their straddling the political, legal, and moral, it is clear that the obligations principle must play some role in justifying (or criticising) these elements of international criminal justice. Above all this area involves the limiting of law by morality. The traditional principle of *lex iniusta non est lex* informs the entire functioning of international courts. The fact that this is hidden in the form of a defence (that one cannot claim superior orders as a defence to criminal activity (ICC Statute 2002, Article 33)) should make it no less central to our thinking about international criminal justice. Nevertheless, we are likely to confront considerable problems if we were to attempt to reconstruct this area as a positivist one whose justification and powers were defined purely by positive law (see Heller 2016 for discussion of these challenges). Part of the point of connecting human dignity to this area of law is not, then, to describe the outrages that the crimes involve but to describe our justified negation of domestic law. Were the ICC to have, within its constitutive rules an explicit Radbruch principle (for further discussion see Chapter 6) directly negating national legal authority rather than only functionally adopting this principle through the negation of superior orders, we might see a more coherent account of state responsibility generally and of the grounds on which the actions of states can be reviewed.

We are also concerned with the limiting of politics by law. These courts require the participation of states for their functioning, and they inevitably involve states enforcing jurisdiction over states whose populace and leaders are weakened by conflict. Arguably our concern should not be that stronger states are referring weaker ones, but rather the problem that stronger states are not referring themselves. The ICC should have the power to determine criminality through direct review (or advisory opinions) on the actions of any states (severing the link between the Court and the Security Council). States should (as above) be engaging in humanitarian intervention, but they should also be subjecting themselves to the jurisdictions of the ICC to confirm the justification of those actions. At the same time, it should be possible to investigate culpable omissions on the part of the Security Council where the Council, through the use of veto, has failed to prevent humanitarian catastrophe. We need the rule of law developed through state action but reviewed autonomously by international institutions like the ICC.

How, in essence, is this field related to, and justified by, human dignity? There is a predominantly substantive argument that can be made here about the international community's particular responsibility to protect plurality. While 'humanity' remains ambiguous as a standard and as a constituency, human diversity is an implication of human dignity and one which is assaulted by the major international crimes. It is along these lines that Arendt defends the otherwise problematic prosecution of Eichmann, problematic because of the apparent lack of *mens rea* on his part and on the apparent problem of Jews standing in judgement on crimes against themselves. Arendt addresses Eichmann as a judge:

> just as you supported and carried out a policy of not wanting to share the earth with the Jewish people and the people of a number of other nations – as though you and your superiors had any right to determine who should and who should not inhabit the world – we find that no one, that, is, no member of the human race, can be expected to want to share the earth with you. This is the reason, and the only reason, you must hang.
>
> (Arendt 2006, 279)

While it is right that international courts no longer use the death penalty, the insistence that attacks on human plurality should be tried and punished in international courts remains a powerful, dignitarian argument. Underlying the crimes of genocide and crimes against humanity is a substantive link between human dignity, the human condition, and justice.

Alternatively, we could insist that humanity is the proper normative foundation for justifying international courts. We can make a claim for the moral authority of the international community (representatives of, or substitutes for, humanity) as the only constituency to whom international criminals can properly answer. Nonetheless, it is difficult to presume that the international community has a privileged relationship with humanity or human dignity – and a special right to prosecute their diminution – without a better theory of international crime and of the international community itself. If the international community claims to be wronged by a crime against humanity of which they are the victim, in that case the victim is *standing in judgment over a wrong perpetrated against themselves* and it is therefore a violation of natural justice. So, despite the substantive link between human dignity and justice, is there no possibility of legitimate *legal judgment* in this context?

Heath demonstrated (see Chapter 1) that human dignity serves a gap-filling function in international criminal justice, a function that appears increasingly unattractive to judges and legal commentators because of its inconsistency and contribution to violations of *nulla crimen sine lege*. My response is that these justice-based concerns are justified, but that nonetheless human dignity must have this function. Something has to play a principled or gap-filling role in the context of international criminal justice because of the under-development of the field but also because this is legality *in extremis*. The application of law to warfare is difficult precisely because law is meant to serve a lawful condition or civil condition and legal judgment is meant to take place where certain normal or reasonable assumptions about agency can be presumed. The application of law to states of war must include principled elements that not only fill gaps in positive law but allow an all-things-considered judgment without this simply being casuistry or purely moral judgement. Human dignity legitimately fills this role because it is our normative bedrock: it holds good even when the circumstances of justice do not, and because it concerns the links between our normative orders, not the playing-out of those normative orders.

Consequently, the problems of international criminal justice (outlined above) could be crudely but effectively summarised as follows: international criminal justice is an area of law where law itself is minimal and patchy, where politics intrudes all too frequently, and where moral claims (with questionable legal pedigree) often have to take the role of strictly defensible legal reasoning. This is precisely the kind of interstitial problem where human dignity has its characteristic application. We do indeed fill 'legal' gaps with certain 'moral' principles; we certainly need some 'political' input to make international criminal institutions work, but we also need certain kinds of 'political' self-limitation to maintain the appearance of justice. Human dignity in this context is equivalent to the ongoing attempt to harmonise these three problematic normative orders. It is the essence of human dignity that we should assume they can be harmonised. Thus in international criminal judgments we should expect to see human dignity (as opposed to outrages on personal dignity) playing a synthesising role in the material and procedural aspects of international justice. Human dignity could be rightly invoked to demand that major political powers give themselves over to international criminal jurisdiction. It could equally correctly be used in material and substantive decisions about how a judgment can be reached in the absence of clear positive law. This is not a *carte blanche* to replace positive law with moral judgment. It is recognition that, in this unique legal and institutional context, we are in need precisely of unified, principled thinking at a procedural and substantive level.

References

Alekovski. (1999) *Prosecutor v. Zlatko Aleksovski*, International Criminal Tribunal for the former Yugoslavia (ICTY) Trial Chamber I, Case number IT-95–14/1-T, 1999.

Allott, P. (2001) *Eunomia: New Order for a New World*, 2nd edition. Oxford, Oxford University Press.

Al-Skeini. (2011) *Al-Skeini and Others v. United Kingdom*, Application no. 55721/07, [ECtHR], July 7, 2011, Available at: www.refworld.org/cases,ECHR,4e2545502.html, accessed March 27, 2017.

Ambos, K. (2013) 'Punishment without a Sovereign? The *Ius Puniendi* Issue of International Criminal Law: A First Contribution towards a Consistent Theory of International Criminal Law' *Oxford Journal of Legal Studies*, 33(2), 293–315.

Appazov, A. (2015) '"Judicial Activism" and the International Criminal Court', iCourts Working Paper Series, No. 17, Available at: https://ssrn.com/abstract=2566136, accessed March 2017.

Arendt, H. (2006) *Eichmann in Jerusalem: A Report on the Banality of Evil*. Harmondsworth, Penguin Books.

Bantekas, I. and Oette, L. (2013) *International Human Rights Law and Practice*. Cambridge, Cambridge University Press.

Barak, A. (2015) *Human Dignity: The Constitutional Value and the Constitutional Right*. Cambridge, Cambridge University Press.
Beitz, C. (2013) 'Human Dignity in the Theory of Human Rights: Nothing But a Phrase?' *Philosophy and Public Affairs*, 41(3), 259–290.
Bennett, G.L. (2009) 'Defamation of Religions: The End of Pluralism' *Emory International Law Review*, 23, 69–84.
Buchanan, A. (1997) 'Theories of Secession' *Philosophy and Public Affairs*, 26(1), 31–61.
Buchanan, A. (2001) 'From Nuremburg to Kosovo: The Morality of Illegal International Legal Reform' *Ethics*, 111(4), 673–705.
Bull, H. (2012) *The Anarchical Society: A Study of Order in World Politics*. Basingstoke, Palgrave Macmillan.
Caney, S. (2005) *Justice Beyond Borders: A Global Political Theory*. Oxford, Oxford University Press.
Capps, P. (2009) *Human Dignity and the Foundations of International Law*. Oxford, Bloomsbury Publishing.
'Charter of the United Nations', October 24, 1945, 1 UNTS XVI, Available at: www.refworld.org/docid/3ae6b3930.html, accessed March 2017.
Fabre, C. (2008) 'Cosmopolitanism, Just War Theory and Legitimate Authority' *International Affairs*, 84(5), 963–976.
Fabre, C. (2012) *Cosmopolitan War*. Oxford, Oxford University Press.
Fabre, C. (2016) *Cosmopolitan Peace*. Oxford, Oxford University Press.
'Geneva Conventions Common Article 3'. (1949) Available at: https://ihl-databases.icrc.org/applic/ihl/ihl.nsf/vwTreaties1949.xsp, accessed March 2017.
Gewirth, A. (1981) *Reason and Morality*. Chicago, University of Chicago Press.
Green, M. (2001) 'What We Talk About When We Talk About Indicators: Current Approaches to Human Rights Measurement' *Human Rights Quarterly*, 23(4), 1062–1097.
Gross, L. (1948) 'The Peace of Westphalia, 1648–1948' *American Journal of International Law*, 42, 20–41.
Hart, H.L.A. (1994) *The Concept of Law*, 2nd edition. Oxford, Oxford University Press.
Heath, J.B. (2012) 'Human Dignity at Trial: Hard Cases and Broad Concepts in International Criminal Law' *George Washington International Law Review*, 44(2), 317–366.
Held, D. (2002) 'Law of States, Law of Peoples' *Legal Theory*, 8(1), 1–44.
Heller, K.J. (2016) 'What Is an International Crime? (A Revisionist History)', Available at: http://ssrn.com/abstract=2836889, accessed March 2017.
Hoyle, C. and Ullrich, L. (2014) 'New Court, New Justice? The Evolution of "Justice for Victims" at Domestic Courts and at the International Criminal Court' *Journal of International Criminal Justice*, 12(4), 681–703.
ICC Forum. (2017) 'Is the ICC Targeting Africa Inappropriately?' Available at: http://iccforum.com/africa, accessed March 2017.
ICC Statute. (2002) 'Rome Statute of the International Criminal Court', Available at: www.icc-cpi.int/nr/rdonlyres/ea9aeff7-5752-4f84-be94-0a655eb30e16/0/rome_statute_english.pdf, accessed March 2017.
ICCPR. (1966) International Covenant on Civil and Political Rights, GA res. 2200A (XXI), 21 UN GAOR Supp. (No. 16) at 52.
ICISS Report. (2001), 'Responsibility to Protect', Available at: http://responsibilitytoprotect.org/ICISS%20Report.pdf, accessed March 2014.

Joerden, J.C. (2014) 'The Promise of Human Dignity' in Van Beers, B., Corrias, L. and Werner, W. eds., *Humanity Across International Law and Biolaw*. Cambridge, Cambridge University Press, 196–219.

Kant, I. (1991) 'Perpetual Peace' in *Kant: Political Writings*. Cambridge, Cambridge University Press, 93–130.

Khen, H.M-E. (2016) 'Aidōs and Dikē in International Humanitarian Law: Is IHL a Legal or a Moral System?' *The Monist*, 99(1), 26–39.

Koskenniemi, M. (2004) 'What Should International Lawyers Learn From Karl Marx?' *Leiden Journal of International Law*, 17(2), 229–246.

Koskenniemi, M. (2006) *From Apology to Utopia: The Structure of International Legal Argument*. Cambridge, Cambridge University Press.

Krieger, H. and Nolte, G. (2016) 'The International Rule of Law – Rise or Decline? Points of Departure', KFG Working Paper Series, No. 1, October 2016, Available at: https://ssrn.com/abstract=2866940, accessed March 2017.

Lagon, M.P. and Arend, A.C. eds. (2014) *Human Dignity and the Future of Global Institutions*. Washington, DC, Georgetown University Press.

Macklin, R. (1977) 'Moral Progress' *Ethics*, 87(4), 370–382.

McCrudden, C. (2008) 'Human Dignity and Judicial Interpretation of Human Rights' *European Journal of International Law*, 19(4), 655–724.

McDougal, M.S., Lasswell, H.D. and Chen, L-C. (1969) 'Human Rights and World Public Order: A Framework for Policy-Oriented Inquiry' *American Journal of International Law*, 63(2), 237–269.

McGinnis, J.O. (2003) 'The Limits of International Law in Protecting Dignity' *Harvard Journal of Law and Public Policy*, 27(1), 137–144.

Megret, F. (2015) 'In Whose Name? The ICC and the Search for Constituency' in Stahn, C., Kendall, S. and de Vos, C. eds., *Contested Justice: The Politics and Practice of International Criminal Court Interventions*. Cambridge, Cambridge University Press, 23–45.

Nickel, J.W. (1987) *Making Sense of Human Rights: Philosophical Reflections on the Universal Declaration of Human Rights*. CA, University of California Press.

Nickel, J.W. (2008) 'Rethinking Indivisibility: Towards a Theory of Supporting Relations Between Human Rights' *Human Rights Quarterly*, 30(4), 984–1001.

OHCHR. (2017a) 'Universal Periodic Review', Office of the High Commissioner for Human Rights, Available at: www.ohchr.org/EN/HRBodies/UPR/Pages/UPRMain.aspx, accessed March 2017.

OHCHR. (2017b) 'General Comments', Office of the High Commissioner for Human Rights, Available at: www.ohchr.org/EN/HRBodies/Pages/TBGeneralComments.aspx, accessed March 2017.

Peters, A. (2009) 'Humanity as the A and Ω of Sovereignty' *European Journal of International Law*, 20(3), 513–544.

Petersen, N. (2012) 'Human Dignity, International Protection' in *Max Planck Encyclopedia of Public International Law*. Oxford, Oxford University Press, paragraphs 1–37.

Prosecutor v. Furundzija. (1998) 'ICTY IT-95-17/1-T', Available at: www.icty.org/x/cases/furundzija/tjug/en/fur-tj981210e.pdf, accessed March 2017.

Radbruch, G. (2006) 'Statutory Lawlessness and Supra-Statutory Law (1946)' *Oxford Journal of Legal Studies*, 26(1), 1–11.

Rao, N. (2011) 'Three Concepts of Dignity in Constitutional Law' *Notre Dame Law Review*, 86(1), 183–271.

Rawls, J. (1999) *The Law of Peoples: With 'The Idea of Public Reason Revisited*. Cambridge, MA, Harvard University Press.

Raz, J. (2007) 'Human Rights Without Foundations', Oxford Legal Studies Research Paper No. 14/2007, Available at: http://ssrn.com/abstract=999874, accessed March 2017.

Reisman, W.M. (2013) *The Quest for World Order and Human Dignity in the Twenty-first Century Constitutive Process and Individual Commitment*. The Netherlands, Brill; Nijhoff.

Riley, S. (2016) 'Architectures of Intergenerational Justice: Human Dignity, International Law, and Duties to Future Generations' *Journal of Human Rights*, 15(2), 272–290.

Schachter, O. (1983) 'Human Dignity as a Normative Concept' *The American Journal of International Law*, 77(4), 848–854.

Shaffer, G. and Pollack, M.A. (2012) 'Hard and Soft Law' in Dunoff, J.L. and Pollack, M.A. eds., *Interdisciplinary Perspectives on International Law and International Relations: The State of the Art*. New York, Cambridge University Press, 197–222.

Shue, H. (2010) 'Laws of War' in Besson, S. and Tasioulas, J. eds., *The Philosophy of International Law*. Oxford, Oxford University Press, 511–530.

Slaughter, A-M. (2012) 'International Law and International Relations Theory: Twenty Year Later' in Dunoff, J.L. and Pollack, M.A. eds., *Interdisciplinary Perspectives on International Law and International Relations: The State of the Art*. New York, Cambridge University Press, 613–625.

Tasioulas, J. (2009) 'Are Human Rights Essentially Triggers for Intervention?' *Philosophy Compass*, 4(6), 938–950.

Teitel, R.G. (2011) *Humanity's Law*. Oxford, Oxford University Press.

Tsagourias, N.K. (2000) *Jurisprudence of International Law: The Humanitarian Dimension*. Manchester, Manchester University Press.

Tuck, R. (2001) *The Rights of War and Peace: Political Thought and the International Order From Grotius to Kant*. Oxford, Oxford University Press.

UDHR. (1948) 'Universal Declaration of Human Rights', Adopted by General Assembly Resolution 217 A(III) of December 10, 1948.

'UN (Draft) Declaration on Human Rights International Solidarity'. (2016) Available at: www.ohchr.org/Documents/Issues/Solidarity/ProposedDraftDeclaration Solidarity.pdf, accessed March 2017.

UN Rule of Law Indicators. (2011) Available at: www.un.org/ruleoflaw/blog/document/the-united-nations-rule-of-law-indicators-implementation-guide-and-project-tools/, accessed March 2017.

Walzer, M. (2015) *Just and Unjust Wars: A Moral Argument with Historical Illustrations*. New York, Basic Books.

Weil, P. (1983) 'Towards Relative Normativity in International Law' *American Journal of International Law*, 77(3), 413–442.

Weinert, M.S. (2015) *Making Human: World Order and the Global Governance of Human Dignity*. Ann Arbor, University of Michigan Press.

WHO Advisory Opinion. (1986) ("Legality of the Threat or Use of Nuclear Weapons") Advisory Opinion [International Court of Justice] of July 8, 1996 – General List No. 95 (1995–1998).

Zolo, D. (2010) 'Humanitarian Militarism?' in Besson, S. and Tasioulas, J. eds., *The Philosophy of International Law*. Oxford, Oxford University Press, 549–568.

5 Transnational law

> The [French] court [*tribunal de grande instance*] noted that the parties had submitted differing accounts concerning the allegations that the working and living conditions were incompatible with human dignity. It found that the applicant clearly worked long hours and did not enjoy a day off as such, although she was given permission to attend mass. [. . .] The [French] court concluded that, while it seemed established that employment regulations had not been observed in respect of working hours and rest time, this did not suffice to consider that the working conditions were incompatible with human dignity, which would have implied, for example, a furious pace, frequent insults and harassment, the need for particular physical strength that was disproportionate to the employee's constitution and having to work in unhealthy premises, which had not been the case in this instance.
>
> —(*Siliadin* [2005], paragraphs 25–26)

> [R]especting the dignity of the human person and the integrity of the groups that constitute his or her personhood [. . .] requires that all forms of society be oriented toward the freedom of 'lower' forms of association, and ultimately toward the freedom of the individual. In short, subsidiarity takes the freedom necessary to human dignity and extends it to a regard for freedom at all levels of social organization.
>
> —(Carozza 2003, 43)

Introduction

In contrast to public international law, transnational law is neither a clearly defined area of law nor one in which the application of human dignity is common. This patchwork of soft regulation and self-regulation, of statal and non-statal practices, is an important legal phenomenon born in circumstances of globalisation. It is also a form of law whose normative underpinnings are opaque, even questionable. This is law made by and for 'international actors', actors constituted by commerce and globalisation, not welfare or nationhood. These actors are norm entrepreneurs, consciously and deliberately creating networks of regulation outside the traditional institutional structures of state law. Human dignity appears to stand very much outside this network in a critical or oppositional position, opposing not only dehumanising unregulated practices (some of which will be our concern here) but also partly critical of unregulated practices *per se*. Thus, human dignity can serve as an analytical and normative tool, insisting that the norms, regulations, and institutions of transnational law be brought within the ambit of a morality of governance and of moral cosmopolitanism.

The analytical task must be grasped from the outset. The nature and scope of transnational law is contested, and it is a matter of debate which phenomena are distinctively transnational or are merely an extension of international, domestic, or commercial law. My principal concern will be with what might be called the *inter-statal* institutions of the European Union and the European Court of Human Rights, and with the *trans-statal* patterns of (on the one hand) labour and migration and (on the other) multi-national commercial activities. It is the latter network of private commercial practices that is most commonly associated with 'transnational law'. However I construe 'transnational law' in a wider sense, reflecting broader dignitarian concerns about law in a globalised context. The relationship between these phenomena and human dignity can therefore range from the emphatic and explicit (regional human rights courts), to the ambiguous (regional trading blocs), to the questionable (labour in global commercial networks), to the positively hostile (collective responses to 'merely' economic migrants).

This chapter ultimately argues for a form of subsidiarity-based constitutionalism, taking subsidiarity – the movement of power 'downwards' towards groups and individuals – as essential to the morality of governance and moral cosmopolitanism required in this area. This connects the constitutive and regulative in a way consistent with human dignity. At a constitutive level we should be defending only transnational legal arrangements that are capable of being brought within institutions of accountability at a state or inter-statal level (democratic subsidiarity). This means, at a regulative level, that we should be allocating legal competence or self-regulation to non-state actors with special expertise (epistemic subsidiarity) only if they can guarantee democratic oversight for all individuals falling within their authority. We therefore have to specify with some care what would count as democratic oversight and accountability for actors in complex transnational processes and practices; and we have to assume that mere diffusion of power away from public authorities towards private actors, however competent in their field of activity, requires clear justification.

First we consider the meaning and challenges of transnational law; then we turn to the ways in which this law, and globalisation more generally, has produced tensions with human rights law. The particular challenge of social and economic rights leads to sustained analysis of the European Union and the constitutionalisation of human rights. It is against the background of these studies that an overall analysis of the importance of subsidiarity can be conducted.

5.1 Defining transnational law

Definition is important not only for analytical and legal clarity but also because the conceptual and the normative are difficult to distinguish in this area. To the extent that conventional (domestic) public law tends to claim legitimate authority and democratic accountability, the distance between transnational law and public law immediately provokes questions of how we might restore, or find alternatives to, conventional authority and accountability.

The term 'transnational' has been used to capture a number of important regulatory or practical networks that can be distinguished from each other: first, practices at the *supra-national* level where sovereignty is pooled, for example in the European Union; second, practices at a *cross-national* level where, for example, a common body of human rights jurisprudence is shared but not uniformly codified in national law; and *extra-national* regulatory regimes and transnational processes, processes existing outside, or at least beyond the easy reach, of the jurisdiction of states. These extra-national regimes can exist either through states deliberately ceding authority (e.g. to regulatory – standard-setting – bodies) or because the nature of the processes in question is such that they are inconsistent with regulation by a single state (e.g. the regulation and taxation of large multinational entities). These kinds of sub-divisions are not rigidly adhered to here, but they are useful for indicating differences from conventional legal jurisdiction typically associated with the territorial state.

Why should we see a distinctive legal phenomenon here? Putting aside for the moment the ECHR and EU, cutting across these transnational practices are the *de facto* emergence of (commercial, labour, migratory) practices for which *de jure* regulation has been reactive rather than proactive. Any description of the legal and regulatory practices that have emerged in the late twentieth century must include the emergence of social and commercial practices that are outside conventional structures of authority and reflect a globalised economic context. The globalisation(s) of labour, capital, and commodities, as well as of culture and society, are distinct and mean that we should be suspicious of addressing globalisation as a unified phenomenon (see Donnelly 2002). By extension, attempts to understand these practices and processes from a regulatory point of view have inevitably embraced the plural and dynamic nature of these processes (for example, van der Burg 2014). So, a coherent and unified conception of these novel practices demands a new focus on 'alternative' forms of judicial and non-judicial adjudication, dispute settlement, and standard setting. (For an overview of the many international judicial fora and alternatives to courts, see Pluricourts 2017.) The recurrence of the language of 'plurality' in this context reflects an attempt to refine our concept of law such that it maps the globalised nature of modern commerce and regulation driven by private actors. And conceptualisations of transnational law and its formation have been addressed as ideas of 'legal pluralism' or alternatively 'interactionism'.

Building on Lon Fuller's later work on 'eunomics' (Fuller 1981) – i.e. good self-ordering built upon social interactions – new principles of global administrative governance have been sought in the interaction of actors, be they states or private individuals engaged in common endeavours. Moving away from a conception of law from the point of view of legislator, such interactionism turns towards the interacting and contracting between individuals, private parties, and the state as equally important actors. Developed fully in the 'interactionist model' of law, this seeks a more plural approach to law treating the normative force of law as residing in the self-ordering capacities of individuals and other actors (van der Burg 2014). This interactionism has a pragmatic attraction. Moving attention away from states and legislation towards actors and the expectations they generate, interactionism is a methodological tool for capturing the complexities of globalised transactions. This produces a model of law based on social expectation, cooperation, and self-regulation as opposed to 'top-down' authority, a model that has historical antecedents and wider significance:

> The history of sociology shows us that insight into the human situation is to be found in the study of the way in which forms of normativity have developed and changed, and particularly how formal structures of regulation and channeling have grown out informal interaction. There is, therefore, a double lesson in the importance of concept formation here and a curious twist in the attraction of a 'pragmatic' approach. It is, after all, Fuller who points out that that there is at least as much to be learned from the informal demands of justice than from the official declaration of it. A concept of law admitting exclusively into its ambit, for example, only appellate decision-making would ignore entirely this vital ontological link with wider social practices.
>
> (Olsen and Toddington 2007, 30)

Interactionism's conception of the sources and function of law has supported new conceptions of law as a whole (for instance, Shapiro's 'planning' conception of law (Shapiro 2011)). But its importance is not merely methodological and descriptive.

Interactionism is usually accompanied by *legal* pluralism, the acceptance of different kinds of national and non-national forms of law appropriate for understanding law in a post-statal or at least globalised world (Berman 2007). Indeed, transnational law has been treated as synonymous with pluralism: "Transnational law is another name for transnational legal pluralism, for an – inherently interdisciplinary – inquiry into the nature of legal regulation of problems, which have long been extending beyond the confines of jurisdiction – both 'inside' and 'outside' of the nation state" (Zumbansen quoted in Garcia 2016, 17). More fully, legal pluralism concerns

> a multiplicity of legal orders that exists in every social arena. There are village, town, and municipal laws of various types; there are state, district, and regional laws of various types; there are national, transnational, and international laws of various types. An array of courts or tribunals supports these bodies of law, often lacking explicit coordination with one another. There are soft forms of law with binding effects, like codes of conduct, model practices, standard contractual terms for business transactions and employment, and uniform workplace rules. In addition to these familiar bodies of laws and rules, in many societies there are more exotic forms of law, like customary law, indigenous law, religious law, or law connected to distinct ethnic or

> cultural groups within a society. There is also an evident increase in quasi-legal activities, from private policing (security in gated communities, universities, malls, public entertainment, and corporate headquarters) and private courts (arbitration), to privately run prisons, to the new *lex mercatoria*, a thriving body of transnational commercial law created through private law making by lawyers and parties.
>
> (Tamanaha in Patterson ed. 2010, 376; reference removed)

With a reorientation of legal scholarship towards non-state-based forms of interaction and the plural forms of law, we are far better able to capture the many regulatory practices that take place across different states and societies. And better able, for instance, to make sense of the hybrid – public and private, state and non-state, indigenous and international – complexes of regulation that govern our social systems in conditions of globalisation.

This way of looking at law in a global context has, of course, normative implications. Transnational processes are often commercial practices which bypass state control and use complex supply chains which optimise profit by evading working regulations and union rights, which seek and rely on the migration of profit, and which involve evasion of tax and accountability by 'treaty shopping' (ECOSOC 2006). These are the practices of actors who will clearly favour self-regulation and standard-setting from within the private sector over public oversight. We could insist that this is a form of emerging customary law. But it is important to stress that transnational law is a pattern of *consciously created* non-public, non-statal approaches to regulation. This movement away from the state is a move towards the interests of commercial and financial actors. The related normative loss is democratic accountability and with it loss of the democratisation of wealth. Indeed, we cannot assume that such order will generate principles and practices consonant with democracy:

> actors that are deeply embedded in transnational networks are notoriously difficult to hold democratically accountable on a national level. The great institutional loser in the shift from classical international law to international law as governance is the national legislature and the national electoral process, the very institutions believed to be at the heart of liberal constitutional democracy.
>
> (Kumm 2004, 915–916)

However, to find a more precise link with the normative principles derived from human dignity, we have to look again at the coordinates of time and territory we take to be the presuppositions of any public law.

The traditional assumption of public international law – that states are territorially bounded entities whose jurisdiction is spatial – is challenged by transnational processes that are not, or cannot be, tied to territory (for example, governance of the internet or certain forms of electronic financial transaction). Transnational chains of production, construction, and provision of goods and services bypass state territories, and different components of these chains shift and migrate depending upon where profit is to be made. The 'distantiation' of space, or 'deterritorialisation' of processes means effective negation of territorial borders, at least for certain kinds of actors (Liste 2014; Sullivan 2014). There are countless ways in which a state can seek to draw these actors and processes back within their jurisdictional reach and institutional oversight. But these attempts often face a gap between the legal assumptions that conventional territorial jurisdiction and the fluid, cross-border nature of the actor (see Kumm 2004).

It is in their relationship with time that we see some of the more striking regulative and normative aspects of this area of law. Transnational law seems to involve phenomena and processes that exist outside or subvert human time. The speed of electronic processes and electronic commerce means that they are beyond the immediate comprehension of human actors; the contracting of multinational actors with overseas partners, and their direct investment in states, takes place in timescales within which national law and legislation cannot easily respond. The links here with human dignity are well explored by Catherine Dupré (2015). For Dupré a principal function of human dignity is to restore a human timescale, to put a human conception of time back into our constitutions and practices. We should think here of the limitations that human dignity places on certain activities (for instance in terms of working time). We should think, too, of the cumbersome, 'articulated', practices and processes of constitutional democracy which lack the rapidity of pure executive power, but which ensure participation, oversight, and consent. But we should also think of our understanding of legal instruments as 'living instruments' reflecting our ongoing processes of collective self-understanding. Even human rights laws can become beholden to their origins and their accreted bodies of case laws. Human dignity helps to wrest our understanding of those rights from their past and ensure they are applicable to present circumstances. Dupré's ideas concerning constitutional time suggest a unique constitutive role for human dignity:

> Human dignity [. . .] enjoys a privileged relationship with time. As the foundation of post-war constitutionalism, it carries the memory of the inhuman times and the promise of a better future. [. . .] It is suggested here that this apparently inflationary increase in dignity uses in relation to constitutionalism and human rights echoes deep changes in time, both in its perception and its construction by constitutionalism.
>
> (Dupré 2015, 141–142; footnote removed)

Dupré rightly argues that the constitutional commitments to human dignity which feature in post-war constitutions globally (and post-communist Europe specially) cannot be merely understood as turnings away from an inhuman past but were very deliberately new beginnings intending a new constitutional epoch. A newly constituted *demos* is separated from the past and projects itself as a dignity-defending polity into the future. This is reflected in the kinds of constitutional eternity clauses that make human dignity irrevocable (see also Weinrib 2016, 184f). The fact that such provisions inhabit the same conditional status as any other constitution – liable to constitutional and executive suspension or destruction – need not detract from the intention, expressed in such 'permanent' constitutional measures, to build a polity anew. Dupré rightly stresses the constructive, constitutive commitment reflected in these constitutional and judicial developments, not merely rejection of the past. But even with this specific constitutional orientation, arising human dignity and the human condition, we still face the problem that transnational law seems to fall outside our conception of public law at all. One way that the transnational has been drawn into public discourse and public governance is as an aspect of our commitment to 'global justice'. Is this an adequate link between constitutionalism, human dignity, and transnational practices?

Discourses of global justice have for several decades now captured many of the distributive questions raised by transnational law as well as some of the regulative ones. We have been concerned with building global institutions and a global civil society able to monitor and hold transnational actors accountable. And legal instruments have been developed to impose basic civil and political regulations (if not distributive responsibilities) on global actors. But it is human dignity, less clearly justice, that demands we draw multi-nation actors back within comprehensive legal oversight. This flows from both its connection to economic and social rights, but also its connection with governance, cosmopolitanism, and constitutionalism. What we will arrive at is a conception of a transnational morality of governance that insists on a proper distribution of legal competence such that any and all transnational processes can be drawn within structures of democratic accountability. (The consideration of those *individuals* who fall between jurisdictions for other reasons – refugees, migrants, and the stateless – will be addressed via moral cosmopolitanism.) Justice, to the extent that its principal manifestation in this context is for global distributive fairness, faces considerable philosophical and practical problems here (for a survey of the limits of justice-discourse in this context, see Forst 2005). The defence of human dignity in transnational law must be a defence of the legal justice itself in the face of private resistance to public regulation. The nature of that 'private resistance' requires further analysis.

5.2 *Lex mercatoria*

The creation of law 'beyond' the state creates a challenge for the idea of public law. If public law is defined by democratic accountability, the formation of networks of commercial regulations by the parties themselves is a kind of private law for publicly important actors and challenges both democracy and natural justice. It also produces a point of tension between democratic and epistemological authority – whether authority lies in, or must ultimately be defined by, 'the people' or 'expertise'.

The idea of a *lex mercatoria* as the partial self-governance of commercial actors (more recently multi-national entities, or MNEs) is not new.

> Thus in these early years [of international law], the public/private, domestic/ international categories that later came to dominate classical international

> legal theory had not been developed. The law of nations was thought to embrace private as well as public, domestic as well as transborder transactions, and to encompass not simply the 'law of states', such as rules relating to passports and ambassadors, but also the law between states and individuals, including the 'law maritime' (affecting prizes, shipwrecks, admiralty, and the like) and the 'law merchant' (lex mercatoria) applicable to transnational commercial transactions. The system was 'monistic' inasmuch as international and domestic law together constituted a unified legal system, with domestic institutions acting as important interpreters and enforcers of international legal norms.
>
> (Koh 1997, 2605; footnotes removed)

Note that this paints a picture both of plural sources of law *and* a unified system. That is to say, there may be law generated in specific fields of activity where various different actors, in different environments, bring their expertise to bear. But there is also a 'monism' to the extent that all routes of power lead ultimately to the state as final arbiter of disputes. There is, under contemporary conditions, continuity and change with regard to this picture. Plurality, as we have seen, is still apparent not only in the continued creation of international law through customary practices but also in the relative autonomy of self-regulated commercial and financial practices. Monism – in the original legal sense of international and domestic law being continuous – is now the exception rather than the rule, and most states are dualist in their selective incorporation of international law. More fundamentally, however, the monism of all competence and accountability lying, ultimately, with states has been challenged by the ability of international actors to choose their fora for disputes and in having the power to contractually compel individuals (and indeed states) to accept forms of dispute resolution and arbitration on terms congenial to the MNE itself. What is the nature of these actors?

Multi-national entities are international actors characterised by having their legal identity, production, and trade in any number of centres globally. MNEs will often be characterised by production and manufacturing processes in less developed countries but sale and contract in developed countries. MNEs associated with financial services will be concentrated in the developed world but migratory in pursuit of favourable tax locations; actors associated with the internet and social networking will be more clearly global but pursue similar migratory patterns. The activities of these entities are characteristic of globalisation, because while the traditional *lex mercatoria* would certainly show many of these flexible, migratory characteristics (dedicated judges would be able to hear the cases of merchants and build their own body of rulings), here we are concerned with territorially complex but temporally rapid global patterns of activity: cheap international labour put to work in ceaseless chains of supply and production.

These MNEs are 'norm entrepreneurs'. They have developed new approaches to contract, dispute, and litigation through the development of practices they themselves have pursued in conjunction with similar agents with similar concerns. Thus we are confronting not merely the emergence of practices methodologically captured by 'interactionism' but the conscious creation of normative structures and normative principles in their own image: arbitration that avoids the risk of significant financial penalties and imposition, on less powerful partners, of jurisdictional fora that favour the stronger party. So, norm entrepreneurship has two related facets. On the one hand, MNEs avoid conventional labour law in their manufacture and supply chains; these practices take place in jurisdictions chosen not only for cheap labour but favourable labour and union laws. Given the power of these actors it is possible for them to lobby national governments to pass or import regulations on labour that are congenial to continued investment in the country. On the other hand, regarding sales and commerce in the developed world, there are uses of conventional but non-statal forms of alternative dispute resolution and 'forum choice' such that the reach of aggressive national courts is, as far as possible, avoided. These favourable fora are likely to apply standards that the MNEs themselves have created or influenced.

We can add to this the additional problem of 'regulatory capture' whereby experts from within their field of practice are part of the regulators setting standards, be it in manufacture or indeed in the accountancy standards to which they are held. Capps gives us examples of where 'norm entrepreneurship' and 'regulatory capture' are conjoined. "GLOBALG.A.P. is a private sector body, whose membership is dominated by European producers and retailers of agricultural produce, and which sets ostensibly voluntary standards for the safety certification of agricultural production processes" (Capps and Pattinson 2017, 214). Other examples include international standard-setting in financial services, insurance, securities market regulation, corporate governance, and auditing (a full list of private, but internationally recognised, standard-setting bodies is provided by the International Monetary Fund (2017)). These examples are important for what they reveal about the regulatory complexity of transnational actors and processes. On the one hand, we see a transnational body imposing standards on national bodies, in the process bypassing national standard-setting. On the other, we see a claim to expertise in the setting of standards, one based on expertise itself, not on a connection with the authority of the state. Rather than answering to the (democratically established) standard setting of states, groups of MNEs create the standards themselves and their expertise (and interests) go into forming the regulations that states will in turn enforce. In essence we again find the epistemic and the democratic in a problematic tension here.

Is this 'law of merchants' (or 'by merchants') purely a problem of regulation, of capturing certain processes or abuses within the jurisdiction of domestic courts? We should see it, in more fundamental terms, as a question of authority. We can conceive the problems created by the *lex mercatoria* as a problem of distribution of competence, i.e. of the courts and other bodies having the power to render practices justiciable. In conventional statist contexts the distribution of competence is not problematic. A hierarchy of courts, governed by the constitution or a group of administrative laws, would always be able to determine the proper level and forum at which a dispute should be heard, thereby also assuring a link back to the authority of the constitution and state. In contemporary transnational regulation, no such connection is assured and competence itself is determined by the actors. Two attitudes could be adopted to this. Either, from a pluralist perspective, we could accept that such actors must be allowed to determine the regulations that govern them; competence should be assumed to be technocratic competence and a connection with constitutional structures treated as optional. Or, we could insist that legal competence must always be traced to a constituted authority that is the final determinant of authority in any legal dispute. Indeed, the language of authority helps to capture this equivocation insofar as authority can be assumed to be reducible in the final analysis to power or to epistemological authority: the 'authority' of the state is either its monopoly on force or its claim to superior knowledge and superior coordination abilities (see Raz 1999). The inflection we choose in this context is crucial. We could insist that authority must be traceable to a constituent authority – an original power-conferring group of people – to which all actors are accountable. This is not, however, a conclusive position on competence or authority. After all, such constituent authority is imaginary, or if not imaginary by now overtaken by the authority of existing institutions and electorates, and it could be said to represent mere power in contrast to the epistemological authority that various (public and private) actors possess. We have, ultimately, to resolve the tension between accountability and expertise if we are to make sense of subjecting transnational practices to 'authority'.

It is also important, however, to make sense of the broadly dignitarian concerns that are produced by the activities of MNEs and make sense, in particular, of what it is that human dignity implies that is not already captured in a concern with global justice. Labour regulation provides one useful point of analysis. The exploitation of labour, and the bypassing or subverting of union rights, by MNEs is well documented (see Pagnattaro 2013). Low wages, labour flexibility, and an un-unionised labour force mean that 'offshore outsourcing' of labour is attractive to MNEs and can be valorised as the movement of wealth and capital into developing countries. While international regulations under the auspices of the International Labour Organisation, and latterly the UN, have sought to harmonise regulation into something like a transnational labour law, there remains a race to the bottom to secure cheap labour under the minimum of regulatory oversight (see Hepple 2005). The failure of the umbrella provisions of the World Trade Organisation – provisions drawing together international standards on commerce and trade – to ensure that human rights laws are not subverted in this race to the bottom means that the governance of labour practices is piecemeal and secondary to the freedom of trade and competition sustained by the WTO arrangements (Hepple 2005, 11f). Robust democracy at a domestic level is certainly part of seeking justice in face of these failures to regulate transnational law: "strengthening democracy where production occurs will give labor advocates a way to hold governments accountable for effective enforcement of labor standards" (Pagnattaro 2013, 43, n. 252). Would there also be value in conceptualising the abuse of labour as a distinctive, even paradigmatic, abuse of human dignity?

It is helpful to revisit, but problematise, what has traditionally been termed the 'dignity of labour' (see Bonefeld and Psychopedis (2005); also Dupré's work

(2015) on the governance of labour in a European context). The term itself is probably unhelpful because (as Arendt's sympathetic critique of Marx implies) what has often been valorised in the traditions of the Left is *work* (the forming of objects, be they artworks or basic commodities) rather than *labour* (the repetitive and mechanical processing of nature for the purposes of survival) (Arendt 1958). The connection of dignity and labour, then, has often failed to be specific about the type of work we should be defending: whether we should celebrate the offer of any employment or rather only that which contributes to the formation of certain kinds of consciousness. In response, and more specifically, we might argue that the defence of labour rights and union rights is a contribution to human dignity to the extent that it accords with the obligations principle. Given the possibility of exploitation through work (be it the privatisation of profit, surplus value, or under-remuneration in state-run industries), work presents distinctive dangers with regard to obligations and status. Private obligations, created through contract, can conflict with public obligations to ensure equality between workers; the legal protections and political commitments of an individual might be waived through such contracting. Under these circumstances an individual's obligations fail to form a harmonious whole. It is, to put it another way, a dignitarian failure in the morality of governance to allow individuals' rights to be negated simply through the assumption of the importance of freedom of contract. Here human dignity and justice clash in a way familiar from debates about liberty of contract and libertarianism (although their contemporary resonances with regard to transnational labour can be found in Zumbansen 2013). The essence of a dignitarian response to concerns about transnational labour is, then, partly the construction of actual standards of legitimate (safe, non-degrading) labour (see, e.g., Mitchell 2016) but, as importantly, it must lie in a critique of libertarian valorisation of freedom of contract regarding labour. Justice implies freedom of contract, but human dignity implies the impermissibility of unconscionable contracts which degrade the individual and encourage a race to the bottom in wages and conditions.

What, more broadly, can be done to draw these entities and their practices into the regulatory ambit of the state? Here public and private law can be divided, and the limits of the one expose the other. Public law – international law, national constitutional law – has frequently been seen to fail in the face of the technocratic and profit-generating promises of MNEs. Indeed, even the dedicated work of the International Labour Organisation and of ECOSOC (the UN body with oversight of economic and social rights) have failed to turn the regulatory, or the ideological, tide against MNEs. Remedies in private law, including private international law, offer some promise here. For instance, the US Alien Tort Statute (1980) in its modern form provides that "[t]he district courts shall have original jurisdiction of any civil action by an alien for a tort only, committed in violation of the law of nations or a treaty of the United States." The act has been used to bring claims against US corporations, in US courts, against abusive or criminally negligent corporations (Dagan and Dorfmann 2016). The ongoing failure in this respect on the Union Carbide claim regarding the Bhopal disaster (see Engel and

Martin 2006) should not obscure the fact that some such claims can be successfully brought in domestic courts. The invitation for private actors or groups of private actors to bring claims has not necessarily been in spite of human rights but has, it can be argued, complemented human rights:

> This strategy, of extending individual rights from the vertical dimension – as rights against the state – to the horizontal dimension, in which they operate at the interpersonal level, typifies recent efforts of human rights lawyers. These efforts, to be sure, are not unique to the transnational context. Quite the contrary: they seem to piggyback on the domestic laws of some jurisdictions that go beyond the state action doctrine [. . .] and conceptualize constitutional rights as fundamental 'to the whole legal system including private law enacted by the State'.
>
> (Dagan and Dorfman 2016, 14; reference removed)

And that indeed captures the complex of public and private concerns that are unified here under the rubric of human dignity. This is accomplished not simply through the invocation of higher constitutional norms but of the individual those norms are intended to serve. Thus human dignity has rightly been invoked to challenge the dehumanising aspects of global capitalism. It has been used to expand the oversight of courts concerned with such processes. And it has been adopted, perhaps ambiguously, by major transnational endeavours like the European Union to express values but less clearly to guide the identification of duties both internal and external to the Union. In each case the obligations flowing from human dignity have not been purely regulatory and they have not been conditioned by the traditional categories imposed by legal justice. They have demanded careful harmonisation of obligations to place human dignity at their centre.

This gives us two further directions of enquiry regarding transnational law. The first is the significance of human rights law. The second is democracy and institutions. Finally, these themes are brought together in a discussion of subsidiarity.

5.3 Human rights and globalisation

Characterised by a tumultuous mixture of geopolitical and national, ideological and economic forces, the first decades of the twenty-first century have falsified the idea of an 'end of history'. Accompanying this, some commentators anticipate an end to international human rights law in the classic, liberal, cosmopolitan form that has become the *lingua franca* of international legal and political discourse (an idea explored, but not endorsed, by Dagan and Dorfman 2016). Because of shifts in the priorities of existing world powers, the emergence of new powers, and the puncturing of globalisation with renewed forms of nationalism, we are likely to see a renewed focus on the regionalisation and nationalisation of rights discourse. In Africa, we see evidence of the influence of the African Charter on Human and Peoples' Rights (ACHPR 2017) and, conversely, rejection of the

International Criminal Court; in European states, we see a concern with forging indigenous bodies of rights to replace international ones and pessimism concerning the very continuation of the European Union. In reflecting on human rights practice, it has been argued that the universalism of human rights has become

> the problem rather than the solution to the complexities of modern politics. Analysts of the politics of identity and difference have forced universalists to reflect carefully on the particularisms which run through their normative commitments and aspirations. Few now need reminding of the importance of the charge that universalists always carry with them 'a clump of (their) native soil'; few need lessons in the need to ensure that universalism must mean greater justice between different cultures.
>
> (Linklater 1999, 481; footnotes removed)

At the very least, even to those sympathetic to human rights, there is concern that the discourse of *obligations* that arises from human rights claims is displacing important discourses of 'benevolence' and 'generosity' that are more attractive normative discourses at grass-roots levels (Ignatieff 2017).

Human rights have never meant global homogeneity in culture or obligations. A body like the European Court of Human Rights [ECtHR], along with the Council of Europe, retains its traditional justification of drawing states together through the rule of law generally and human rights harmonisation specifically. This has meant, for instance, providing direct standards or conditions for states leaving political authoritarianism (e.g. Greece) or wishing to join other supernational bodies (e.g. Turkey). So, just as human rights have never meant absolute harmonisation of laws, nor has there ever been a time at which human rights were not political in important respects. My present concern is to think through the structural and political nature of the ECtHR and consider what it can contribute to human dignity in a context of globalisation, specifically whether it is dynamic enough for an era of globalisation. One worry in this respect is a familiar one, that the Court's jurisprudence of human dignity is particularly flavoured by its connection with degradation. A focus on degradation (particularly via Article 3, prohibiting torture, inhuman, and degrading treatment) is not surprising given that this is a persistent feature of the legal conceptualisation of human dignity in general. Nevertheless, the importance of not letting this over-determine the scope of human dignity is particularly acute where we are concerned with novel, and often morally ambiguous, transnational phenomena.

The ECtHR as we find it today is the product of a distinctive kind of post-war ambivalence. On the one hand the creation of a pan-European court was already mooted at the time of the drafting of the main international instruments. The explicit intention of the Court is to give effect to that 'international bill of human rights'. Conversely, the Court, it was presumed, would do its work relatively unobtrusively and would deal only with very few cases, predominantly cases brought by one state against another (Bates 2010, 8f). Neither the present number of signatories was anticipated, nor the quantity of cases, nor that inter-statal claims would be very rare relative to the many thousands of individual petitions.

Its structure lies in a treaty (the Convention) containing the core rights along with the organisational norms of the Court; it is augmented by additional protocols expanding and reforming the Court's work. In turn, the Court and the Convention sit within the wider work of the Council of Europe, intended to foster the rule of law in Europe. The Court's decisions automatically bind the signatory states and demand remedial action to change laws inconsistent with the Court's reading of the rights and their legitimate qualifications. Occasional resistance to the Court takes two forms: a concern with the sovereignty of domestic parliaments (UK) and direct challenges at the level of the primacy of the Court's law (Russia) (for discussion of both see Hillebrecht 2012). Political interference to lessen the impact of the Court might be expected. Nevertheless, at a broadly political level, the more or less uniform enforcement of judgements, and the insulation of the Court itself from domestic politics, have all reached an unexpectedly consistent level.

We should also note the importance, at a politico-legal level, of the Court's use of a 'margin of appreciation' in deciding how the qualification of rights should be realised in different states (see Letsas 2006). In other words, the function of the Court is not to produce uniformity, at least in those circumstances where rights are legitimately 'qualified' (i.e. limited in pursuit of just ends, in ways which are proportionate to those ends and would be acceptable within other democratic states). The margin of appreciation is important because it makes the jurisprudence of the Convention rights include a certain *inherent* flexibility. Rights, especially those with a strongly social element like privacy and expression, must be understood in the context of concrete social and political contexts. The margin of appreciation allotted to states in the context of qualified rights is important in allowing variations in the implementation (or 'enjoyment') of rights to privacy, expression, assembly, and religious belief, amongst others. That reasonable variation is possible here is not merely pragmatic. It is of the essence of human rights *laws* that they be tailored to the circumstances they will be applied in. This links to two themes to be addressed elsewhere: subsidiarity as respecting the expertise or democratic mandate of other groups (see below), and the fact that it is essential to human rights law that it be tailored (at least to some extent) to find harmony between human dignity principles and the forms of justice characteristic of individual states (see Chapter 6). The important point to note here is that the sharing of principles is possible without also demanding uniformity in law. And the merit of regional human rights institutions is their creating regional standards without compromising basic principles. Where, then, does the Court sit within our concerns with the institutional implications of human dignity and globalisation?

Regarding moral cosmopolitanism, the development of cross-constitutional laws is important. Alongside the rights already mentioned, we could also note the burgeoning importance of Article 4 (the prohibition on slavery and servitude), which is increasingly being used, employing the language of human dignity, to address abuses related to global trafficking and unpaid labour (see *Rantsev v. Cyprus and Russia* [2010]; *Chowdury and Others v. Greece* [2017]). But we find that a more complex set of concerns inevitably arises in asylum and migration cases. The ECtHR faces the challenge of ensuring the right normative balance between the protections that should attach to any individuals, the jurisdictional limits of the Court, and the EU treaty obligations that govern migration into and within Europe. A discourse of human dignity is easy to use in this context but rarely decisive in the final judgment of cases:

> while it is clearly desirable that every human being have a place where he or she can live in dignity and which he or she can call home, there are unfortunately in the Contracting States many persons who have no home. Whether the State provides funds to enable everyone to have a home is a matter for political not judicial decision.
>
> (*Chapman v. The UK* [1995], paragraph 99)

In contrast, it can be decisive in cases of Article 3 violations concerning degradation:

> The Court considers that the applicant has been the victim of humiliating treatment showing a lack of respect for his dignity and that this situation has, without doubt, aroused in him feelings of fear, anguish or inferiority capable of inducing desperation. It considers that such living conditions, combined with the prolonged uncertainty in which he has remained and the total lack of any prospects of his situation improving, have attained the level of severity required to fall within the scope of Article 3 of the Convention.
>
> (*MSS v. Belgium and Greece* [2011], paragraph 263)

In that case a regulative function for human dignity achieves a valuable end (for further discussion of Article 3 see Chapter 6). But what should be crucial in this kind of case is not mere prohibition but a mixture of dignitarian principles: sovereignty to insist that individuals can exercise their basic rights, permission to ensure that their status is not reduced to any particular administrative or legal role or position, and the obligation principle, ensuring that their protections are not lost in a putative clash of basic normative commitments. This, then, is the full articulation of what in other contexts is intelligibly, but not always clearly, articulated as human dignity (or, particularly with regard to statelessness, the 'right to have rights').

What does the Court contribute to our understanding of a morality of governance in the context of globalisation? There is an important link to forge here between human dignity's interpretive role (the broadly 'heuristic' function attributed to human dignity) and the 'autonomy' of law (of decision-making but also autonomy in the meaning of legal concepts) which the Court takes to be central to its role. The point of connecting human dignity and human rights law is to make positive law reflect underlying principles of human status but to do so in a way that is responsive to the internal jurisprudential logic of institutions as well as changing circumstances of justice more generally. Thus it is both 'politically' and 'philosophically' that human dignity assists in the autonomy of human rights law. These meet in a resistance to positivism that would make human rights conditional – for their enforcement and their construction – on the will of the state or polity. The reduction of human dignity to (on the one hand) an opaque 'foundational' role and (on the other) a regulative role (concerning dignitarian harm) fails to precisely articulate this autonomy or connect with status principles more generally. As a consequence, the *politics* of European human rights law looks crude and unprincipled (isolation and disdain for individual states and domestic law). What it should be communicating is that the most complex, modern, interstitial problems that face our societies can and must be addressed through human dignity and that this may therefore require radical rethinking of the positive law of human rights and principled implementation of that law by political actors. We need radically new interpretations of norms (like Article 8 on privacy) that require re-working in the light of technology, norms (like Article 10 on expression) that require reworking in the light of clearly pluralistic societies, or norms (like Article 4 on slavery) that require reworking in the light of contemporary forms of labour.

The burden of history that animates a limited and prohibitive conception of human dignity is nowhere more pronounced than in the Court's grappling with social and economic entitlements. These are not clearly represented in the Convention and only partly in the additional protocols attached to the Convention. The Court has been able to broadly defend such entitlements to the extent that they concern *property* and the entitlement to a home to the extent that it is an implication of the right to a private life (see Costa 2013). We have to look elsewhere for clear demands, and a clear jurisprudence, of social and economic rights.

5.4 Social and economic rights

Both good governance and moral cosmopolitanism meet in concern for social and economic rights. Defending and implementing these rights requires concern for the generic conditions of human agency and for our entitlement-conferring principles, principles that are not exhausted by distributive justice but concern human dignity itself. Promulgated in the UDHR, the separate legal development of economic and social human rights is often explained (in part) as a concession, during the Cold War, to the Soviet Bloc and the communist world (Bantekas and Oette 2013, 367–368). These rights were divided from the civil and political rights (rights developed in and prioritised by liberal states) so that championing one group might not be hampered by suspicion of the other. Partly as a consequence of this, the rights to work, to health, to join and form trade unions, and to the protection of an individual's wider cultural and natural heritage, have suffered under a shadow of suspicion that they are aspirational rights or manifesto rights. It is frequently argued that they either fail to be rights at all, or represent promises that cannot be committed to in good faith on the part of the state.

The importance of economic and social rights in relation to human dignity is not, then, a simple concern with the fulfilment of basic needs. These rights represent pre-eminently interstitial concerns: irreducibly political as well as moral, and requiring coherence between distributive justice and human dignity itself. Reduction of these rights to the fulfilment of basic needs would, amongst other things, leave unanswered human dignity's relationship with autonomy and self-constitution. The brute material fact that self-constitution (or anything else) could not be accomplished without access to material minimums still fails to capture why we should have health or education as rights and why they speak to our status and not simply our interests. It is as interstitial rights that human dignity becomes pertinent to the interpretation of these rights: we cannot understand these rights other than through their problematic but inevitable straddling of legal, moral, and political; the rights often engage vexed questions at the meeting point of public and private responsibilities. And nor can we understand the dynamism of these laws – their proper interpretation now and in the future – other than as a demand to preserve the human condition. Preserving the human condition means that plurality and sustainability must be amongst the principal interpretive perspectives we bring to bear on these rights. The specific economic and social rights arise from our generic needs, agency, and vulnerability. But the proper interpretive perspective on them lies in ensuring that there is human diversity into the future and securing the conditions for the realisation of human rights as a whole.

As interstitial rights, economic and social rights have to be coherently protected across our normative orders. This means that it is not enough to create coherent bodies of declarations (of hard and soft law) through international and domestic *legal* institutions. These rights also have to be given political form and political support. Particularly with respect to transnational law and abuses of economic and social rights, it is not enough for states to adhere to (on the one hand) WTO rules and (on the other) avoid violating economic and social rights at home. Concerted legal and political efforts are required to regulate transnational abuses of those rights. This is why, moreover, we should be suspicious of the idea that globalisation has been accompanied by the emergence of a new *ius commune* (an international common law) centred on human dignity which will allow human rights to be harmonised across constitutions and capture the international actors, and international abuses, characteristic of globalisation (as argued for by Carozza 2008). Sharing of regulations is insufficient without commitment to a more fundamental obligation and competence distributing arrangement. (Again, this will have to await further discussion with regard to subsidiarity, below.)

Why could we not simply appeal to 'justice in allocating basic goods' as the essence of these rights? The integration of social and economic rights into constitutional and transnational thinking has required concern with the nature of the standards being set – that is, whether they demand the object of the right at the highest attainable standard, at the highest standard *all things considered*, or that these rights simply demand the fair allocation of whatever resource is available. These variations are often reduced to constraints related to *feasibility*, but this is an opaque and pragmatic rather than principled standard (Gilabert 2009). In fact, the object of any social and economic right will be constructed (alongside any UN General Comments on the right) through various discursive, participatory, and broadly democratic means. Undoubtedly, complete failure to realise a right might be observable in some circumstances: denial to education to girls, denial of health care to the poor, denial of workers' rights under inadequate labour law. But the construction of the object of a right, the relevant standard, and the basis of fair allocation will be inseparable from wider concerns about justice, i.e. the particular allocation of benefits and burdens within a state. But we need to identify why it is that such a human right can become an exclusionary reason within public reason, displacing other distributive arguments.

We can explore these ideas through the example of a right to health. The human right to health has been an important focus for analysis for its moral, legal and political complexity. At a moral level we have to consider what the extent of the moral right is: for individuals to access to health care provision, to have the best possible health care provision, or to health itself (see Hassoun 2015). Where the right has been construed in terms of equitable access to treatments and resources whose provision is subject to the contingencies of politics and economics, the right appears to be an extension of a right against discrimination only (see *Soobramoney* [1997]). The right to a 'decent minimum level of health care' would be a more substantive right, not only to equitable access, but to entitlement on the basis of need (Buchanan 1984). A wider theory of justice would be needed to capture the contents of such a right. Indeed, the need to consider general distributive responsibilities here could be taken as vindication of libertarian positions that would treat such a right – strongly distributive and poorly correlative – as reflecting a failed conception of (human) rights common to liberal rights theory more generally. Why, then, is the libertarian wrong?

The right, as a right to minimum, is governed by a dignitarian principle that insists that the individual's entitlements are to displace a general rule if that is necessary to protect their status. In what circumstances will that apply? Certainly in those circumstances where the utilitarian political claim is not made in good faith and decent health care provision is available to the individual at no excessive cost to others in a society. The requirement to benefit the least well off when this is at no significant cost to others may well be considered a principle of justice, e.g. Rawls's concern with requiring Pareto optimality in justifying differences of treatment (1999, 58f). But the conceptualisation here concerns human dignity, not justice. That is, we are not designing institutions or allocating burdens but rather identifying the principles that apply in those circumstances where an individual *claims a decent minimum of health care but is denied it*. More specifically, where a state denies health care on the basis of lack of availability or affordability, human dignity is rightly invoked as a functional standard related to the claimant him- or herself excluding or displacing an overall calculation of the state's resources and duties. The individual's entitlement must be "[c]onstrued by reference to a person's material capacity to live a dignified life. This means that where people are indigent or unable to pay for medical and other socio-economic necessities, lest they be deprived of a dignified life, then the state must offer these free of charge" (Bantekas and Oette 2013, 391). This, admittedly, begins to blur the line between human dignity as a principal underpinning of the right and the substantive *content* of the right. But the standard of 'dignified life' can be construed as a life where a full range of human rights can be enjoyed; it need not be construed as a minimal humanitarian standard. And, more to the point, the invocation of human dignity in this context is meant to render irrelevant any difference in what is actually or potentially provided by the state or by private actors. The specific arrangement of public and private provision for health care is important for overcoming the limitations of the state's resources and ensuring just distribution of knowledge and treatment where power rests in the hands of private actors. The right to health does not preclude private actors being involved in securing the highest attainable levels of health for individuals. But it does imply a positive responsibility on the state to ensure formal equality amongst recipients and the use of claim rights (and not merely an assessment of interests) to identify individual entitlements regardless of any other wider political or economic calculation.

Economic, social and cultural rights (like other human rights) provide the means by which we give individuals the power to assert their claims *qua* individual, not as representative of class with particular interests. They are then a contribution to the preservation of plurality within our practical reasoning and challenge the assumption that human needs and entitlements are uniform. The right to education is particularly important in that respect for supporting the self-constitution (and not merely economic readiness) of individuals. The right to cultural heritage supports the same kind of function at a group level. These rights, as a class, have a special function to play in supporting the human condition as one of diversity and plurality. And, regardless of whether we consider the right to a healthy environment to be one right or a cluster of human rights, this class of rights protects the condition of the enjoyment of any human rights in the future. So, again, the attempt to unify economic and social rights around basic material interests struggles to explain the common denominators of the existing rights, let alone their basis as rights. It is as a dignitarian defence of the human condition – which in turn is premised on dignitarian principles – that these rights need to interpreted.

Economic, social, and cultural rights also stand at an intersection between concerns with international human rights, global justice, and the duties of the state. But when we think in these more general, global terms, then the more political discourse of 'global justice' often becomes dominant. While this is intelligible, and flows from the distinction between human dignity and justice I have been defending, it is tempting to draw the implication that because the object of these rights cannot be determined precisely and must stand in a kind of equilibrium with the demands of distributive justice, then human dignity – 'by default' – is no longer applicable and by extension, economic, social, and cultural rights are not human rights proper. But this implication need not be drawn, and instances where dignitarian principles appear to be exhausted either represent entrenched political barriers (poor governance) or lack of an established body of jurisprudence. These problems are replicated as we turn to the European Union. On the one hand, an institution explicitly concerned with social and economic rights is able to impose standards and clarify rights both legislatively and through adjudication. On the other, the strengthening of such rights can come at costs: both the marginalising of civil and political rights (including direct representative democracy) and, relatedly, the erosion of public powers rendering technocratic, not democratic, practices the major determinants of those social and economic rights.

5.5 Constitutionalising Europe

The 'constitutionalisation' of Europe through the ECHR and the EU offer an important, but no doubt specific, lesson in constitutionalisation. If the ECHR has afforded a kind of cosmopolitanism consistent with the independence of European states, the European Union has aspired to coordinate the good economic governance necessary to underpin a kind of federal unity. In other words, Europe (broadly understood) has at least two different institutional frameworks that have sought to constitute it as a principled political unity. But this has been pursued through different legal and economic means. And, importantly, it has been constitutionalisation through evolving practices rather than through the adoption of an explicit constitutional document. This is not a pure example of 'interactionism' given the social and political engineering that was consciously pursued after the Second World War. But it is a crucial example of constitutionalisation on principled grounds and constitutionalisation largely in the absence of efforts to make Europe into a single *demos* (Williams 2003; Habermas 2012).

Nevertheless, through the European Union, Europe has been constituted as both a space of economic and social freedom and as a fortress. We consider, first, that 'free space', then the 'fortress'. The basic freedoms of the European Union – of goods, labour, capital – were not envisaged as ends in themselves but means of overcoming antagonism amongst Europe's major powers and, in time, fostering 'ever-closer union'. *Unifying* was not intended to mean *centralising* and the principle of subsidiarity was intended to clarify the relative competences of the EU and the Member States, with the EU assuming power only in those circumstances where unified action at a European level was best able to achieve collective goals (EU Protocol on Subsidiarity 2007). The re-envisaging of the European Communities as the European Union reflected a concern with the social functions that could be served at this higher European level. This includes the stalled commitment to have the Union accede as a Signatory State to the ECHR (Treaty of Lisbon Article 59, paragraph 2). It also includes a Charter of Rights about which we should endorse Dupré's positive assessment:

> [T]he European Union Charter of Rights, which came into force with the Lisbon Treaty in 2009 [. . .] is headed by a resounding commitment to the protection and respect of human dignity under title 1 of the Charter. The Charter provisions on dignity reflect the whole history of this concept and its connections with democracy. Under the Charter, dignity is definitely

> not a 'vacuous' concept, rather it encapsulates the substance of European democracy as a regime where 'the individual is at the heart of its activities' (preamble); the death penalty is abolished (art. 2), eugenic practices, human cloning and making the human body the source of financial gain are prohibited (art. 3); torture, inhuman or degrading treatment are prohibited (art. 4); slavery, forced labour and human trafficking are prohibited (art. 5); and finally working conditions have to respect workers' dignity (as well as their health and safety) under art. 31.
>
> (Dupré 2012, 266)

The implications of human dignity move beyond those traditionally found in EU law:

> In addition, the Charter acknowledges two new concerns of 21st century European constitutionalism by giving dignity special protection in the field of medicine and biology (art. 3) and in relation to the elderly (art. 25). This cluster of rights arguably forms a thick definition of dignity and gives 21st century European democracy its distinctive feature as a system of government which claims to place at its centre a multidimensional definition of human beings and endeavours to control power so that it may not be exercised in an unjust way, such as reducing individuals to mere objects.
>
> (Dupré 2012, 266)

This useful overview (as might be anticipated) slightly obscures the different levels at which human dignity might be connected with the charter and with the EU as a whole. After all, we need an account of how human dignity's primary position in the charter implies or informs (for example) workers' rights and care of the elderly. We need to know how these multifarious areas of regulation are connected by anything other than family resemblances. This is not to say that these constitutional and regulative commitments should not be conjoined, but we should be wary of celebrating the whole instrument as a dignitarian one without a more fine-grained analysis of where and how it can be used in core constitutional debates.

Before pursuing that analysis, however, it is important to note that at a constitutional level there is continuing contestation over the relative powers of the Union and Member States. Subsidiarity partly accomplishes a reconciliation, but its effectiveness and reasonableness depends upon the right choice and application of burdens of proof concerning who or what is competent to allocate power. There is, of course, a continuing and increasing crisis in the Union occasioned by the resurgence of nationalism. But there is also a related specific concern with what (in the context of the ECHR) would be called 'the margin of appreciation', namely the more nuanced normative concerns about what must be decided by the democratic bodies of Member States given their bond of *democratic authority* with the polity (democratic subsidiarity) and with their special claim to *understand* the indigenous mores and indigenous claims understanding of justice in each Member State (epistemic subsidiarity). As the German Constitutional Court said of the Lisbon Treaty,

> European unification on the basis of a treaty union of sovereign states may not be achieved in such a way that not sufficient space is left to the Member States for the political formation of economic, cultural and social living conditions. This applies in particular to areas which shape the citizens' living conditions, in particular the private sphere of their own responsibility and of political and social security, protected by fundamental rights, as well as to political decisions that rely especially on cultural, historical and linguistic perceptions and which develop within public discourse in the party political and parliamentary sphere of public politics.
>
> (*Organstreit Proceedings* [2009], headnote paragraph 4)

The German and other constitutional courts do indeed have competence to decide welfare rights over which they claim expertise in contrast to the interpretation of EU economic duties over which the Union maintains competence. It is legitimate to claim the primacy of one's own democratic institutions against the assumption that 'genuine expertise' in governance lies elsewhere. It is also legitimate, conversely, to claim that complex regulatory issues of common concern are better coordinated at a pan-European level and that in certain circumstances long-term thinking at that level should trump the short-term thinking of domestic politics.

In the EU we see a distinctive variation on the charge that the regulative and constitutive aspects of human dignity are inadequately conceptualised. On the one hand, given the European Union's explicit commitment to human dignity in its treaties and supporting instruments, there is an apparent failure to include human dignity in its core constitutional thinking at all. The development of the EU is at present driven by crisis and preservation of economic stability in the bloc; we see little evidence of pursuit of fundamental democratic reform of the EU or the ability to adopt a principled stance as an international actor challenging the international influence of the United States or of large multi-national entities (MNEs). At the same time, the regulatory uses of human dignity we find in the EU are examples of prohibitive constraining uses. They are often close to the idea of sanctity, and functionally human dignity is a prohibitive norm intending (partly as a pure norm prohibiting anything violating sanctity and partly as a precautionary principle) to estop actions that symbolically denigrate humanity regardless of their concrete outcomes. *Omega* (2004) is instructive in this respect. Concerning the German prohibition on 'Laser Quest' games because of their putative, and impermissible, imitation of killing, the European Court of Justice upheld Germany's human dignity–based ban:

> The referring court states that human dignity is a constitutional principle which may be infringed either by the degrading treatment of an adversary, which is not the case here, or by the awakening or strengthening in the player of an attitude denying the fundamental right of each person to be

> acknowledged and respected, such as the representation, as in this case, of fictitious acts of violence for the purposes of a game. It states that a cardinal constitutional principle such as human dignity cannot be waived in the context of an entertainment, and that, in national law, the fundamental rights invoked by Omega cannot alter that assessment.
>
> (*Omega* [2004], paragraph 12)

That a national constitutional commitment to human dignity should trump certain economic rights is, of course, defensible assuming that a human rights violation is involved. That human dignity is actually *harmed* in computer-based games is less easy to see except in the light of Germany's own historical memory of militarisation. But this is a narrow basis on which to make a decision with pan-European significance. Again, the relative authority and competence of the EU and national courts is not possible to determine *a priori*. But the decision reflects a familiar theme of the constitutional collapsing into the regulative.

On the other hand, aside from any explicit commitments to human dignity, the defence of economic freedoms, a social charter, and the harmonisation of legal systems in Europe has produced a novel commercial foundation for cross-statal commerce and with it a new conception of the rights and status of individuals in Europe more generally. The attractions of the European Union to, for instance, Ukrainians prior to partial annexation by Russia lay not merely in economic prosperity but a space of opportunities and an alternative to the nationalism of existing political discourse (Open Democracy 2015). The idea of producing a European *demos* out of these processes, if this were ever a coherent objective, has been harmed by the recent resurgence of nationalism in Europe. But the conception of Europe as a space characterised by economic freedoms and rights, a choice for citizens between states (including exit from more repressive into less repressive states), and with it a rejection of the reduction of the obligations given by any particular culture, represent a dignitarian aspiration – a general structural alignment of both social systems and normative orders with the permission and normative protection characteristically found in human rights.

In what follows we should begin to assess whether this conclusion about the dignitarian value of the EU's freedoms is defensible. This means imposing a division between what they might mean for the EU's internal sovereignty (its internal constitution and governance) and its external sovereignty (its relationship with the rest of the world as a sovereign actor). Internally, were we to 'constitutionalise' Europe more systematically using human dignity, we would have to think beyond the crude division of labour already implied by the economic union and the quasi-constitutional ECtHR. Europe could constitute itself as a polity with principled commitment not only to human rights but to a permissive principle. This, recall, demands a robust conception of private sphere, protection of liberties, and the limitation of state (and private) power such that, in the domain of technology and data, the private sphere and the presumption of innocence are preserved. The sharing of jurisprudence on privacy between the ECtHR and the

EU has pointed in this direction but is very far from a coherent vision of public authority and private autonomy in Europe.

Putting that more generally (and in anticipation of the themes of Chapter 6) the constitutionalisation of Europe requires us to rethink what should be the nature of 'public reason' in Europe. Public reason is the demand that we synthesise justice and human dignity within and across our democratic institutions. It requires understanding what is excluded and demanded by human dignity at a constitutional level while also acknowledging both the 'normal' demands of judicial decision-making (and judicial review) and the reasonable variation that exists between states, especially regarding differences in culture and resources. Public reason amounts to the constraints placed on public decision-making by 'reasonableness', but reasonableness construed as dignitarian principles, human rights, and the rule of law, each of which represents relatively substantive demands (and constraints) on any institutional or constitutional arrangement.

Let us compare, then, justice and human dignity here. With regard to *justice* in Europe, it is a reasonable or just demand that there should be subsidiarity to respect the independence and expertise of individual states. (There is no reason why there should be, for example, further harmonisation of private law across Europe; this is desirable from the point of view of economic efficiency but not demanded by justice or by the constitutional framework of the Union.) But, by extension, the legal framework within which that competence is allocated should be the higher level of the European Union itself. With regard to *human dignity*, it was an inevitable and valuable demand that the Union become a signatory to the European Convention on Human Rights; the EU needed to make civil liberties, not just economic rights, justiciable. At the same time, of course, the EU needs to retain the permissive approach to labour, goods, and services that is its economic bedrock. Free movement is the inevitable corollary of this, and it follows from the obligations principle as well as from moral cosmopolitanism: if the legal, moral, and political aspects of Europe's existing treaty commitments are to be harmonised, they inexorably require free movement as a matter of reason and not just reasonableness. However, free movement is part of Europe's internal sovereignty.

Turning then to external sovereignty and the union's relationship with states and citizens beyond Europe, we find a greater challenge to undo Europe's 'fortress'. The basic principles for migration, as a matter of justice, should already be clear on the basis of Europe's recent failures: eradication of illegal networks of migration; creation of humanitarian corridors so that those with the entitlements of refugees have clear and safe passage; and coherent resettlement policies across Europe. Moreover, the disproportionate burdens carried by Greece and Italy, and the reintroduction of internal barriers in Europe, are inconsistent not only with existing treaties and constitutional commitments but with human rights law (*MSS v. Belgium and Greece* [2011]). However, in the context of migration and asylum, and regarding the specific function of human dignity, there is often recourse to a vague *standard* of human dignity, a standard which has failed in the state from which a migrant originates, or a standard fulfilled upon reception in

Europe (see *MSS v. Belgium and Greece* [2011]). On the basis of the dignitarian principles – particularly the obligations and permissive principles – we would be better advised to look at the categories and processes being used and ask to what extent individuals are being reduced to particular administrative categories and therefore denied rights. For example, the distinction between refugee, asylum seeker, and economic migrant cannot be clearly drawn, and indeed a strict division between those with a well-founded fear of persecution and those seeking better social systems, greater respect, and more freedoms is an administrative aspiration but not one with sound normative foundations. Prior to those classifications we need to affirm the more basic rights of exit and entry.

The 'right of exit' and 'right of entry' are moral rights, and they are not necessarily symmetrical rights. It is uncontroversial that we have a right to leave the states we inhabit, but equally uncontroversial that limits are placed on if and how we are received in other states (see Kleingeld's discussion of Kant and 'hospitality rights' (Kleingeld 1998)). The right to exit is derived from a basic right to liberty but also the principled demand that our rights should not be jeopardised by political authority. Qualification on a right of *entry* can take any number of legal, political, or moral grounds, with general justification of such conditions arising from the state's responsibility to govern and serve a populace using limited resources, and more specific limits arising from security issues. The countervailing arguments for open borders point to the fact that membership of a state is morally arbitrary (place of birth) and that a principled reconstruction of rights of entry can be easily made out given states' ability to protect rights and provide basic entitlements with no comparably burdensome costs to existing citizens. The open borders position is, then, the most consistent with the moral cosmopolitanism of human dignity and indeed the most coherent position on its own terms. Nevertheless, public reason, as the ongoing harmonisation of human dignity and justice certainly requires that we attend to the demands of global justice and the political and economic dynamics of migration. Given that much future migration will be the consequence of resource shortages and resource conflict, the preservation of the human condition must outside and within Europe must be a central plank of any coherent migration policy.

With all of the foregoing points in mind, what would a more complete, dignitarian constitutionalisation of Europe look like? There is no doubt that any idea of a 'European super-state' is more a confection of its enemies than an aspiration of European politicians. Rather, a federation of states preserving their own constitutional identities has always been the sole model for ever-closer union in Europe. That is, a cosmopolitan of basic entitlements, and a morality of governance distributing power in pursuit of the basic economic rights, defended by the union but nevertheless admitting variation in the justice provided in each state. What power is properly assumed by the EU? Those policy areas that inexorably require a unified voice and resistance to political short-termism – foreign policy and sustainability – must fall within the purview of pan-European institutions. At the level of sustainability this need not preclude 'common but differentiated responsibilities' as we find in the UN governance of sustainability and climate change (see Gardiner 2004), but it does require, *a fortiori*, long-term thinking separated from the normal political cycles of individual states, and it requires grasping the opportunity to create sustainable institutions because of (not in spite of) the economic crisis facing several Member States. Unified foreign policy is not merely pragmatic but the only way to ensure principled response to emergency; it is also a means to overcome the inconsistencies created by competing bilateral treaties between the Member States and various non-EU states. While accession to the ECHR is at present unattractive to the EU, the adoption and enforcement of these civil and political rights alongside the social and economic rights that are the building blocks of the EU would mean the first attempt to truly mesh the 'indivisible' branches of human rights. It would also mean that the privatisation of state practices and services within Member States would come under greater scrutiny as potential challenges to the ECHR rights to, for instance, liberty, a fair trial, and the prohibition on slavery and servitude. The essence of these concerns lies in dignitarian principles applied to a complex organisation with a distinctive history and facing specific challenges. Nevertheless, the EU has an opportunity to sustain constitutional momentum, momentum stymied by nationalism but also by its own failure to decide what a constitutional commitment to human dignity entails.

5.6 Subsidiarity

Throughout the foregoing analysis different kinds of subsidiarity have been appealed to. This is not surprising. We are dealing with an area of law that sits uncomfortably between international and statal, public and private, and between the claims of democracy and of expertise amongst private actors. Subsidiarity is, in other terms, the meeting point between a morality of governance, of cosmopolitanism, and (fundamentally) of finding a distribution of power and authority consistent with human dignity. Subsidiarity certainly has a *prima facie* claim to a relationship with human dignity (Carozza 2003; Kanetake 2016) because it concerns respecting individuals as bearers of authority and knowledge. But more needs to be done before this can be treated as the core application of human dignity to transnational law.

The principle finds its most modern expression in the Treaty of European Union:

> Under the principle of subsidiarity, in areas which do not fall within its exclusive competence, the Union shall act only if and insofar as the objectives of the proposed action cannot be sufficiently achieved by the Member States, either at central level or at regional and local level, but can rather, by reason of the scale or effects of the proposed action, be better achieved at Union level.
>
> The Treaty of Lisbon (2007), Article 5(3)

The principle has a pedigree far older than the European Union, namely in Catholic social thought and the presumption (found in a certain form in Aquinas) that power should be diffused to communities as those equipped to understand and solve their own local problems (Follesdal 2013). It can be articulated with different emphases. We could say it is essentially democratic, demanding decision-making carried out as close to the citizen as possible. We could, with Carozza, put greater emphasis on when assistance should be extended to those with less power: "the principle that each social and political group should help smaller or more local ones accomplish their respective ends without, however, arrogating those tasks to itself" (Carozza 2003, 38). A different emphasis could be purely instrumental or a general principle of practical rationality: downwards diffusion of power is simply means–end rationality because those close to a problem will be better able to diagnose and solve it.

For present purposes I will treat the general principle, at the heart of these different iterations, as the idea that *given any particular social problem or need for political or social accountability, decision-making power should (all things being equal) be diffused to the lowest institutional unit competent to deal with it.* For its implementation there must be use of burdens and standards of proof. The burden will (usually) be on the stronger or 'higher' organisation to prove its entitlement to exercise power. The standard of proof it will need to discharge will vary. In the EU, for example, that is a mixed and variable standard: "The reasons for concluding that a Union objective can be better achieved at Union level shall be substantiated by qualitative and, wherever possible, quantitative indicators" (EU Protocol on Subsidiarity (2007), Article 5). As I have indicated (and the EU principles broadly reflect), there are certain kinds of phenomena that are more likely to satisfy the standard of proof (e.g. governance of sustainability). Nevertheless, this will be a case-by-case, not *a priori*, judgement of where authority, or expertise, or both, are to be located.

Two general features of this are important to note before we move any further. It is clear that some kind of principle like this is needed to marry complex organisations, institutions, and agencies. We need a principle that assists in assigning roles to national, transnational, and subnational bodies. We cannot presume that upwards movement of power is always valuable. Second, subsidiarity does seem in some instances to rely on ideas of democratic legitimacy, i.e. political power must be assumed to reside in the individual (or their community) and this must inform the conceptualisation of large-scale collective problems. If true, this creates an interesting tension with certain conceptualisations of cosmopolitanism that presume the normative priority of the general and the international.

Two questions therefore arise: first, whether we should see a simple justificatory relationship between human dignity and subsidiarity; second, even if so, whether we can treat this as essential for governing transnational institutional practices. Carozza's position is the most fully worked out dignitarian defence. His broad articulation is as follows:

> Subsidiarity is applicable whenever a community cannot be said to be capable of achieving that common good in a self-sufficient manner. If a political community is capable of being a complete or perfect community, encompassing

> the sum total of the requirements for the common good, then it has no need for the subsidium of any larger human association, and subsidiarity could be considered inapplicable.
>
> (Carozza 2003, 57)

The normative justification lies, however, not in reference to the common good but to individual-based authority. Its justification is

> personalistic, rather than contractual or utilitarian. [. . .] That is, its first foundation is a conviction that each human individual is endowed with an inherent and inalienable worth, or dignity, and thus that the value of the individual human person is ontologically and morally prior to the state or other social groupings. Because of this value, all other forms of society, from the family to the state and the international order, ought ultimately to be at the service of the human person. Their end must be the flourishing of the individual.
>
> (Carozza 2003, 42; footnotes removed)

Clearly this eschews the purely pragmatic or instrumental conception of subsidiarity. It is not simply that we are concerned with a practical-rational principle of knowledge and problem-solving competence. Nor is this a democratic principle in the sense of diffusing power to all and only those bodies that are democratically appointed (it leaves open the possibility that non-democratic states could in some instances be better defenders of human status at least in terms of provision of goods or protections of interests). Rather there is an assumption that power becomes more legitimate the closer it gets to individuals. Is this true?

In fact this places us back at the heart of an antinomy already touched upon: whether legitimacy or authority flow from individuals *per se* or from individuals as holders of knowledge. Subsidiarity could, on the one hand, concern the movement of power as far as possible towards individuals. It could, on the other, concern the proper place for judgments to be made about the nature of and solution to problems. These are significantly different foci. The democratic justification concerns the circumstances where it is proper for a higher authority to displace a lower one, i.e. when assistance and exercise of authority is justified given the assumption against paternalist exercises of power. Epistemologically, this concerns who is better placed to understand and define a problem. So, these ideas come apart to the extent that the democratic justification concerns who is to *solve* a problem, whereas the epistemological one concerns who is to *define* it. At the same time, if the democratic principle concerns resistance to paternalism, then it hinges on higher authorities not always *knowing best*, and as such collapses into an epistemological claim.

A distinction between democratic and epistemological subsidiarity is important not only to get at the different principles that might be at work here, but also to clearly resist the idea that migration of power downwards away (from the state or other body) is necessarily a good thing. Indeed, the epistemic and democratic are potentially at odds here. We want power to move towards 'the people' and towards 'experts'. But these claims need unpacking and may mean different things in different circumstances. The demand for democratic *oversight* means that experts are not always the final arbiter of the justified. Equally, the demand to centralise technocratic competence in some sectors means that *majoritarian decision making* is not always the final arbiter of the justified. (These are competing discourses that were poorly distinguished in political discourse around 'Brexit', for example.)

A basic, normative, and dignitarian position would then be that democratic accountability – the drawing of actors and processes into positions such that their actions can be reviewed by democratic institutions – follows from the obligations principle and from a morality of governance. But there is, I would argue, an additional argument against accepting epistemic subsidiarity here, one related to what Fricker calls 'epistemic injustice' (Fricker 2007). Claims about knowledge and technocratic expertise are not simple or susceptible to a single form of evaluation. More importantly, certain classes of people and actors can be and have been denigrated as knowers (particularly minority groups). As such we should not assume that claims to expertise are necessarily value neutral: they often come at the cost of disparaging other groups as knowers. Respect for the expertise of private commercial actors has involved disparaging indigenous groups and indigenous knowledge in ways that have meant financial gains for the private sector. Not only are claims to expertise questionable if they are intended to displace democratic authority, they are also characteristically problematic if they arise from MNEs challenging claims to knowledge that fall outside the boundaries of scientific and economic rationality congenial to profit-making companies.

If subsidiarity provides the principled underpinning of obligation and competence distribution in a transnational context, what concrete commitments are likely to flow from it? The main consequences of globalisation (privatisation of profit, public assumption of risk) represent failures of clarity on where we should draw practices into public accountability and where and to what extent we should be respecting technocratic expertise. A tamed and sustainable globalisation will require international agreement on the distribution of accountability and competence for MNEs. It will also require different institutions for the monitoring and implementation of economic and social rights. The prevailing UN bodies are prey to a form of regulatory capture whereby states can reduce these to developmental aspirations. This is exacerbated by accepting that quasi human rights claims can arise from the interests of corporations (see Grear 2007). Assigning greater power of monitoring over economic and social rights to regional human rights courts is one necessary condition of ending this, as is the continuing socialisation and democratisation of regional blocs like the EU. While these developments could be defended independently of concern with human dignity, human dignity provides two normative elements that are unifying but overlooked. We are concerned with human rights that can be negated by transnational practices; a commitment to human dignity and human rights demands remedies in our institutions such that rights cannot be ignored in favour of efficient self-regulation. And we are required, by human dignity, to maintain commitment to public reason such that justice and human dignity are brought into proper agreement; meaning, *inter alia*, that the rights of individuals cannot be ignored because of the limits of our existing legal institutions. It is to that conception of public reason that we now turn.

References

ACHPR. (2017) 'African Charter on Human and Peoples' Rights', Available at: www.achpr.org/, accessed March 2017.

Alien Tort Statute. (1980) (28 U.S.C. § 1350; ATS).

Arendt, H. (1958) *The Human Condition*. Chicago, The University of Chicago Press.

Bantekas, I. and Oette, L. (2013) *International Human Rights Law and Practice*. Cambridge, Cambridge University Press.

Bates, E. (2010) *The Evolution of the European Convention on Human Rights: From Its Inception to the Creation of a Permanent Court of Human Rights*. Oxford, Oxford University Press.

Berman, P.S. (2007) 'Global Legal Pluralism', Princeton Law and Public Affairs Working Paper No. 08–001, Available at: https://ssrn.com/abstract=985340, accessed March 2017.

Bonefeld, W. and Psychopedis, K. (2005) *Human Dignity: Social Autonomy and the Critique of Capitalism*. Aldershot, Ashgate Publishing.

Buchanan, A. (1984) 'The Right to a Decent Minimum of Health Care' *Philosophy and Public Affairs*, 13(1), 55–78.

Capps, P. and Pattinson, S. (2017) *Ethical Rationalism and the Law*. Oxford, Bloomsbury.

Carozza, P.G. (2003) 'Subsidiarity as a Structural Principle of International Human Rights Law' *American Journal of International Law*, 97(1), 38–79.

Carozza, P.G. (2008) 'Human Dignity and Judicial Interpretation of Human Rights: A Reply' *European Journal of International Law*, 19(5), 931–944.

Chapman v. UK. (1995) ECHR (Application no. 27238/95).

Chowdury and Others v. Greece. (2017) ECHR (Application no. 21884/15) judgment of 30 March 2017.

Costa, J-P. (2013) 'Human Dignity in the Jurisprudence of the European Court of Human Rights' in McCrudden, C. ed., *Understanding Human Dignity*. Oxford, Oxford University Press, 393–402.

Dagan, H. and Dorfman, A. (2016) 'Interpersonal Human Rights and Transnational Private Law', October 27, 2016, Available at: https://ssrn.com/abstract=2860275, accessed March 2017.

Dembour, M-B. (2006) *Who Believes in Human Rights? Reflections on the European Convention*. Cambridge, Cambridge University Press.

Donnelly, J. (2002) 'Human Rights, Globalizing Flows, and State Power' in Brysk, A. ed., *Globalization and Human Rights*. CA, University of California Press, 226–241.

Dupré, C. (2012) 'Dignity, Democracy, Civilisation' *Liverpool Law Review*, 33(3), 263–280.

Dupré, C. (2015) *The Age of Dignity: Human Rights and Constitutionalism in Europe*. Oxford, Bloomsbury Publishing.

ECOSOC. (2006) 'Committee of Experts on International Cooperation in Tax Matters Abuse of Tax Treaties and Treaty Shopping', Available at: www.un.org/esa/ffd/tax/secondsession/Taxation-Treaty%20Abuse.doc, accessed March 2017.
Engel, S. and Martin, B. (2006) 'Union Carbide and James Hardie: Lessons in Politics and Power' *Global Society*, 20(4), 475–490.
EU Protocol on Subsidiarity. (2007) Available at: http://eur-lex.europa.eu/legal-content/EN/TXT/?uri=CELEX%3A12008E%2FPRO%2F02, accessed April 2017.
Follesdal, A. (2013) 'The Principle of Subsidiarity as a Constitutional Principle in International Law' *Global Constitutionalism*, 2(1), 37–62.
Forst, R. (2005) 'Justice, Morality and Power in the Global Context' in Follesdal, A. and Pogge, T. eds., *Real World Justice: Volume 1*. The Netherlands, Springer, 27–36.
Fricker, M. (2007) *Epistemic Injustice: Power and the Ethics of Knowing*. Oxford, Oxford University Press.
Fuller, L.L. (1981) *The Principles of Social Order*. Durham, Duke University Press.
Garcia, F.J. (2016) 'Law and Globalization: Conceptual Issues', June 28, 2016. TLI Think! Paper No. 33/2016, Available at: http://ssrn.com/abstract=2834299, accessed March 2017.
Gardiner, S.M. (2004) 'Ethics and Global Climate Change' *Ethics*, 114(3), 555–600.
Gilabert, P. (2009) 'The Feasibility of Basic Socioeconomic Rights: A Conceptual Exploration' *The Philosophical Quarterly*, 59(237), 659–681.
Grear, A. (2007) 'Challenging Corporate 'Humanity': Legal Disembodiment, Embodiment and Human Rights' *Human Rights Law Review*, 7(3), 511–543.
Habermas, J. (2012) 'The Crisis of the European Union in the Light of a Constitutionalization of International Law' *European Journal of International Law*, 23(2), 335–348.
Hassoun, N. (2015) 'The Human Right to Health' *Philosophy Compass*, 10(4), 275–283.
Hepple, B. (2005) *Labour Laws and Global Trade*. Oxford, Bloomsbury Publishing.
Hillebrecht, C. (2012) 'Implementing International Human Rights Law at Home: Domestic Politics and the European Court of Human Rights' *Human Rights Review*, 13(3), 279–301.
Ignatieff, M. (2017) 'Human Rights, Global Ethics, and the Ordinary Virtues' *Ethics and International Affairs*, 31(1), 3–16.
International Monetary Fund. (2017) 'Standard Setting Agencies', Available at: www.imf.org/external/standards/agency.htm, accessed April 2017.
Kanetake, M. (2016) 'Subsidiarity in the Maintenance of International Peace and Security' *Law and Contemporary Problems*, 79(2), 165–187.
Kleingeld, P. (1998) 'Kant's Cosmopolitan Law: World Citizenship for a Global Order' *Kantian Review*, 2, 72–90.
Koh, H.H. (1997) 'Why Do Nations Obey International Law?' Faculty Scholarship Series. 2101, Available at: http://digitalcommons.law.yale.edu/fss_papers/2101, accessed March 2017.
Kumm, M. (2004) 'The Legitimacy of International Law: A Constitutionalist Framework of Analysis' *European Journal of International Law*, 15(5), 907–931.
Letsas, G. (2006) 'Two Concepts of the Margin of Appreciation' *Oxford Journal of Legal Studies*, 26(4), 705–732.

Linklater, A. (1999) 'The Evolving Spheres of International Justice' *International Affairs*, 75(3), 473–482.

Liste, P. (2014) 'Transnational Human Rights Litigation and Territorialised Knowledge: Kiobel and the "Politics of Space"' *Transnational Legal Theory*, 5(1), 1–19.

Mitchell, L. (2016) 'Dignity as De-Alienation: A Critique' *Academy of Management Proceedings*, 2016(1), doi:10.5465/AMBPP.2016.14161abstract, accessed March 2017.

MSS v. Belgium and Greece. (2011) ECHR (Application no. 30696/09).

Omega. (2004) Omega Spielhallen- und Automatenaufstellungs-GmbH v. Oberbürger- meisterin der Bundesstadt Bonn, [ECJ] Judgment (First Chamber) of October 14.

Olsen, H. and Toddington, S. (2007) *Architectures of Justice: Legal Theory and the Idea of Institutional Design*, Ashgate, Aldershot.

Open Democracy. (2015) 'Ukraine's European Integration', Available at: www.opendemocracy.net/od-russia/devin-ackles/ukraine%E2%80%99s-european-integration, accessed March 2017.

Organstreit Proceedings. (2009) '(German Constitutional Court) BVerfG, Judgment of the Second Senate of 30 June 2009–2002 BvE 2/08', Available at: www.bundesverfassungsgericht.de/SharedDocs/Entscheidungen/EN/2009/06/es20090630_2bve000208en.html, accessed March 2017.

Pagnattaro, M.A. (2013) 'Labor Rights Are Human Rights: Direct Action Is Critical in Supply Chains and Trade Policy' *South Carolina Journal of International Law and Business*, 10(1), 1–62.

Pluricourts. (2017) Available at: www.jus.uio.no/pluricourts/english/, accessed March 2017.

Rantsev v. Cyprus and Russia. (2010) *Rantsev v. Cyprus and Russia* ECHR (Application no. 25965) judgement of January 7, 2010, Available at: www.refworld.org/cases,ECHR,4b4f0b5a2.html, accessed April 2017.

Rawls, J. (1999) *A Theory of Justice*, Revised edition. Oxford, Oxford University Press.

Raz, J. (1999 [1975]) *Practical Reason and Norms*. Oxford, Oxford University Press.

Shapiro, S. (2011) *Legality*. Cambridge, MA, Harvard University Press.

Siliadin. (2005) *Siliadin v. France*, Application no. 73316/01 [ECHR] 26 July 2005, Available at: www.refworld.org/cases,ECHR,4406f0df4.html, accessed April 2017.

Soobramoney. (1997) *Soobramoney v. Minister of Health, KwaZulu-Natal* ZACC 17, 1998 (1) SA 765 (CC), 1997 (12) BCLR 1696 (CC), November 27, 1997, Constitutional Court (South Africa).

Sullivan, G. (2014) 'Transnational Legal Assemblages and Global Security Law: Topologies and Temporalities of the List' *Transnational Legal Theory*, 5(1), 81–127.

Tamanaha, B.Z. (2010) 'Law and Society' in Patterson, D. ed., *A Companion to Philosophy of Law and Legal Theory*. Oxford, John Wiley and Sons, 368–380.

The Treaty of Lisbon. (2007) 'Treaty of Lisbon Amending the Treaty on European Union and the Treaty Establishing the European Community', December 13, 2007, 2007/C 306/01, Available at: www.refworld.org/docid/476258d32.html, accessed April 2017.

van der Burg, W. (2014) *The Dynamics of Law and Morality: A Pluralist Account of Legal Interactionism*. Farnham, Ashgate.

Weinrib, J. (2016) *Dimensions of Dignity: The Theory and Practice of Modern Constitutional Law*. Cambridge, Cambridge University Press.
Williams, A. (2003) 'Mapping Human Rights, Reading the European Union' *European Law Journal*, 9(5), 659–676.
Zumbansen, P. (2013) 'Lochner Disembedded: The Anxieties of Law in a Global Context' *Indiana Journal of Global Legal Studies*, 20(1), 29–69.

6 Public law

> The Constitution is forward-looking and guarantees to every citizen fundamental rights in such a manner that the ordinary person-in-the-street, who is aware of these guarantees, immediately claims them without further ado and assumes that every right so guaranteed is available to him or her on demand. Some rights in the Constitution are the ideal and something to be strived for. They amount to a promise, in some cases, and an indication of what a democratic society aiming to salvage lost dignity, freedom and equality should embark upon. They are values which the Constitution seeks to provide, nurture and protect for a future South Africa.
>
> —(*Soobramoney* [1997], paragraph 42)

Introduction

Public law, the constitutional and administrative governance of a state, presents a large and complex phenomenon within which to find the applications of human dignity. It requires finding distinctions between commitment to justice and commitment to human dignity within the multiple responsibilities of the constitutional state. It requires attention to the historical particularity, and sociological dynamism, of the contemporary state. And it requires normative precision concerning the use of coercive force against individuals in the morally conflicted context of criminal justice.

Many common ways of linking human dignity and the state are unsatisfactory or incomplete for reasons we have already encountered. On the one hand, human dignity is a general, foundational commitment, and there is symbolic significance in a state committing itself to human dignity as a value. Thus, as Eberle says of the German Constitution, a constitution can be "anchored in the architectonic value of human dignity, meaning, at least, that each person is valuable *per se* as an end in himself, which government and fellow citizens must give due respect" (2008, 4; footnote removed). On the other hand, that 'architectonic' commitment might as well be expressed in the language of flourishing, or liberty, or democracy, or any other principle with a similarly individuating and protective function. The precise contribution human dignity makes to the *self-conception* of a modern democracy remains opaque. Moreover, in a well-functioning system of public law with equality law and a prohibition on degradation, it is simply not clear what human dignity serving a *regulative* function would add to that self-conception. The use of human dignity for regulative purposes tends at best to unhelpfully reopen conceptual and normative confusions about the nature of the concept and at worst denies it any constitutional significance at all.

The main challenge of conceptualising human dignity in public law is, then, to explain its distinctive constitutional significance and its contribution to our understanding of public reason. There are, I would suggest, three crucial principles of public governance that are not merely issues of justice but of human dignity: constitutionalising human rights, maintaining the division between public and private, and implementing criminal justice in a way that preserves liberties for society while respecting the human dignity of criminals. As we have seen before, human rights law is a useful starting point. But in this context it is especially important that we sharpen a distinction between constitutional rights and human rights. Human rights are not only a set of entitlements arising from the innate right of individuals but, in practice, they have to be interpreted and balanced in a distinctive way: they should have a relatively independent jurisprudential life driven by a dynamic, principled core in human dignity. More widely, human rights and human dignity furnish a state with the general principles of human status from *within which* justice – consistency and coherence in granting remedies – takes its basic moral orientation. Accordingly, my conception of 'public reason' is as the ongoing *reconciliation of human dignity and justice* within and across the organs of government. Defending this conception of public reason requires concern with both the institutional arrangements of democracies and with the nature and demands of the 'reasonable' within a constitutional state.

We look first at the defensibility of the state as a form of social organisation; this ties human dignity to democratic authority but also the demands of public reason. Then we look to the links between human rights and the rule of law; operationalising human rights within a constitutional state not only requires limits on the power of the organs of the state but also necessitates acting upon a certain conception of public reason. Then the public-private divide is defended as an essential permissive condition of human dignity; this requires a resistance to the 'colonisation of the lifeworld' by technocratic reason. Thereafter we turn to criminal justice concerns; the proper scope of criminal law, the conduct of criminal justice, and the dignitarian constraints on punishment.

6.1 The responsibilities of the state

Our immediate concern will be to identify the force, and limits, of a functional understanding of the state. This concerns certain common arguments for the state's claim to authority. Working through these arguments is necessary to clearly situate the responsibilities of the state in relation to the wider cosmopolitan responsibilities implied by human dignity. We must secure the status of the state as a morally defensible, indeed morally required, form of social arrangement despite the cosmopolitanism that human dignity is rightly associated with.

The role and justification of the state can be put purely in terms of the ends it serves. These functionalist arguments would typically point to the state being a necessary condition of the rule of law providing coordination between actors and providing regulation of power. Its specific functions include provision of institutions, governance of resources, and collective security, functions necessary for the coexistence and flourishing of groups and of individuals. 'Functionalist' here denotes the sociological idea of the state producing a social whole by maintaining social order and a division of labour (Cotterrell 2011; Verschraegen 2002). This sociological position has been drawn upon in various guises in political theory including both utilitarian and socialist theory (Bosanquet 1920), and is also found in the roots of legal positivism (Bentham 2007). Functionalism can also be defined by what it is opposed to. It should be thought to stand in opposition to nationalist arguments insisting on an 'organic' link between nations and states. Such organicist positions stand in contrast to a dignitarian defence of the state as an agent whose authority derives from democracy and from its capacity for public reason.

Before we reach those conclusions, however, note that from functionalist foundations significantly different, plausible political positions can be defended. Libertarian and liberal theorists draw different conclusions about the function of the state as a basic rights-defending, or welfare-providing, entity respectively. Nevertheless, such positions will tend to agree that the 'modern' or 'Westphalian' state is a *territorial* state with the power to exercise exclusive control over space, with its basic territorial functions existing regardless of any organic, nationalistic link between a body of people and land:

> Individuals' rights, the stability of individuals' expectations, and ultimately their physical security, depend upon the effective enforcement of a legal order. Effective enforcement requires effective *jurisdiction*, and this in turn requires a clearly bounded territory that is recognized to be the domain of an identified political authority. Even if political authority strictly speaking is exercised only over persons, not land, the effective exercise of political authority over persons, depends ultimately upon the establishment and maintenance of jurisdiction in the territorial sense. This fact rests upon an obvious but deep truth about human beings: They have bodies that occupy space, and the materials for living upon which they depend do so as well. Furthermore, if an effective legal order is to be possible, both the boundaries that define the jurisdiction and the identified political authority whose jurisdiction it is must persist over time.
>
> (Buchanan 1997, 47; emphasis in original)

As with other forms of public law, territory and time remain core components of the justification of state authority. Control of space plus persistence through time are functionally necessary for the discharge of both security and welfare roles. The territorial control exercised by states, and their continuing legal personality through time (despite changes in the natural persons who inhabit roles within the state), are functional presuppositions shared across a spectrum of philosophical defences of the state and political philosophies.

However, if these were the limits of the justification of the state they would face a fundamental critique from cosmopolitanism: territorial states require borders that impose arbitrary differences of treatment, and impose arbitrary variations in the enjoyment of rights. This cosmopolitan critique (already partly addressed in Chapter 3) can also be joined to other dignitarian criticisms of functionalism. These other, normative, deficiencies of functionalism become clearer if we consider what it would be to fully privatise key functions of the state. Assuming (for argument) that the state continues to maintain the military forces necessary for the existential maintenance of the state, states could privatise prisons, schools, and the core administrative responsibilities of central and local government. We should assume that private actors can discharge these responsibilities lawfully and efficiently. The residual problem is that we can still question their *authority* to do this. For Alon Harel, "[t]here are certain goods that are 'intrinsically public'; they cannot be provided by private individuals" (2014b, 51). This argument is linked directly to human dignity. "Dignity, I argue, demands that decisions and actions be based on certain reasons. Dignity imposes constraints on the deliberation of the agents; it dictates not what agents ought to decide or do but primarily how they ought to reason" (Harel 2014b, 51). This idea of 'reasoning consistent with human dignity' is found in legislative and adjudicative practices that take individuals' rights to be inexorable, i.e. that any reasoning by the state must assume the existence of human rights. Such reasoning can only be undertaken by a state given its independence from private interest. The reasoning of state actors, as public actors, is intrinsically rights-protecting in a way that the reasoning of private actors cannot be. This amounts to a dual assault on functionalism. First, it ascribes rights to individuals *as* human rights, not as rights simply acquired through choice; private corporate persons can neither possess such rights nor recognise their value. Second, and relatedly, the state discharges what I term an obligations principle as part of its morality of governance: it has a responsibility to ensure that normative orders – law, morality, and politics – are harmonised in such a way as to ensure that the status of human persons is not compromised by competing contradictory obligations. Private provision of certain functions of the state would produce precisely such contradictions, with the imperatives issued by a private provider of (say) prison facilities of a different order to those of the state itself. The imprisoned individual may have a legal responsibility to obey the commands of a private security provider, but it is far less clear that they have a moral one.

This critique of functionalism via human dignity and public reason will be further defended below when we turn to the special demands of the rule of law and the idea of public reason itself. First, however, there needs to be clarity on where this dignitarian reasoning based on human rights sits: in one particular organ of government, or across the workings of the state? On this question the work of Jacob Weinrib (2016) can be usefully contrasted with Harel's. Weinrib also uses human dignity to propose limits on the power of the state, and draws upon both Kant's 'Doctrine of Right' and Gustav Radbruch's inclusive positivist argument that any system of positive law is morally constrained by the potential for the *judiciary* to negate the validity of unconscionable or anti-democratic law as law (Radbruch 2006). Indeed, Weinrib's account places considerable weight on the 'justiciable constraints' produced by human dignity:

> By modern constitutional practice, I refer to the sum of conditions that legal systems in the postwar era have introduced to make the exercise of public authority accountable to the human dignity of all who are subject to it. These conditions include: a constitution that establishes the terms for the lawful exercise of all public authority; a set of constitutional rights that bind all branches of government; an accessible judicial body authorized and obligated to respond to constitutional complaints by reviewing the conformity of government conduct to constitutional norms; substantive constraints on the amending power that preserve the essentials of the constitutional order; and doctrines that determine the protections that constitutional rights afford and the limits to which rights are subject in reference to the overarching idea of human dignity. Together these conditions create, refine, and sustain a legal order in which the human dignity of each person forms a justiciable constraint on the exercise of all public authority.
>
> (Weinrib 2016, 2)

Weinrib goes on to make an important distinction between different kinds of moral failures a state can exhibit and their different implications for law, namely failures of 'injustice' and of 'barbarism' (2016, 86f). The first is a failure of distribution and remedies, the latter a more fundamental assault on human dignity. And while the normal constitutional functioning of the state will be broadly informed by human dignity, the latter 'barbaric' failures alone permit judicial resistance to the authority of the other organs of the state on grounds of human dignity. This distinction strongly echoes the division between justice and human dignity and their implications that I have drawn elsewhere (see Chapter 3). The distinction that Weinrib draws allows him a useful distinction between our general situation vis-à-vis the authority of the state where occasional failures of justice do not negate its claim to authority and the cases (over which Weinrib and Radbruch would concur) when the justified authority of the executive and legislature runs out. He, however, goes on to tie this distinction to the different spheres of ***public and private law*** (2016, 64) and the obligations placed on public and private actors; private law is ultimately concerned with justice and public law with our protection from barbarism. This division is more difficult to defend without more sustained analysis of the public-private divide. More specifically, it presupposes a strict normative distinction between public and private *law* which I will not endorse. These are themes that will be returned to.

Weinrib does, however, put pressure on Harel's account of where human dignity sits within our wider constitutional concerns:

> On the one hand, [Harel's] justification of constitutional rights holds that a legal system is defective if the freedom of any individual within it is 'contingent on the good will of the legislator'. On the other, Harel's justification of judicial review holds that the commonwealth model [giving especially strong powers to the legislature] is acceptable even though it leaves the task of determining whether to conform with right 'to the legislature and its good will'.
>
> (Weinrib 2016, 166)

In other words, we should expect more precision concerning both where the ultimate authoritative application of human dignity is to be found: Weinrib places it in the courts, Harel divides it between judicial and legislative organs. Harel's division not only means that the ultimate *locus* of human dignity's significance for the state is uncertain, but it means that public reason – the conditioning of public choices by commitment to rights and dignity – is itself conditioned by democratic will. So, we are owed a clearer account of where and how human rights can be conditioned (qualified, balanced, defeated, etc.) – in the courts like other legal norms, or in parliament like other principles and policies? If the latter, then it no longer seems possible to divide constitutional from human rights – meaning, in turn, that the distinctive relationship between public authority and human rights that is central to Harel's position would be lost. These are important questions. But it is worth noting that Weinrib's contrary emphasis on justiciability creates a kindred set of problems. If the constitutional commitment of a state to human dignity is found predominantly (or most characteristically) in its judicial, rather than legislative, functions, how is a fully constitutional vision of human dignity possible given the judiciary's responsibility to respond to disputes, show fidelity to the text of a constitution, and exercise a conservative force on the dynamics of the political? Is human dignity ultimately justiciable only in Radbruch cases of barbaric (unconscionable or constitution-dissolving) laws? Or should we expect more frequent uses, as in the US Constitution's Eighth Amendment jurisprudence? And is Weinrib able to draw lines between public and private authority in the state such that public law and public reason is given a legitimating role in the coercion of individuals? Harel, I think, is correct in encouraging us to look beyond the important, but limited, 'Radbruch formula' to connect human dignity and the authority of the state. But is a more complete argument connecting authority, public law, and human dignity possible? More specifically, is public *law* sufficiently political, and sufficiently far-reaching in its scope, to fulfil my (and Harel's) demand that each of the organs of government have a constitutional relationship with human dignity?

First the scope of public law itself needs clarification. Public law, Harel writes,

> consists of constitutional law, administrative law, criminal law, and tax law. It contains both norms governing horizontal relations between different

> branches of the government and norms governing vertical relations between the government and individuals or private entities. In contrast, private law contains norms governing the horizontal relationships among private entities. The fields of law that are most paradigmatically classified as private law are contract law, property law, and tort law. This classification is valuable because allegedly it has normative (or even political or ideological) consequences. It is believed that public law is a sphere designed to promote the public good or the common good of the community while private law protects individual freedom, typically negative freedom – the freedom to follow one's objectives without intrusion.
>
> (Harel 2014a, 1042)

In the background of such a division are countless accidents and variants in the drawing of the divide and no *a priori* or systematic line between the two can be drawn (*pace*, for example, Beever 2013). There are certainly intuitive divisions between these spheres of law and longstanding differences in remedies and evidential standards. But the content of both public and private law, as a matter of justice, admits a great deal of reasonable variation.

Are there any non-contingent connections between human dignity and private law? Certainly constitutional practice, and juridical commentary, has sometimes drawn public and private law together through human dignity itself:

> Since human dignity constitutes the architectonic principle of the German legal system, it radiates into and affects private law and, indeed, the whole legal system. Under this doctrine, known as Third Party Effect (*Drittwirkung*), the norms of the [Constitution] enter into and influence the norms of private law, as the norms of private law can do the same with respect to constitutional law. The legal system as a whole operates in tandem.
>
> (Eberle 2008, 5)

The field of 'personality rights' in civil law jurisdictions has also encompassed the discourse of dignity within concerns that are both public (constitutional rights) and private (individual reputation claims). More fundamentally, however, we would want to say that human dignity *demands* both spheres of law: general governance of the public sphere and the ability to bring claims as a private citizen against other citizens. The latter must be amongst the rights demanded by innate right, or innate sovereign equality, and include the entitlement to enter into contracts and have standing as legal persons. The precise division between the two spheres of public and private law is not, however, implied by innate right. Kant himself commences his reflections with property and private right and thereafter deduces public right as a necessary condition of private justice (see Ripstein 2006). This is not an implication or line of argument I think we need to follow. What is important is that both are drawn from innate right and that the state can and will have some role to play in private law, in deciding distributions of property and the scope of private law claims. Attempts to remove the state from private law, and to purify it of distributive concerns, do not have any foundation in human dignity.

The analysis so far has problematised any simple relationship between public law, authority, and human dignity. Unlike Weinrib I do not think a strict normative distinction between public and private law can be drawn, nor, more fundamentally, do I argue that the constitutional function of human dignity centres on judicial activity, constitutional interpretation, and the prevention of barbarity. But I do not think we are yet in a position to show how human dignity, the legal, and the political should interact in a state. First, human dignity must inform our conception of the rule of law, the application of human rights, and reason-giving by the state. Second, we need a more comprehensive understanding of what it is we are doing when we draw a distinction between public and private, both as 'spheres' and as forms of authority.

6.2 The rule of law and public reason

The rule of law is not only a broad aspiration of good governance. It serves as an internal critique of law expressing ideals for legal systems (as institutionalised systems), an ideal for governance (treating law as a system with a governmental purpose), or requires law to be a rational purposive social activity needing clear means-ends rationality. Human dignity can be used to support each of these ideas by stressing the general orientation of systems towards *agency*: laws should address agents as rational actors; it should be coordinating and not simply controlling; it should rely upon, and not simply bypass, rational individual agency. For those reasons, in the context of the rule of law, human dignity can be separated from specific regulative practices like human rights law and relates to the moral orientation of legal systems, i.e. their relationship with freedom, integrity, and respect (see Riley 2015).

These are familiar themes in Fullerean philosophy of law where the formal aspects of law-making are governed by an 'internal morality of law' (Fuller 1964). The canons or *desiderata* of legislation include generality, clarity, publicity, consistency, feasibility, constancy, prospectivity, and congruence. These ensure that law is (at a minimum) fulfillable and (in a more substantive sense) maximises the possibility of its own self-execution. Legislation that fulfils these demands not only successfully guides our actions but is law properly so-called: law as opposed to arbitrary governance or mere 'commands backed up by force'. Luban glosses the implications of Fuller's position:

> Fuller believes that the rule of law enhances human dignity. The point is not that the rule of law is logically incompatible with despotic government or harsh laws. Rather, the point is that the rule of law robs despotism of some of its most characteristic devices, and in this way it is practically incompatible with despotism. Why would repressive governments want to burden themselves by restricting the laws they enact to those permitted by Fuller's

> canons? It seems overwhelmingly likely that they would not, because their power to intimidate their subjects would diminish.
>
> (Luban 2010, 40)

However, as discussed elsewhere (see Chapter 3) this risks treating the rule of law as a sufficient condition of human dignity, an over-reach identified by Raz:

> If the rule of law is the rule of good law then to explain its nature is to propound a complete social philosophy. But if so the term lacks any useful function. We have no need to be converted to the rule of law just in order to discover that to believe in it is to believe that good should triumph. The rule of law is a political ideal which a legal system may lack or may possess to a greater or lesser degree. That much is common ground. It is also to be insisted that the rule of law is just one of the virtues which a legal system may possess and by which it is to be judged. It is not to be confused with democracy, justice, equality (before the law or otherwise), human rights of any kind or respect for persons or for the dignity of man.
>
> (Raz 1979, 211)

There is a temptation, as Raz sees it, to assume that aspiring to and fulfilling the rule of law is equivalent to fulfilling the demands of human dignity (such a position might be attributed to Fuller). In fact, we should contrast the rule of law – the separation of powers and checks and balances in a state – from what I have termed the obligations principle. The latter would be much closer to a sufficient condition for human dignity: the obligation to ensure that different normative orders (law, morality, and politics) are harmonised in such a way as to protect the status of the human person. Put another way, while Fuller's position could ultimately (as Hart argued (1958)) be reduced to one of instrumental rationality – means-ends rationality demands a certain clarity and consistency in legislation – the obligations principle makes human status primary: the individual is denied their basic status if conflicting normative orders make competing claims upon them. Nevertheless, the obligations principle itself should not be treated as a sufficient condition of human dignity; we need other dignitarian principles, as well as human rights, for human dignity to be protected in a state. But Fuller is right to link law, morality, and politics in our understanding of law as such.

The connection is explored by Habermas who turns our attention, rightly, towards the interplay of human rights, human dignity, and democratic rule of law.

> The idea of human dignity is the conceptual hinge which connects the morality of equal respect for everyone with positive law and democratic law-making in such a way that that their interplay could give rise to a political order founded upon human rights [. . .]. Because the moral promise of equal respect for everyone is supposed to be cashed out in legal currency, human rights exhibit a Janus face turned simultaneously to morality and to

> law. Notwithstanding their exclusive moral content, they have the form of positive, enforceable subjective rights which guarantee specific liberties and claims. They are designed to be spelled out in concrete terms through democratic legislation, to be specified from case to case in adjudication and to be enforced with public sanction.
>
> (Habermas 2010, 469)

Habermas, we should note, is happy to maintain a certain equivocation between which of the judicial and the legislative organs is the primary driver of the development of human rights and interpreter of human dignity. And the 'political order' created by, or founded upon, human rights is additionally uncertain insofar as human rights certainly offer important regulations but do not exhaust the constitutional demands of a modern state. These demands, we might assume, are for Habermas determined elsewhere through discursive democratic practices (Habermas 2001). In comparison, a more fulsome connection between democracy and the rule of law is offered by Fox-Decent and Criddle in their analysis of the state and human rights (2010). Using a 'fiduciary' conception of the state, he insists on a direct and necessary relationship between human rights and the rule of law.

> Within the fiduciary framework, human rights emerge as entitlements to be treated in certain ways by public institutions. In particular, public institutions are duty-bound to secure individuals against arbitrary power by promoting the republican ideal of nondomination. [. . .] the human rights enshrined in international law provide a normative structure conducive to nondomination. They are mid-range or intermediary norms that reside between the amorphous demands of dignity and the concrete institutionalization of sovereign power, and they are susceptible to modification pursuant to democratic deliberation. In short, human rights under the fiduciary theory are normative consequences of the state's assumption of sovereign powers and are thus constitutive of sovereignty's normative dimension. [. . .] Put another way, human rights are correlates of the state's duty to secure conditions of noninstrumentalization and nondomination. We see below that instrumentalization and domination are distinct, but both reflect an ideal of independent agency.
>
> (Fox-Decent and Criddle 2010, 310)

Fox-Decent makes important points, especially in characterising human rights laws as 'intermediary' and 'modifiable'. In his view human rights are 'intermediary' between the international law of human rights and other domestic laws. (Which, as a matter of doctrinal interpretation, is certainly true.) But I would prefer to see human rights law as intermediary between the principles implied by human dignity, and the justice (the disputes and adjudications) that make up the quotidian functioning of law. Moreover, the fiduciary responsibility of the state remains potentially ambiguous. While it is uncontroversial that human rights entail limitations on the power of the state, a stronger claim making the state's authority conditional on the delivery of certain or all human rights requires a much more fulsome justification. Be that as it may, Fox-Decent's separation of instrumentalisation and non-domination is broadly correct, insofar as the former is a regulative and the latter a constitutive function for human dignity. Most importantly, if the moral, legal, and political are to be brought into harmony, then we should have a set of *dynamic, modifiable, sovereignty-protecting laws*, namely human rights laws. Such laws should be governed – applied but also modified – by the normal canons of legal reasoning because this ensures that they are delivered equally and impartially. In that sense, human rights and the rule of law are connected, but we should not be looking for a single source of implication of one by the other, rather principled unity around human dignity. That principled unity is expressible as the pursuit of 'public reason'.

From John Rawls's influential perspective, public reason is principally articulated in opposition to 'comprehensive' political or philosophical positions. The latter would claim to possess the whole truth about the arrangement of public affairs (or the whole truth in other domains of knowledge and practice). Public reason represents the reasoning within a democratic polity, reasoning that involves reining in comprehensive doctrines. It must certainly be *rational* and therefore reject knowledge that transcends what is generally knowable (therefore rejecting religious claims). But it must be *reasonable* in that it must involve acting upon reasons that we can expect people to endorse; reasonable grounds for action would include the maintenance of the democratic system of governance itself and include those grounds for action that can be followed by everyone regardless of their own comprehensive doctrines. There are two ways we can use this as orientation for our own enquiry into the constitutive place of human dignity in the state. First, we could treat public reason as a set of 'publicity tests' for reasons that can be legitimately proffered in a democratic state. Second, we could treat public reason as a wider demand for principled governance and the rule of law.

The translation of public reason into certain kinds of tests (or side constraints) on the conduct of democratic polities (across the separated powers of government) takes several forms. It could mean shareable reasons or clear justifications for every act of government (see Forst 2011). It could mean (at a more epistemological level) 'followability' in the reasons that are given for public acts (O'Neill 1996). It could mean something like 'fulfilability' (Fuller 1964). These entwine the ideas of 'ought implies can' (that public reason is essentially a demand for rational governance) and of justification to rational actors prepared to put aside their comprehensive doctrines (that public reason is essentially a demand for reasonableness in governance). These are all encompassed in Capps's account:

> The success of a legal order in stabilising expectations relies upon some conception of public practical reasons upon which law and legal institutions can rest in light of moral pluralism. Without this, law, instrumentally, cannot regulate social interaction and, as such, becomes inert. But what are these

> public practical reasons? [. . .] To speculate, we might say that such reasons are justified to the extent that they reflect fundamental principles of public or civil association, and these, we might presume, cash out into a series of civil rights. Equally, the idea that such reasons are public, rather than private, suggests that they should stand a test of publicity. Such reasons are those that all members of a community can accept as reasonable. Private reasons are ones which cannot survive this test because they are reasonable to the individual holding them in a subjective sense only.
>
> (Capps 2009, 153)

If the 'rational' typically captures only means-end rationality, the 'reasonable' is reasoning that makes the concerns of social co-existence a side constraint. Thus the reasonable would prohibit certain courses of action that would otherwise be rational; the extermination of a state's enemies may be rational in the circumstances but unlikely to be accepted as reasonable if brought into the light of public discourse. However, if public reason requires the test of publicity, it cannot be exhausted by such publicity. Rather – if we think of the Arendtian public realm and the morality of governance – it should be thought to include commitment to both permissiveness and contingency ('fundamental principles of civil association', as Capps puts it). Public reason is not the mere existence of a space of public discourse; it also keeps open the possibility of conflict and change in a polity. Equally, if we narrowed public reason to the preservation of 'civil rights' we would miss the underlying general principles we associate with human dignity and with it the special normative force of human rights.

Accordingly, I think we need to take a dignitarian conception of public reason to require human dignity (principled governance), human rights (the institutionalised legal defence of human dignity), and alongside them the normal functioning of justice and the rule of law. Again, Dworkin and Brugger's judiciary-focussed positions are instructive. The judiciary's fidelity to law embraces rationality (consistency in reasoning) and reasonableness (the determination of which reasons are permissible in the light of their reconstruction of the constitution and other authoritative doctrine). This means (on the one hand) it is a conservative force in determining what is reasonable; this means (on the other) that the counter-majoritarian critique is ill-founded because the judiciary show fidelity to the constituent power of the people as source of the original constitution ('We the People'). And, as Dworkin and Brugger insist, judicial interpretation is forward- as well as backward-looking and (as Dupré insists) this dual perspective encompasses a conception of human dignity itself. Thus we see a conservative fidelity to a conception of human dignity as prohibitive of atrocity and discrimination (in Germany and South Africa, for instance). But the judiciary also have to reconstruct a forward-looking conception of human dignity as the living or vital core of the constitution. All of this, of course, takes place within the conventional (reasoning and doctrinal) constraints that are constitutive of legal institutions *per se*. We do not abandon justice when we defend human dignity; public reason has to mean the reconciliation of the two.

By an alternative route we have returned to the centrality of human rights for the realisation of public reason and a morality of governance. The judiciary, but not the judiciary alone, are required to limit their decision-making freedom by human dignity, human rights, and justice. Where human rights are concerned, the judiciary has a specific (and by now familiar) role to conceive of human rights as 'indivisible' and as part of 'living instruments'. To put it another way, we would expect the judiciary to invoke human dignity only where there are extensive or dangerous break-downs in the realisation of human dignity: systematic failure to realise human rights, systematic reduction in our natural permissions, systematic contradictions between the law and the conscience of a considerable part of the populace. Human dignity can be used as a heuristic within the normal jurisprudence of human rights, but experience has shown that this tends to involve a conservative and backwards-looking concern with basic protections and degradation. What indivisibility and a living instrument do is to translate dignitarian principles into tools for 'normal' human rights jurisprudence under 'normal conditions'. They force the judiciary to look for principled connections and principled justifications within the protections afforded by human rights law as a whole (indivisibility) and they encourage a future and not just backwards-looking concern with the development of the law. Human dignity keeps human rights dynamic, but to reach legal judgments human dignity takes specific jurisprudential forms that have no need to invoke the language of human dignity directly.

The point of this account of dignitarian reasoning in the judiciary is not to locate the dignitarian responsibilities of the state purely within the judiciary. It is constraints on their reasoning that are crucial: fidelity to the constitution but also future-orientated interpretation; commitment to the 'indivisibility' of human rights as a distinctive body of laws where the moral, legal, and political meet in relative isolation from day-to-day politics. This isolation or insulation is precisely what is hinted at in invocations of the 'reasonable' aspects of public reason: constitutive side constraints on the political that ensure the maintenance of the polity, the protection of basic values, and resistance to sacrificing individual status to collective gains. These are responsibilities we can place on the executive and legislature as well as the judiciary (see Chapter 3). The fact that this must be undertaken in an ongoing dialogue with justice – with normal judicial and political practices ensuring representation, accountability, and redress for wrongs – means that public reason is an ongoing task of self-governance and self-understanding by a polity. This is, I think, an unusual way of expressing a common intuition, namely that a good state has the rule of law: it not only has laws, but it has laws governed by status-protecting principles.

6.3 The public-private divide

One of the areas of normative concern that has an important but confused role in discourses of human dignity and the rule of law is the public-private divide. We assume that the rule of law will protect such a divide, but it is rarely considered an explicit aspect of the rule of law. It is, perhaps, too substantive, dynamic, or historically contingent to be a definitive political or moral commitment. With regard to human dignity, we are familiar with specific cases where the violation of the body or home are treated as violations of the fundamentally or inalienably private and therefore of dignitarian concern. But, as Marmor puts it, the existence of the private sphere must one way or another be of wider, more general concern:

> [H]aving a reasonable measure of control over ways in which we present ourselves to others is an important aspect of our well-being. It enables a whole range of choices about the constitution of one's social environment, without which life would be either too stifling or too alienated. People need to be able to determine, at least to some extent, the amount and the kind of personal distance they maintain with others. That is not because everyone has something to hide (though that may be true as well), but because everyone needs some choice about how close or how distant they want to be from different others. A reasonable amount of control over ways in which we present ourselves to others is necessary for the kind of choices we want to make about the social interactions we have with different people. It is part of what enables us to shape the social life we want to have.
>
> (Marmor 2015, 10–11; footnote removed)

But thereafter it is unclear whether the divide as such should be the concern of human rights law, specific prohibitive dignitarian norms protecting the body and the home, or a more complex mixture of political, legal, and moral concerns. We must (recalling discussions in Chapter 3) consider the nature of the divide itself and how the existence of both spheres is important. We also (recalling the merits of Harel's account) need to think of the divide as a division between two different kinds of authority and how this interacts with the rule of law and with our natural liberties. We also need, finally, to consider the sociological dynamics of the divide and consider what the permissive principles demand as we consider technological changes in the modern state.

The public-private divide is complex and dialectical. We understand these two spheres in contradistinction to the other, by excluding the public from the private and vice versa. In the public law of the state, this complex dialectical process is played out clearly in the uncertain and apparently disordered law of privacy. In common law systems we do not find (until at least the twentieth century) statutory or constitutional protection of privacy. Protection of the private was constructed out of various components of the constitution and the common law (see Solove 2002). In the US this complex, piecemeal approach has proven extremely flexible, meaning privacy could, for example, be extended to include a right to abortion. In the UK, the previously patchwork law of privacy has been considerably enhanced under the influence of European human rights law. Despite that, however, the underlying principles in privacy law remain unclear. First, the meaning of public (as a space, or as an authority) remains vague and context-specific. And, second, the historical legacy of the law concerning the private sphere has betrayed protection or insulation of the private sphere from public scrutiny such that forms of labour and forms of abuse have been hidden. Thus, the public and private do remain in a dialectical relationship at the heart of law, with the 'private' meaning the exclusion of public scrutiny, and the 'public' broadly meaning the exclusion of private self-interest. But a unified, principled body of law remains elusive.

One major consequence of this is that there is no clear rejoinder, either in the language of human dignity or justice, to the privatisation of the public sphere: the adoption of public roles by private bodies or the domination of the public sphere of discourse by private commercial actors. A dignitarian response to this should be that the withdrawal of the state from the governance of certain aspects of public life does not mean the expansion of liberty. It can mean the expansion of lawlessness, and it can mean the governance of practices and places by private and quasi-public actors (e.g. private security firms or multi-national corporations). This points again to the limits of a functional conception of public authority and public reason. The existence of public authority means individuals cannot be judges in their own cases; it does not simply mean 'equal treatment before the law' but also means the more basic natural justice of having our actions judged by a third party who is not (for judicial purposes) our equal but an independent superior. And the existence of public reason is different to the mere imperative to govern as efficiently as possible; it means a preservation of liberties and preservation of a public sphere. Just as the emergence of the state meant the illegitimacy of vigilante justice, a well-governed polity should be able to question the right to institute private security and semi-autonomous policing zones within its boundaries.

This has further connections with public reason. By excluding private interests in order to defend a purely public reason, we are insisting on the priority of 'public interest' over 'private interest' and insisting on the exclusive power of the public realm to include human rights as a necessary, not just *pro tanto*, aspect of reasoning (as Harel argues). But again, I would want to see public reason here not only as a side constraint on the reason that can be given for action but as encompassing wider dignitarian principles. After all, the permissive principle – preserving natural and social permissions, and maintaining contingency within our social systems – also draws into what is 'reasonable' certain kinds of exclusions of technocratic claims and resistance to excessive governance. Public reason, in essence, is opposed to the 'colonisation of the lifeworld' by regulation and technocratic or bureaucratic regulations (see below). Thereby, the constitutive implications of human dignity become much clearer: it demands a certain kind of public reason encompassing human rights but also encompassing permissiveness, a permissiveness regarding our conduct and self-determination, but also the permissiveness of reducing the intrusion of private actors into public discourse even where these have claim to technocratic expertise. The links with subsidiarity here are clear, as is the fact that human dignity (unlike justice) entails far more substantive implications than flow from the public-private divide. The divide, as Arendt and others insist, is not an accident of modernity but structurally essential to public reason.

Accordingly, part of the problem of reforming this area of law is that the public and private *as forms of authority* blur with a second phenomenon: the public and private as 'spheres' in which different forms of life and different social practices are to be found. Recall that the permissive principle concerns natural, social, and moral liberties; the preservation of natural liberties, including our natural or innate right, but also natural entitlements arising from a shared environment and shared public spaces. The permissive principle concerns the preservation of social liberties, those permissions that come from the silence of law which seek to minimise the burden of the law and which resist the 'colonisation of the human lifeworld' (below). It also concerns the preservation of moral liberty, those permissions that come from the public-private divide, strong permissions legally limiting the power of the state and public actors. In the first instance, the principle directly opposes the totalitarian state that destroys the public sphere and the possibility of public self-determination other than through violent revolution. It also means preventing the destruction of public spaces such that the right to public assembly can be maintained (Open Democracy 2014).

At the same time, broadly leftist critiques of the divide become important. What originated in Marx's critique of Hegel's bourgeois conception of the public-private divide (Marx 1977) turned into a radical conception of the abolition of private property and private sphere as we currently think of it. It also, more recently, took the form of a critique of the divide as hindering distributive justice or shielding abuse. With the dignitarian principles as a starting point, the more radical positions would have to be rejected – at least as basic conceptualisations of the public-private divide – because of their failure to include the normative and dignitarian significance of the divide as a contribution to both private autonomy and an autonomous public space. The permissive principle has the potential to transcend these problematic debates. The concern is with natural liberties. This is particularly clear when we consider the wider, modern phenomena of the 'colonisation of the lifeworld' (derived from the work of Habermas) and of functional differentiation (derived from the work of Durkheim and Luhmann).

The colonisation of the lifeworld concerns the saturation of human life and culture with technocratic efficiency as opposed to public reason proper. Technocratic rationality exchanges proper deliberation of our collective ends for the pursuit of efficiency regardless of ends; the bureaucratic discharge of government becomes, therefore, more attractive than the deliberation of democracy and 'regulation' replaces law-making:

> We are seeing what has been called the 'juridification' of social life, or also, in Habermas's words, the "colonization of the life-world," but this overproduction of laws and decrees, this instrumental and 'situational' use of law, does not do any good to the legislator's prestige. The mass production of laws necessarily escapes discussion of principles or pondered public debate, obeying instead more corporative, not to say clientelist, logic. The 'public reason' thus driven out of legislative assemblies is often transferred to courtrooms, and democracy – in order to escape the corrupt and corrupting logics

> of part clientelism and technobureaucratic opacity – tends to become, so to speak, 'judicial'.
>
> (Torre 2002, 381)

These critiques are important and reflect both the need for an expanded conception of public reason (as I have defended it) and the particular importance of seeing public reason as permissive in a specific dignitarian sense. My conception of public reason is not 'judicial'; this would be better levelled at positions that impose procedural tests of publicity on grounds for action. On the contrary, Habermas rightly stresses the importance of public discourse, by a range of actors, in the public sphere broadly construed. Moreover, we should agree that public authority is never merely a technocratic status but an authoritative role required to deliver justice, respect rights, and preserve freedoms. Public reason must be thought to include the preservation of natural liberties in the face of demands for more efficient government. To the extent that there is also, as part of this critique, a criticism of the movement of power from parliament to the courts and with it a more fundamental 'judicialisation' of democratic questions, further clarity is needed on what problems and forms of law are at issue here. That weak permission (the absence of law) is being eroded by the creation of multiple new grounds for legal action is as much a problem for legislatures as it is for the courts themselves. That human rights law is expanding its reach and brings with it weaker or stronger forms of judicial review should not, on my account, be seen as problematic. Habermas has, more broadly, called into question any neat connection between the protection of human dignity and contemporary liberal political philosophy. Prevailing positions would be unable to capture the phenomenology, and normative complexity, of this 'colonisation'. This critique, and disconnect between human dignity and liberal politics, can be deepened.

The idea of 'functional differentiation', built upon Luhmann's work on social systems, challenges us to think in terms of individuals' movement between different social systems and their not being confined to a limited group of (often private) social systems. Through social and economic pressures, like those articulated by Habermas, individuals can be progressively confined to a social system like the economy (as worker) or the private sphere (as consumer). Pressures to confine individuals to these spheres or roles runs contrary to the movement between social roles and social systems characteristic of modernity. This, for Lindemann, has dignitarian aspects:

> [H]uman dignity [is] the right to present oneself as an individual. Human dignity in this sense is an ongoing social accomplishment. Individuals have dignity insofar as they are able to present themselves to others as a coherent personality, which as an individual integrates diverse communicative obligations of different societal subsystems in a consistent way. A person should not only be able to act as a family member, a sales person or a member of a political party and so on, but should also be able to indicate that he/she does so as an individual in his/her particular way. [. . .] The individual integrates the

> diversity of functionally differentiated role expectations and thereby becomes a structural feature of modern society. As such, each individual has to be respected in principle and generally.
>
> (Lindemann 2015, 12)

This is an important response to the (originally) Durkheimean idea that human dignity is merely the expression of certain formal assumptions required by the impersonal encounters of modernity (Chapter 3). Human dignity lies in the preservation of possibilities, for an individual, within these different systems or processes of a society. The normative challenge of human dignity is to preserve these options when they are being shut down.

> Nevertheless, functional differentiation is also a potentially self-destructive process, which itself can become a threat to the normative institution of human dignity. Luhmann has described this primarily with respect to the political realm, but other functional domains can also become potentially destructive. One even has to take into account a liberal threat to functional differentiation that would tie recognition as a person with dignity to a particular personal performance – for example the performance of the rational actor following his or her own self-interest that is demanded in the economic sphere. In this case, human dignity would be threatened by a dominance of the functional domain of the economy.
>
> (Lindemann 2014, 198–199)

Again this seems to me correct and especially important as a rejoinder to virtue-based conceptions of human dignity that both make human dignity conditional on certain practices (of self-respect, typically) and which champion a virtue ethics without regard for the distinctive structures and challenges of modernity. It acts as a corrective to seeing the distinctive or authentic manifestation of human dignity as 'giving consent' or making a 'consumer choice'. And it also provokes additional reflections, outside the immediate scope of our concerns, with the challenge of linking human dignity not only with autonomy but with authenticity. Functional differentiation does not merely concern the preservation of liberties or autonomy in complex societies but also the very possibility of maintaining identity under the pressures of the colonisation of the lifeworld and the progressive intrusion of private actors into the public sphere.

By shifting from authority to forms of life, we have begun to entwine the themes of public authority, public governance, the public and private spheres, and the institutional concerns initially addressed in Chapter 3. The points of linkage take in all three dignitarian principles: individual sovereignty and human rights as the positive, enforceable, face of human dignity; permissions and permissiveness within the prevailing social systems of modernity and their challenge to both public and private spheres; and the recurrent challenge to combine our normative orders in such a way as to preserve the other principles. These together form a morality of governance, and a distinctive conception of moral cosmopolitanism, appropriate for the governance of modern states. It remains to be determined what can or should be said about the violent elements of those societies, namely exercise of coercion and the challenge of punishment.

6.4 Criminal law

The relationship between criminal law and human dignity has to be drawn carefully, both because from a certain perspective any form of punishment appears to be a *prima facie* dignitarian wrong and because (human dignity notwithstanding) all criminalisation is potentially harmful or repressive. It is tempting to allow human dignity to become a standard with which to draw a line between defensible and indefensible coercive conduct by the state. That function is important and will be defended. Indeed, such a standard already has an extensive regulatory life of its own in, for instance, the jurisprudence of the ECHR and in the jurisprudence of the Eighth Amendment of the US Constitution (Daly 2012). But the relationship must be a deeper one. It is as much in the conceptualisation of *criminalisation* as the regulation of punishment that we find the constitutive importance of human dignity. Criminal law and criminal prohibitions do not merely mark the minimum standards of civility necessary for the maintenance of law and order. The choice of the boundaries of criminalisation forms the point at which natural sovereignty, natural permissions, and coherent obligations find their most pressing and practical point of contact. In other words, only through a clear, principled criminalisation can we hope maintain human dignity in a state, and that principled criminalisation presumes the coalescing of individual freedom, collective liberties, and justice.

Criminalisation is necessary to maintain the freedoms and therefore the innate rights of individuals across a society. Human rights, as ever, provide a guide to where we can find those wrongful acts that should be the object of coercive power by the state; human rights encompass the general and generic entitlements of individuals, their welfare and autonomy, and criminal law protects these entitlements. Human rights and criminal prohibitions characteristically include concern for the integrity of the body but also concern with the welfare conditions of the individual (economic and familial concerns) and the social being of the individual (their property and their social status).

At the same time, human rights law is amongst the most important constitutive frameworks for understanding criminalisation, insisting upon the necessity of certain criminal norms and practices (including positive duties on the part of the state to investigate their violation) and on the impermissibility of criminalisation where this is an unwarranted intrusion into autonomy and civil liberties. Taking these contributions of human dignity together – a constitutive commitment to rights-preserving criminalisation, and the linking of human rights norms with criminal norms – we have the outline of a dignitarian defence of existing forms of criminalisation that would not be considered especially revisionist or radical. Conversely, to the extent that certain criminal statutes are 'administrative' or 'communicative', they do not clearly protect the generic interests associated with human rights or they concern prohibiting actions in the absence of fault – then we could also argue that a burden of justification is against them from the point of view of human rights. At the very least, we should be able to use human rights to review and indeed revoke criminal law that fails to protect (or goes beyond) measures protecting core, or generic, human interest. Moreover, the obligations principle concerns the ongoing governance of systems of norms and procedures such that balances can be struck: between state and citizen, but also between political, moral, and legal imperatives. In other words, the political and the moral often point in two different directions regarding the creation and imposition of criminal laws: the politically expressive value of criminalising, and a moral hesitancy against excessive use of criminal sanctions. We have, I would argue, a dignitarian obligation to resolve that tension in a way favourable to individuals' status.

Thus one core, recurrent theme will be that the content of criminal law must be determined in a way that maximises permissions. But, as has already been suggested (Chapter 3), this does not mean accepting the harm principle (Feinberg 1990; Mill 1998) as the foundation of criminalisation. The permissive principle makes the preservation of liberties the bedrock of an approach to criminalisation. But this is in concert with other the other principles concerned with the preservation of rights and with a morality of governance. Permissiveness has to be combined with rights, otherwise we have only negative grounds for determining what should be criminalised (i.e. not criminalising purely self-regarding duties). So, we should be able to support the expansion of criminal offences into social practices that have evaded regulation through respect for individual sovereignty. But we should be concerned with the reduction of the range of offences where these are (increasingly) of purely 'expressive' or 'communicative' value and therefore political rather than freedom-maximising. We reach that conclusion by comparison with the harm principle.

The simplest imputation from the permissive principle is that criminal regulation should be minimised as far as possible to preserve the natural liberties of the individual and maximise as far as possible the space of choice open to them. This would be close to the Millian harm principle (Mill 1998) and its variants (see Feinberg 1990) which represent, at their core, both an eagerness to preserve natural liberties and a revulsion against paternalism:

> [T]he only purpose for which power can be rightfully exercised over any member of a civilized community, against his will, is to prevent harm to others. His own good, either physical or moral, is not a sufficient warrant. He cannot rightfully be compelled to do or forbear because it will be better for him to do so, because it will make him happier, because, in the opinions of others, to do so would be wise, or even right. These are good reasons for remonstrating with him, or reasoning with him, or persuading him, or entreating him, but not for compelling him, or visiting him with any evil in case he do otherwise. To justify that, the conduct from which it is desired to deter him, must be calculated to produce evil to some one else. The only part of the conduct of any one, for which he is amenable to society, is that which

> concerns others. In the part which merely concerns himself, his independence is, of right, absolute. Over himself, over his own body and mind, the individual is sovereign.
>
> (Mill 1998, 14)

Under the present analysis, Mill's combination of protecting liberties and preventing paternalism, under the aegis of sovereignty, is undoubtedly attractive. But it is questionable whether this blending of liberties and resistance to paternalism is as coherent and functionally applicable to criminal law as it seems (see Kleinig 2017 for further analysis of human dignity, paternalism, and criminalisation). Resistance to paternalism is (in a certain sense) already included within my defence of dignitarian claim-rights, claim-rights understood in light of the will theory of rights which makes independent choice an end in itself and the core of respect for individuals (Chapter 2). But in conceptualising criminalisation *purely* through resistance to paternalism we face problems from two directions. First, (as already discussed), we face the phenomenon of the state bypassing our rational agency through refinements to our 'choice architecture' ('nudging') undertaken for good ends (and in part as a corrective to the intrusion of private commercial actors in the public sphere); there are, in other words, ambiguous examples of paternalism that require more careful analysis (and indeed some defensible forms of paternalism *per se* (see Enoch 2016)). Second, there are necessary intrusions into the private sphere to protect the vulnerable. A mechanism for producing justified criminal norms cannot depend upon a harm principle without specificity about liberty itself and without a better account of the public-private divide.

Mill undoubtedly has a richer conception of the public-private divide than the analysis so far suggests. His defence of 'experiments in living' (and expansion of the franchise) connects to his epistemology and normative theory, meaning the private sphere is characterised by individuals being free (but not compelled) to cultivate the 'higher pleasures' that he includes in his utilitarian calculus. Accordingly, "If a person possesses any tolerable amount of common sense and experience, his own mode of laying out his existence is the best, not because it is the best in itself, but because it is his own mode" (Mill 1998, 87). With this comes a requirement to resist the use of criminal law to intrude into the private sphere and to determine the mode of life chosen by individuals. The idea, now more commonly expressed as the priority of the right over the good, is echoed in Rawls's own permissive liberalism. Rawls argues that:

> the state has a responsibility to see to it that people have the resources and opportunities necessary in order for each of them to take responsibility for their own lives. What they then go on to make of those lives is entirely up to them: provided that they do not interfere with the choices of others, or the capacity of others to make such choices, the state takes no interest in any particular person's decisions about how to live his or her life. That is the sense in which Rawlsian liberalism is 'neutral' with respect to conceptions of the

> good. Neutrality is the consequence of a commitment to human freedom, rather than a premise in some argument in favor of granting freedoms.
> (Ripstein 2006, 1397–1398)

The defensibility of this way of approaching the public-private divide and the bases of criminalisation depends upon resistance to perfectionism and a division between self- and other-regarding duties. Even refined in Rawls's work, then, we do not find a simple normative dividing line between what can and cannot be criminalised, but a network of further concerns about which obligations can be enforced by the state and why.

There is a conventional legal response to what connects criminal prohibitions, justice, and the responsibilities of the state. That is, the content of criminal law is conventionally divided into *mala in se* and *mala prohibita* prohibitions, being, respectively, those acts that are wrong in themselves and those which are rendered wrong by authority. At a moral level, these are arguably divisible into deontic prohibitions (*mala in se*) and consequentialist concerns (*mala prohibita*), being perfect duties in the first instance and socially important laws (but not perfect moral duties) in the second. Is this division of dignitarian concern? On the one hand, we can see both as falling within the sphere of justice and therefore admitting reasonable variation between states. No neat *a priori* distinction between *mala in se* and *mala prohibita* can be discovered. Rather there is frequent blurring between what is *generally* prohibited by states and offences treated as *universally* wrong. Indeed, the law could be instrumental in forming our conception of what is *mala in se*.

On the other hand, it could be argued that we can broadly align human dignity with *mala in se* norms, and justice with *mala prohibita*. After all, we don't expect a complete and comprehensive moral justification for all of the specific norms of criminal law. Criminality is too complex, and the functions served by criminal justice too pragmatic, for there to be a univocal basis for criminalisation. But we do expect there to be a set of *mala in se* prohibitions that have a common moral underpinning. And when we look at the long-standing connection between human dignity and prohibition of degradation we can see certain regulative function for human dignity which is hard to deny (below).

In fact, in large measure this is likely to return us to our initial starting point, namely the broad but not strict link between what it is essential for the state to criminalise and human rights. And if we are to defend the very notion of *mala in se* offences, we are faced with a choice between accepting that link with human rights or defending a more functional understanding of those offences as prohibitions necessary for the basic continuation of any polity but not otherwise morally necessary (cf. Hart 1958). It is the human rights–based approach, I would argue, that gives us a better fit with the scope of contemporary criminal law, and indeed a better critical perspective on it. However, we still require a justificatory narrative to explain why, even if criminalisation is broadly required to maintain human rights, this authorises *the state* (and the state alone) to exercise coercive force and do so in a way which involves '*hard treatment*' of individuals who violate that law. These are the concerns of the next two sections.

6.5 Criminal justice

The dignitarian position on criminal justice I wish to defend is as follows. We seek the careful attribution of guilt, and careful the quantification of punishment, to uphold *human dignity*: to hold rational individuals to account for their actions while also creating a mechanism for discharging that guilt. At the same time we seek the pursuit of proportionality in punishment because it is *just*: the realisation of criminal justice must quantify an appropriate punishment, not manage an individual relative to their dangerousness. A commitment to public reason is the continued playing out of the relationship between these two commitments and, in the context of criminal justice, is principally a demand to maintain a system of proportionate penalties while excluding moral and political concerns from that system.

Before systematising this, however, we should note that this position helps to clarify the common but puzzling distinction between 'shame cultures' and 'guilt cultures' (a distinction originating in Dodds 1963). In broad terms, shame cultures attribute fundamental moral faults to an individual, faults that demand their expulsion from the polity. Guilt cultures, in contrast, are concerned with specific acts transgressing specific laws, and the guilt arising from those transgressions can be discharged without denoting fundamental flaws in an individual. While the anthropology here might be crude, the division points to a distinction of deep normative importance, namely the distinction between moral guilt and criminal responsibility. The 'dischargeable' nature of criminal responsibility distinguishes it from the possible forms that moral guilt can take: failures of virtue (failures to instil good dispositions in oneself), failures in self-regarding duties (failures to fulfil one's potential or exploit one's good fortune), or indeed of failures in imperfect other-regarding duties (to be generous, to enhance the lives of others). This does not mean that criminal law is defined by perfect other-regarding duties. It does mean that whatever crimes punishment is attached to, the guilt and responsibility we are concerned with is not moral responsibility. This also means, by extension, that we should be concerned, from a dignitarian perspective, with the reduction of criminalisation and punishment where these blur the boundaries of legal and moral. In essence, just as we would decry the *politicisation* of criminal justice we should also, from the perspective of human dignity, be wary of its *moralisation*.

Criminal justice concerns legal, not moral, responsibility. And it is important to note that there is a close link between what should be criminalised in the light of human dignity and the *general procedural and institutional context* in which criminal justice is conducted. The trial process itself, and its relationship with human dignity, might be summarised via the concerns brought under the obligations principle: we need to bring law, morality, and politics into harmony, meaning legal trials should not be *political* trials, nor should they be *moral* trials concerned with failings of moral character. However, criminal justice is wider than trials, and its general relationship with human dignity is best captured in the idea of the presumption of innocence, an idea that we have already seen is at the normative core of our innate right (Chapter 2). The presumption indicates a natural protection from untrammelled attributions of guilt, be they guilt by association or groundless accusation. It reflects the rejection of original sin or metaphysical guilt (Jaspers 2009) attaching to humans or humanity automatically and irrevocably. It reflects the fact that we are juridically equal and, in the first instance blameless, regardless of the contingencies of our life histories and life worlds. And it reflects the importance of keeping the moral and legal apart in our conceptualisation and enforcement of responsibility.

The presumption is also constitutive of criminal trials. There is a large and important body of jurisprudence (particularly from the ECtHR) that explicates the human right to a fair trial (see Mahoney 2004). But it is noteworthy that scholars (including Griffin) have given especial attention to one component of this right, the presumption of innocence, such that the presumption appears as the core of the human right with the implication that other parts of the right to a fair trial are matters of justice only. It rightly raises the possibility that the presumption of innocence is prior to the right to a fair trial, animating the very human right it is usually assumed to be a mere part of. As Griffin puts it:

> [E]veryone has a (human) right to be presumed innocent until proven guilty; if one's guilt were presumed, and action appropriate to that presumption then followed, such as serious loss of liberty or property, then one's capacity to live one's chosen life would be seriously impaired. It is true that not all cases of presumption of guilt need result in diminished personhood, but the line between those that do and those that do not would be hard to draw, and the sort of simplicity needed by both moral norms and civil laws is likely to result in a blanket presumption of innocence.
>
> (Griffin 2008, 198)

This idea is supported by Duff's call for an expansion of our conception of the presumption:

> [W]hile a distinctive PoI [presumption of innocence] operates within the criminal trial to protect defendants from unwarranted conviction and punishment unless guilt is proved 'according to law,' we can also identify another PoI that operates earlier in the process that leads from reported crime to the criminal trial: a PoI that protects all citizens against having the burdensome normative role of defendant imposed on them, unless there is sufficient evidence of their guilt. Perhaps it would be more accurate to say that this PoI protects those suspected of crime (for in any noncorrupt legal system, only those suspected of crime face the prospect of becoming defendants); but it

> can best be understood, I will argue, as expressing a broader PoI *that protects all citizens.*
>
> (Duff 2013, 176; emphasis added)

The principal dignitarian component of the presumption of innocence (and a fair trial) is the permissive principle and the assumption that moral failings should not be of criminal concern. This makes 'evidence of bad character' a particularly problematic aspect of modern criminal trials and of especial dignitarian concern. As Lacey has shown, the evidential centre of criminal trials has shifted from character (as disclosed to a defendant's family and local community) to the total exclusion of such evidence to the more recent return of evidence of bad character (Lacey 2011). While safeguards are in place to insist that only evidence of probative value is included within a trial, it remains problematic that otherwise legally irrelevant failings of moral character might become objects of concern within a criminal trial. Certainly evidence intended to show 'dispositions to act' forms an important and indeed arguably central element to certain conceptions of criminal responsibility (Feinberg 1970). Nevertheless, its inclusion represents a triumph of pragmatism over principle and a dangerous move towards the extension of criminal concern to private conduct. We could compare, in this respect, certain types of anti-social behaviour provisions that provide for rapid escalation from minimally disruptive behaviour, through accretion of civil penalties, to eventual criminalisation (see Hoffman and MacDonald 2010). This, too, represents a certain kind of route from the private to the public and from the moral to the criminal and has a questionable claim to be consistent with human rights. The inclusion of evidence of bad character within a criminal trial provides, perhaps, the more insidious phenomenon given that moral and criminal *responsibility* are being blurred and has a questionable claim to be consistent with human dignity itself (Lacey 2011, 151–178).

The presumption of innocence does not, alone, furnish us with all the principled bases of criminal justice. But it is an important link between innate right and the morality of governance: our natural absence of guilt must form part of more general judgements of public reason. It should also be added that there is an important epistemic aspect to the application of the presumption of innocence. The perception of guilt amongst others is subject to prejudicial preconceptions, prejudices which are a feature of criminal justice practice in particular and social epistemology more generally (see Fricker 2007). Criminal justice is not simply about the state's monopolisation of force, but also monopolisation of the epistemic authority to determine responsibility and the exclusion of private judgments. This in turn relates to innate right and our innate *rightfulness.* And when modern campaign slogans emphasise that 'no person is illegal' it is not merely a question of equality that is operative here but the *natural juridical entitlements* of the individual including the imposition of special burdens before individuals can be considered 'guilty' (Hong 2017).

What then can we treat as underlying principles for criminal justice as a dignitarian practice? I argue that we must reject a semi-formal argument concerning natural justice, and an argument concerning victims' rights, in favour of an argument for the state's exclusive power to create a distinct sphere of legal criminal responsibility. The formal argument, related to natural justice, is that (first, and structurally) a superior must stand in judgment over an inferior and (second) that the superior party must be separated from both victim and criminal. The state's right to judge *qua* superior authority, I would argue, captures an important aspect of what we mean by criminal *justice*. The state, in its role as superior party, does exchange forms of revenge and other forms of recompense for a distinctively authoritative intervention into disputes. The separation from the two parties imposes a finality to that intervention that would otherwise be lacking. But it does not, I would argue, give sufficient attention to the nature of criminal responsibility.

Conversely, the centralising of the rights of victims has a *prima facie* attractiveness in a theory of criminal justice. At one level criminal justice can be seen as instrumentally related to the interests of victims, remedying their harm or re-establishing their status. At another, more abstract, level, conceptions of criminal justice like Hegel's (2008) involve the idea that criminal justice negates a negation: that the harm done to the victim is negated through harm done to the criminal and that, in one abstract sense at least, criminal justice must involve 'two wrongs making a right'. We can find, within this broad position, a spectrum of views from the very direct serving of the retributive and restorative needs of a victim to a more abstract concern with the responsibility of the state to right their wrong. This ambiguity has a (cyclical) historical dimension:

> [T]he emergence and development of criminal law are linked to the substitution of the sovereign for the victim in the role of injured party, the consequence being that the penalty was to be distinguished 'from the reparation of the wrong caused to the victim', we are now compelled to observe that there has been a remarkable change over the past few decades. First, the victim is accorded an increasingly important role in criminal proceedings; secondly, the aim of repairing the damage sustained is occupying an increasingly fundamental position in that context.
>
> (Tulkens 2011, 595)

Protection of human rights could, in fact, be used to support these victim-centred positions. That is, we are concerned with the rights held by victims, or with a wider social responsibility on the part of the state to maintain the conditions for preservation of rights. Elements of both of these must be true if criminal justice (in its contemporary form) is to be justified: we cannot neglect the concrete needs, or legitimate retributive instinct of victims, but neither do those obligations exist outside a wider concern with preservation of rights within a state as a whole. However, there is still a residual and legitimate dignitarian concern that the perpetrator becomes instrumental in such approaches; that they are the means by which a victim is given redress, or their punishment is the means by which the state communicates the importance of rights.

With these deficient positions in mind, we should treat criminal justice as, at root, an obligation on the state and a dignity-defending obligation. That dignitarian foundation concerns the creation of ***a wholly publicly controlled form of responsibility and guilt*** serving criminal, victim, and society. It is not justified by a right to punishment (Kant) but neither is it simply a moral economy of freedoms (Hegel) where harm to a freedom is responded to by the state with a second wrong negating the first (positions discussed further below). The essence of the view defended here is that the imposition of an appropriate quantity of legal responsibility and legal punishment is the best way to respond to the precise level of an offender's guilt while responding publicly, through the state, to their violation of rights. But note that this does not precisely map a justification via ***proportionality***. Both justice and human dignity demand that proportionality be the core of justified punishment, albeit for different reasons. Formal or legal equality demands retributive proportionality: proportionality to the gravity of the crime in question and proportionality to other punishments meted out for the same crime. Human dignity demands that there should be legal quantification of responsibility: creating a quantum of legal guilt proportionate to the crime but limited by respect for individual sovereignty. This is different to determining what is 'owed to victims'. Victims deserve retributive recompense for wrongs, a recompense particularised to nature of the criminal act they were subjected to; they also deserve general or symbolic commitment to their rights through the general workings of criminal justice. Victim's rights do, then, justify punishment of a guilty individual. But they, alone, are neither necessary nor sufficient for legitimate punishment. They cannot capture the dignitarian demand that legitimate punishment be ***mediated by the state and wholly legal***. This retributive demands of the victim are not directly inflicted on the criminal; it also means that retribution by the state cannot be waived by the victim. (The state can choose, through restorative justice, to allow victims to control the process and even the waive the unusual, state-determined quantum of punishment. But this is mediated by the state, and the victim's ability to themselves acknowledge the offender's guilt and waive further punishment remains conditional on no further legally or criminally relevant material coming to light.)

Certain elements of Kant's and Hegel's approach to criminal justice are useful for exploring this position, though full explanation awaits our discussion of punishment itself. Kant's position is broadly that the criminal has a right to be punished on the basis of this being what would be rationally willed by a guilty agent wishing to re-enter the civil condition. On the present account, we can say that it is rational to want to discharge debts of legal guilt, but this is not the same as a 'right to be punished'. The plausibility of a right to be punished lies in it 'respecting rationality' through delivering a foreseen punishment and returning the criminal to the civil condition. Only the latter part is plausible, but it needs reconstruction. Precisely because legal guilt is fungible and limiting – it reflects a quantum of guilt not a state of moral guiltiness – it is rational to will the discharge of one's own legal debt. If the debt can be discharged, the individual returns to a rightful condition with the full protections of the state and full autonomy to exercise their rights and liberties. *The state* as the 'holder' or 'determinant' of legal guilt is uniquely able to treat that guilt as a quantity to be discharged, and can protect the individual from arbitrary punishment (where moral and legal guilt are combined or where an individual is simply victimised or scapegoated). The putative right to be punished cannot be defended as rational or as a right, but the right to discharge guilt can be.

Equally, Hegel's criminal justice model based on rights and the right of the state alone to punish is broadly correct. But in Hegel's economy of wrong and counter-wrong we can lose sight of the dignitarian-based state responsibility *to exchange moral for legal guilt*. Structurally, punishment cannot make sense without its communicating that a grave act is being responded to with something equally grave. But this misses the importance of that response being a purely legal one produced by special social institutions, not a response to the nature of the offender themselves. This should also warn us, in considering the philosophical foundations of criminal justice, against focus on proportionality alone (which does not justify criminal justice *per se*, only fair sentencing) or on the rights and interests of victims.

This does not exhaust, however, our concerns with the *regulative* aspects of human dignity in criminal justice and particularly victim and criminal as participants in criminal justice. There is no doubt that human dignity can be used to turn our attention to more neglected aspects of objectification or instrumentalisation in processes, including criminal justice processes, be it the active participation of defendants or communication to victims. Precisely in having interstitial implications, human dignity is intended to protect the individual against status harms that are incidental to the working out of otherwise legitimate normative orders like the legal system. Accordingly, Paul Roberts provides a powerful and subtle description of the forms of objectification, both dramatic and seemingly incidental, in criminal justice processes (Roberts 2006). There is enormous value in this focus on the phenomenological aspects of the trial though it is hard to square with the reading of human dignity offered here; it is a discourse of dignity (similar those defended by Margalit 2009 or Darwall 2006) that uses the language of dignity to express experiences of disrespect and which concern civility and respect more generally.

The ways in which protection of dignity and rights goes beyond respect is also apparent when we think about the experience of witnesses (including victim-witnesses) in criminal trials. Their experience may well be of instrumentalisation. A trial is not 'for' a victim. Nonetheless, a victim is wronged if procedure does not take account of their interests, both at the level of basic welfare and in terms of respecting their conscious concerns with the conduct and outcome of the trial. To say that victims are merely means to an end in criminal processes would, in the normal course of things, be an exaggeration. After all, the giving of testimony is sometimes valuable as an end in itself. There are, however, principled reasons for concern with the regulation of trials such that they are cognisant of treating each participant as a rational addressee of law and rational participation in processes, a position defended by Waldron (2012) and (with qualification) by Meyerson:

> The essential claim of the dignitarians is that courts should treat defendants as active subjects, not passive objects – ends not means – which involves respecting them as people who can reason, explain themselves and enter into a dialogue with the state. Jeremy Waldron, for instance, argues that the procedures that regulate the conduct of trials, and especially the opportunity they provide for argumentation and contestation, respect human dignity by treating people as 'bearers of reason and intelligence', who have their own view or perspective on the application of legal norms to their situation.
>
> (Meyerson 2014, 13)

I would agree that this is an aspect of respect, the respect that is due on dignitarian grounds, not merely welfare policies on the part of the state. They also flow quite directly from all prevailing conceptions of the human right to a fair trial.

A final important question that has to be raised in this context is how criminal justice systems should respond to civil disobedience. The human rights to assembly and to expression give rise to rights to protest in the public sphere, but the law cannot countenance its own violation. Rather, the standard understanding of the relationship between disobedience and law is that the civil disobedient is the person who publicly resists an unjust law in the pursuit of change in another aspect of the law, but who is and must be prepared to accept the punishment of the law (see Rawls 1999, 326f; also Raz 1979, 262f). If civil disobedience is justified – which indeed it must be, at least *pro tanto*, under the obligations principle because the law cannot exhaust our obligations – then the position regarding the *law* should be relatively straight-forward. That is, the law must mete out whatever punishment is normally deserved for that particular harm to person or property and will thereby deliver the expected (if unwelcome) hard treatment to the disobedient. The paradox of disobedience has always been the competing or incommensurable appeals to justice that can be made on behalf of obedience to the law and following the dictates of conscience. However, we are in a position to confine the appeal of justice to the formal playing-out of the obligations found in a legal system, and the dictates of conscience found within human dignity instead. Given that the present account of human dignity is thin with regard to regulatory norms (as opposed to constitutive implications) it is difficult to point to single ideas that will always justify disobedience. Nevertheless, it seems clear at a principled level that serious or systematic failure to deliver human rights (sovereignty), to protect the public sphere as a permissive sphere (permission), or continual creation of laws that repeatedly clash with the moral dictates felt by a large portion of a population (obligations), will be good candidates for justified disobedience.

With regard to civil disobedience, the nature and challenge of determining guilt and punishment is particularly acute because it questions the judiciary's fidelity to justice on the one hand and human dignity on the other. The delivery of criminal penalties against conscientious law-breakers means respect for justice, the limitation of punishment a respect for human dignity. Weinrib's distinction between the occasions when the law is barbaric or merely unjust, with only the former triggering a Radbruch exception to the rules, seems of little help here. We would be troubled by a judge's inattention to either justice or human dignity. Blindness to the dictates of conscience means morally empty justice; withholding justice from 'defensible' disobedience in some circumstances (but inevitably not in others) upholds neither justice nor human dignity consistently. Public reason therefore inevitably appears contradictory in this context: judges must deliver legal justice under institutional rules and procedures, but at times they can and should respect human dignity by reducing the quantum of punishment otherwise owed.

However, two further points can be made. The first is procedural and concerns the determination of when law-breaking is genuinely conscience-based. There are relatively clear criteria by which disobedience can be judged authentic, namely if the behaviour is conducted publicly, consistently (across different occasions or consistent with publicly professed commitments), and at some personal loss (a richer argument in this vein is provided by Brownlee 2012). This takes as its paradigm public acts of disobedience from those who exhibit consistent commitment to a reformist cause. It excludes opportunist activities for private gain. And it also excludes the claims of individuals who want to dictate certain patterns of behaviour within their own groups or companies but without personal loss (see, for example, *Hobby Lobby* [2014]). Accordingly, the possibility of the judiciary identifying the kinds of acts that should be the beneficiary of leniency is more straightforward than might be assumed. The second point is that we can also draw a distinction between situations where leniency is required and circumstances where the law itself should be set aside. The Radbruch criteria provide some guidance to where law is so unconscionable it should not only not be applied but it should be negated as law by the judiciary. These are circumstances of grave injustice or systematic failure to deliver rights. These would be distinguished from situations where there is persistent contradiction between individual conscience and public law. In the latter circumstances, assuming the criteria above, the judge has a duty to limit but not waive the impact of the law. The Radbruch duties of the judge are much less likely to arise. But they can arise, and in those circumstances would be properly articulated using the language of human dignity (see Alexy 2002).

6.6 Punishment

We should, finally, consider the punishments that are the product of criminal justice. Application of human dignity appears especially problematic in this respect because

> there is a real and irremediable contradiction in avenging the offended human dignity of the victim by violating that of the criminal. The only way,

> not of eliminating the difficulty (for strictly speaking it is insoluble), but of alleviating it, is to lessen the punishment as much as possible.
>
> (Durkheim, quoted in Cotterrell 2011, 11)

As the foregoing argument has indicated, we should not endorse Durkheim's pessimism about the insolubility of the problem here, but we should agree with the conclusion that we should seek to lessen punishment. We need to ask on what basis we are permitted to use hard treatment, and whether there is a clear dividing line between those forms of treatment that do, or do not, produce dignitarian wrongs. As suggested, there are two important alternatives here regarding why punishment might be justified at all: on Kantian grounds (the right to be punished in such a way as to discharge a debt) or on Hegelian grounds (the need for a second wrong to make a right).

One of the most important ways of finding the core of such debates and problems is to ground the justification of punishment in human rationality, both in the sense of holding to account an individual for freely chosen acts and for the use of punishment as a communicative practice speaking to rational agents. Kant, for instance, sees the criminal individual as having freely chosen to have renounced the civil condition and return to a state of nature; their responsibility, and by extension that of the state, is to return to a rightful condition through the discharge of guilt through punishment:

> Thus Kant attempts to establish the claim that some forms of coercion (as opposed to violence) are morally permissible because, contrary to appearance, they are really consistent with rational freedom. The argument, in broad outline, goes in the following way. Coercion may keep people from doing what they desire or want to do on a particular occasion and is thus prima facie wrong. However, such coercion can be shown to be morally justified (and thus not absolutely wrong) if it can be established that the coercion is such that it could have been rationally willed even by the person whose desire is interfered with.
>
> (Murphy 1973, 225)

And, for Kant:

> The criminal himself has no complaint, because he has rationally consented to or willed his own punishment. That is, those very rules which he has broken work, when they are obeyed by others, to his own advantage as a citizen. He would have chosen such rules for himself and others in the original position of choice. And, since he derives and voluntarily accepts benefits from their operation, he owes his own obedience as a debt to his fellow citizens for their sacrifices in maintaining them.
>
> (Murphy 1973, 228)

The putative 'right to be punished' that has been taken to follow from this is difficult to defend (as suggested above). Assuming rational agents cannot will harm to themselves (even though they may rationally will to discharge a debt of guilt they have accrued) means that criminals are unlikely to have a right to punishment *per se* as much as a right to the means to restore their innate rightfulness.

The entitlement to restore an individuals' own state of rightfulness offers a better route to justifying the 'hard treatment' that is characteristic of punishment. That treatment has been defended on communicative grounds (i.e. only hard treatment as opposed to, say, restorative processes, can communicate the community's censure to an individual). A better defence lies, I think, in the need to correlate the (abstract) 'burden' of guilt held by the criminal with a period or form of deprivation. Justice 'seen to be done' is not merely a side constraint on criminal procedure but also a demand for any corrective response to criminals to have some kind of correlate (not merely repentance, however sincere it may be). The public nature of punishment is not merely a demand for a spectacle of punishment but for a link with the openness and authority of the public sphere. Again, Harel (with Gur-Ayre) rightly links with authority, superiority, and agents acting for the right reason:

> Punishment is a public manifestation of condemnation and disapprobation of the criminal deeds. Unlike deterrence or even certain forms of retribution, public condemnation is possible in the first place only if it emanates from the appropriate agent. Condemnation is ineffective unless done by an agent who is in a privileged status to that of the one subjected to the condemnation, one whose judgments concerning the appropriateness of the behaviour is worthy of attention or respect. Otherwise, an infliction of 'a sanction' amounts to an act of violence which cannot express or communicate censure for the culpable and wrongful acts done. Arguably in a liberal society, it is only the state that can make such judgments and as the privatized activities are not the doings of the state, private entities vested with formal authority to execute the activities in question cannot speak and act in the name of the state.
> (Gur-Ayre and Harel 2016, 17)

This position, culminating in a critique of privatised prisons, rightly stresses the special and intermediary relationship played by the state. It is (as above) both the victim and the state whose authority underlies punishment, and the direct link with the state should not be broken through the privatisation of prison services. This should sit within a broader critique of prison provision as hidden from public scrutiny and separated from the public sphere. We should, in other words, be concerned with better oversight of prisons, better efforts to integrate individuals' life in prison with their existing lives, and with the minimisation of incarceration more generally. Punishment is a public responsibility requiring public manifestation (as opposed to secrecy); punishment also requires the preservation of individuals' private life without which their basic human status is drawn into question.

If dignitarian punishment – publicly determined legal responsibility producing a limited quantum of punishment – entails the isolation of legal responsibility from moral responsibility, it also requires reductionism in punishment. Justice requires that there be consistency across different punishments for relevantly similar crimes and wrongdoings. But the essence of dignitarian criminal justice is that an individual can be serving a three-fold symbolic function (asserting the rights of victim to redress, society to protection, and criminal to having their innate right upheld even while their entitlements are suspended) and this is *communicated* through deprivation (punishment) and *constrained* by the justice of proportionality. This means there is no natural quantum of punishments only the need for a consistent system. The communicative efficiency of temporary isolation – communication to society, victim, and offender – means that dignitarian concerns are discharged. The fact that justice demands proportionality and hierarchy is problematic; a graduation of punishments for crimes seems to require a breadth of punishments from short sentences to life imprisonment. But just, proportional punishment requires only consistent equal punishment, and the assumption that such a scale of punishment is both natural and necessary should be resisted.

But what, then, of the established regulatory uses of human dignity in this context? Such uses are not only long-standing but expanding both in terms of the scope of basic bodily integrity protections (that is, the conceptualisation of degradation in law) but also in terms of the richness of our understanding of procedure and the additional indignities that can accompany any institutionalised processes that threaten to instrumentalise the individual (Waldron 2012; Roberts 2006). We consider the expansion of that jurisprudence in the ECHR and conclude with a discussion of 'hope' in this context.

The dignitarian *norm* we find in ECHR jurisprudence concerns a prohibition on dignitarian wrong which is construed in objective terms. Individuals' dignity can be harmed through degrading and disrespectful acts that wrong the individual *irrespective of whether they consciously experience the wrong or an act as a wrong* (*Bouyid* [2015]). The development of a dignitarian wrong as the key regulative function of human dignity is problematic. In the first instance it is clear (certainly to a large number of judges, including the dissenting judges in the *Bouyid* judgment) that this particular dignitarian wrong (encompassing all forms of degradation that arise from the diminution of the individual by the state in situations of disparity of power) does not derive from international human rights law. Indeed, the origin of such an idea is more likely to have arisen from civil law discourses of 'personality rights' that attach particular constitutional importance to the individual being able to protect their personality from degrading wrongs including, but not exclusively, defamation. As to the Convention Article 3 itself, interpreted *noiicistur a sociis*, 'degradation' would have to reach a very high threshold to apply: it would have to have the level of harm typically associated with inhuman treatment or torture. As interpretation of the norm has developed, degradation is increasingly evidenced by objectively wrongful condtions (mistreatment at the hands of the state, or an actor authorised by the state) and no particular threshold of harm has to be met.

What should we conclude about the evolution of a dignitarian wrong? We should I would argue, be wary of a discourse of 'dignity', of *social* dignity and the wrongs that can befall individuals because of inequalities of power. Human dignity proper covers the same territory but does so without positing a kind of *wrong* that is an independent, regulative ground of legal claim against others. We can reject (as I advocate) the idea that we can understand human dignity as producing a special dignitarian wrong, or we can reject the idea that (human) dignity can produce a fully rounded, principle-producing philosophy of human status and related obligations. Criticism of the 'dignitarian turn' in Article 3 jurisprudence is premised on the assumption that we must take seriously the status principles that arise from innate right, and on the assumption that we cannot derive comprehensive constitutional claims from limited regulative ones.

Degradation can take place where the individual is denied hope. A feature of a high-profile German constitutional case (*Life Imprisonment Case* [1977]) is the importance of hope, and not extinguishing hope provides a final but vitally important link with human dignity.

> From Article 1.1. of the Basic Law, in conjunction with the principle to maintain a state based on social justice, one can – and this is particularly true in the execution of criminal punishments – derive the duty of the state to allow [everyone at least] that minimum level of existence at which human dignity is conceived. It would be inconsistent with human dignity perceived in this way if the state were to claim the right to forcefully strip a human of his freedom without [the detainee] having at least the possibility to ever regain freedom.
>
> (*Life Imprisonment Case* [1977], paragraph 1)

Moreover,

> a humane execution of the lifetime imprisonment can only be assured if the sentenced criminal has a concrete and principally attainable possibility to regain freedom at a later point in time; for the core of human dignity is struck if the convicted criminal has to give up any hope of regaining his freedom no matter how his personality develops. In order to assure this perspective [to regain freedom at some point in the future], which is the prerequisite for rendering lifetime imprisonment bearable according to the [court's] understanding of human dignity, in a manner which meets constitutional requirements, the [current] legal rules of parole are not sufficient.
>
> (*Life Imprisonment Case* [1977], paragraph 4)

To place an individual in a situation of hopelessness is to deny them very concrete possibilities: liberty and the goods that come with liberty. The parallels between certain kinds of life imprisonment and the death penalty are (in this respect) clear. The objectionability of the death penalty lies not only in violation of the proper powers of the state, but the removal from individuals of a certain kind of orientation to the future. The fact that individuals outside prisons may themselves be hopeless is not a falsification of this position. It is the *deliberate* removal not only of liberty but of hope – that change or new beginning is possible – that renders certain forms and lengths of imprisonment morally problematic. And the underlying dignitarian premise here is not only a link with the human condition and the human potential for new beginnings, but also the obligations principle that legal responsibility should not permanently displace moral responsibility.

If the dignitarian foundations of criminal justice and punishment concern the creation of a wholly ***publicly controlled*** form of responsibility and guilt serving criminal, victim, and society, the essence of that public control is to main the innate right of the criminal. An individual does not have their rightfulness, their natural sovereignty, negated even in punishment, albeit their exercise of rights is curtailed. One other way to understand that public control of guilt is, then, as the maintenance of hope. When punishment is arbitrary or excessive an individual is deprived of hope: the hope that they will ever discharge their legal guilt. Excessive punishments could be *just* in the limited sense that excessive punishment could be meted out consistently across criminals committing similar crimes. But they could not be consistent with human dignity because they are not contained and conditioned by the understanding that legal guilt and punishment must be finite and dischargeable. 'Hope' has, accordingly, formed an important part of human dignity jurisprudence in this area.

This account of hope distils the essence of the present reconstruction of human dignity. While the regulative link between human dignity and punishment has been assumed to be the prohibition of degradation, this leaves undetermined what it is about human dignity that we assume to be especially or distinctively prohibitive of certain acts. And it leaves undetermined why we can nonetheless coerce others through the conventional, justice-pursuing practices of the state. Without moving beyond the function of prohibition, we may as well abandon human dignity to being a synonym of 'not degrading others'. The link with hope demonstrates that we are concerned with the inexorable sovereignty of the individual, what they are naturally permitted to do, and how the legal, moral, and political must be harmonised to support innate sovereignty and natural permissions. This, then, is the kind of complex, constitutive position that a defence of human dignity must inhabit if it is not to simply signal our opposition to barbarity.

References

Alexy, R. (2002) *The Argument From Injustice: A Reply to Legal Positivism.* Oxford, Oxford University Press.

Beever, A. (2013) *Forgotten Justice: Forms of Justice in the History of Legal and Political Theory.* Oxford, Oxford University Press.

Bentham, J. (2007) *The Principles of Morals and Legislation.* New York, Dover Publications.

Bosanquet, B. (1920) *The Philosophical Theory of the State.* London, Macmillan and Company.

Bouyid v. Belgium. (2015) 23380/09 Judgment (Merits and Just Satisfaction) Court (Grand Chamber) ECHR 819.

Brownlee, K. (2012) *Conscience and Conviction: The Case for Civil Disobedience*. Oxford, Oxford University Press.
Buchanan, A. (1997) 'Theories of Secession' *Philosophy and Public Affairs*, 26(10), 31–61.
Capps, P. (2009) *Human Dignity and the Foundations of International Law*. Oxford, Bloomsbury Publishing.
Cotterrell, R. (2011) 'Justice, Dignity, Torture, Headscarves: Can Durkheim's Sociology Clarify Legal Values?' *Social and Legal Studies*, 20(1), 3–20.
Daly, E. (2012) *Dignity Rights: Courts, Constitutions, and the Worth of the Human Person*. Philadelphia, University of Pennsylvania Press.
Darwall, S.L. (2006) *The Second-Person Standpoint: Morality, Respect, and Accountability*. Cambridge, MA, Harvard University Press.
Dodds, E.R. (1963) *The Greeks and the Irrational*. Berkeley, University of California Press.
Duff, R.A. (2013) 'Who Must Presume Whom to Be Innocent of What?' *Netherlands Journal of Legal Philosophy*, 42(3), 170–192.
Eberle, E.J. (2008) 'The German Idea of Freedom' *Oregon Review of International Law*, 10, 1–76.
Enoch, D. (2016) 'What's Wrong with Paternalism? Autonomy, Belief, and Action' *Proceedings of the Aristotelian Society*, 116(1), The Oxford University Press.
Feinberg, J. (1970) *Doing and Deserving: Essays in the Theory of Responsibility*. Princeton, Princeton University Press.
Feinberg, J. (1990) *Harm to Others*. Oxford, Oxford University Press.
Forst, R. (2011) 'The Ground of Critique: On the Concept of Human Dignity in Social Orders of Justification' *Philosophy and Social Criticism*, 37(9), 965–976.
Fox-Decent, E. and Criddle, E.J. (2010) 'The Fiduciary Constitution of Human Rights' *Legal Theory*, 15(4), 301.
Fricker, M. (2007) *Epistemic Injustice: Power and the Ethics of Knowing*. Oxford, Oxford University Press.
Fuller, L.L. (1964) *The Morality of Law*. New Haven/London, Yale University Press.
Griffin, J. (2008) *On Human Rights*. Oxford, Oxford University Press.
Gur-Arye, M. and Harel, A. (2016) 'Taking Internationalism Seriously: Why International Criminal Law Matters', Hebrew University of Jerusalem Legal Research Paper No. 16–21, Available at: https://ssrn.com/abstract=2774320, accessed March 2017.
Habermas, J. (2001) 'Constitutional Democracy: A Paradoxical Union of Contradictory Principles?' *Political Theory*, 29(6), 766–781.
Habermas, J. (2010) 'The Concept of Human Dignity and the Realistic Utopia of Human Rights' *Metaphilosophy*, 41(4), 464–480.
Harel, A. (2014a) 'Public and Private Law' in Dubber, M.D. and Hörnle, T. eds., *Oxford Handbook of Criminal Law*, Oxford, Oxford University Press, 1040–1063.
Harel, A. (2014b) *Why Law Matters*. Oxford, Oxford University Press.
Hart, H.L.A. (1958) 'Positivism and the Separation of Law and Morals' *Harvard Law Review*, 71(4), 593–629.
Hegel, G.W.F. (2008) *Outlines of the Philosophy of Right*. Oxford, Oxford University Press.
Hobby Lobby. (2014) *Burwell v. Hobby Lobby*, 573 U.S. [US Supreme Court] (2014).
Hoffman, S. and Macdonald, S. (2010) 'Should ASBOs Be Civilized?' *Criminal Law Review*, 6, 457–473.

Hong, K.E. (2017) 'The Ten Parts of "Illegal" in "Illegal Immigration" That I Do Not Understand', Boston College Law School Legal Studies Research Paper No. 444, Available at: https://ssrn.com/abstract=2942303, accessed March 2017.

Jaspers, K. (2009) *The Question of German Guilt*. New York, Fordham University Press.

Kleinig, J. (2017) 'Paternalism and Human Dignity' *Criminal Law and Philosophy*, 11, 19–36.

Lacey, N. (2011) *Philosophical Foundations of Criminal Law*. Oxford, Oxford University Press.

Life Imprisonment Case. (1977) German Constitutional Court 45 BVerfGE 187.

Lindemann, G. (2014) 'Social and Cultural Presuppositions for the Use of the Concept of Human Dignity' in Düwell, M. et al eds., *The Cambridge Handbook of Human Dignity: Interdisciplinary Perspectives*. Cambridge, Cambridge University Press, 191–199.

Lindemann, G. (2015) 'Human Dignity as a Structural Feature of Functional Differentiation: A Precondition for Modern Responsibilization' *Soziale Systeme*, 19(2), 235–258.

Luban, D. (2010) 'The Rule of Law and Human Dignity: Re-Examining Fuller's Canons' *Hague Journal on the Rule of Law*, 2(1), 29–47.

Mahoney, P. (2004) 'Right to a Fair Trial in Criminal Matters Under Article 6 ECHR' *Judicial Studies Institute Journal*, 4(2), 107–129.

Margalit, A. (2009) *The Decent Society*. Cambridge, MA, Harvard University Press.

Marmor, A. (2015) 'What Is the Right to Privacy?' *Philosophy and Public Affairs*, 43(1), 3–26.

Marx, K. (1977) *Marx's Critique of Hegel's 'Philosophy of Right'*. Cambridge, Cambridge University Press.

Meyerson, D. (2014) 'The Moral Justification for the Right to Make Full Answer and Defence' *Oxford Journal of Legal Studies*, 35(2), 1–29.

Mill, J.S. (1998) *On Liberty and Other Essays*. Oxford, Oxford University Press.

Murphy, J.G. (1973) 'Marxism and Retribution' *Philosophy and Public Affairs*, 2(3), 217–243.

O'Neill, O. (1996) *Towards Justice and Virtue: A Constructive Account of Practical Reasoning*. Cambridge, Cambridge University Press.

Open Democracy. (2014) 'The End of Public Space: One Law to Ban Them All', Available at: www.opendemocracy.net/ourkingdom/josie-appleton/end-of-public-space-one-law-to-ban-them-all, accessed April 2017.

Radbruch, G. (2006) 'Statutory Lawlessness and Supra-Statutory Law (1946)' *Oxford Journal of Legal Studies*, 26(1), 1–11.

Rawls, J. (1999) *A Theory of Justice*, Revised edition. Oxford, Oxford University Press.

Raz, J. (1979) *The Authority of Law: Essays on Law and Morality*. Oxford, Oxford University Press.

Riley, S. (2015) 'Human Dignity and the Rule of Law' *Utrecht Law Review*, 11(2), 91–105.

Ripstein, A. (2006) 'Private Order and Public Justice: Kant and Rawls' *Virginia Law Review*, 92(7), 1391–1438.

Roberts, P. (2006) 'Theorising Procedural Tradition: Subjects, Objects and Values in Criminal Adjudication' in Duff, et al eds., *The Trial on Trial, Volume Two*. Oxford, Hart Publishing.

Solove, D.J. (2002) 'Conceptualizing Privacy' *California Law Review*, 1087–1155.

Soobramoney. (1997) *Soobramoney v. Minister of Health, KwaZulu-Natal* ZACC 17, 1998 (1) SA 765 (CC), 1997 (12) BCLR 1696 (CC), November 27, 1997, Constitutional Court (South Africa).

Torre, M. (2002) 'Theories of Legal Argumentation and Concepts of Law: An Approximation' *Ratio Juris*, 15(4), 377–402.

Tulkens, F. (2011) 'The Paradoxical Relationship Between Criminal Law and Human Rights' *Journal of International Criminal Justice*, 9(3), 577–595.

Verschraegen, G. (2002) 'Human Rights and Modern Society: A Sociological Analysis from the Perspective of Systems Theory' *Journal of Law and Society*, 29(2), 258–281.

Waldron, J. (2012) 'How Law Protects Dignity' *The Cambridge Law Journal*, 71(1), 200–222.

Weinrib, J. (2016) *Dimensions of Dignity: The Theory and Practice of Modern Constitutional Law*. Cambridge, Cambridge University Press.

Index

abuse 185; of groups 93; rejection of 19, 21; of state power 70
action, human rights and 51, 75–76, 79–81
African Charter on Human and Peoples' Rights 149
agency 66, 178; bypassing of 89–90; group 116; human rights and 51–52, 54–55, 58, 61; moral 55; politics and 76; protection of 70, 78; rational 62, 89, 178, 191
agency poverty 39–40
aggression 126–127, 131
Alekovski Case 123–124
Alexy, Robert 15
all things considered standard 121, 134, 154
Ambos, K. 58
Ancient Law (Maine) 38
Anthropocene 77
anthropological cross 84
anti-consequentialism 70–71
anti-utilitarianism 70, 82
Arend, A.C. 58
Arendt, Hannah 33–34, 75–81, 133, 148, 185
Aristotle 23, 74–75, 79
asylum 152, 161–162
atrocity 7, 104, 107, 110, 129–130, 182
authority: constituent 147; democratic 158; of democratic institutions 82; freedom from superior 50; judicial power 84; limits on 8, 10; public 185; of the state 173–176; in transnational practices 147
autonomy 43, 47, 58, 89; functional differentiation and 188; of groups 116; of human rights law 152–153
barbarism, protection from 175, 178, 205
basic status 37–40
benevolence 91, 150
Beyleveld, D. 18
Bhopal disaster 148
bodily integrity 7, 44, 51, 53–54, 203
Brownsword, R. 18
Brugger, W. 17, 84–85, 182
Buchanan, A. 31, 37, 55–56, 127–128, 173
Bull, H. 112

Caney, S. 112
capital, globalisation of 140
Capps, Patrick 84, 112–113, 146, 181–182
Carozza, P.G. 138, 164–165
Categorical Imperative 58–59, 62
change, as status principle 46
Chapman v. The UK 152
checkerboard question 83
Chen, L-C. 101
choice: architecture 89, 191; governance of 89–90
Ci, Jiwei 39
Cicero 19
civil disobedience 8, 13, 126–127, 199–200
climate change 77, 86, 88
coercion 44, 82–83, 85, 92, 192
colonisation of the lifeworld 185–186
commodities, globalisation of 140
common good 70, 101, 131, 164–165, 177
comprehensive conceptions of human dignity 24
computer games 159–160

conceptualisations of human dignity 24
condemnation 202
consequentialism, limits to 71
constitutional incoherence 5–6, 15
constitutionalism 143–144
constitutional principle(s): global 109–114; human dignity as 5
constitutional provisions, entrenchment of 87
constitutional rights 54, 61
constitutional rights distinct from human rights 172
constitutionalisation of Europe 157–163
contract 38, 148; contractarian tradition 43, 67, 75; freedom of 46
contradictory component of law, human dignity as 27
corrective justice 72, 78
correlativity in rights, lack of demand for 27
cosmopolitanism: cultural 112; institutional 112; international law and 111–115; moral 66, 90–95, 111–112, 139, 151, 153, 188; state justification 174
Cotterell, R. 49
Council of Europe 150
Criddle, E.J. 180
crimes against humanity 129–131
criminalisation 189–195
criminal justice 130–134, 193–200
criminal law 12, 189–193
cruelty 15
cultural cosmopolitanism 112
cultural rights 156
culture, malleability of human 33
Curthoys, N. 80

Dagan, H. 149
Darwall, S.L. 23
decolonization movements 117
defamation 6, 118, 203
degradation: European Court of Human Rights focus on 150; prohibition on 4–5, 10, 21, 104, 192; punishment and 203–205
democracy: constitutionalism 143–144; rule of law connection 179–180
democratic accountability 142, 144, 166
democratic authority 158
democratic institutions 81–88; executive 85; judicial 84–85; legislative 83–84
democratic subsidiarity 139
deterritorialisation of processes 143
dignitarian principles *see* obligation principle; permissive principle; sovereignty principle
dignitarian rights 53–54
dignity: history of concept 19–20; right to 48
dignity of labour 147–148
discrimination, right against 155
disobedience 8, 13, 126–127, 199–200
disruption, human dignity and 27
distributive justice 78
Doctrine of Right 57, 59, 175
Dorfman, A. 149
Duff, R.A. 194–195
Dupré, Catherine 82, 87, 143–144, 157–158
Durkheim, Emile 49, 186, 188, 201
duties 21, 45, 54
Dworkin, R. 61, 70, 81, 83–85, 182

Eberle, E. J. 171, 177
economic rights 153–157
ECOSOC 148
education, right to 156
Eichmann, Adolf 81, 133
emergency power 85
entitlements: to claim remedy 72; conditioned 70; core 69; corrective justice and 72; human dignity as status 36–37, 43–44; human rights and 51, 60; of the individual 14, 31, 71–72; innate right and 45; juridical 31, 36, 66, 70–72, 194; linking social systems with 31; morality of governance 88–89; rightful standing and 43; static standards of 49; unconditioned 70; universal 52
entrepreneurs, norm 107, 138, 145–146
environment, relationship with 77–78, 86–87
epistemic injustice 166
equality: human dignity as barrier to justification of 5; human rights and 51; innate 42; juridical 41, 45, 51, 69; natural 20, 46; natural sovereign 40–41, 43–46, 49–50, 69; relative 66; of states 107; status, human dignity 25, 37
essentially contested concept, human dignity as 7–8

Etinson, A. 23
eunomics 140
Europe, constitutionalisation of 157–163
European Convention on Human Rights 157, 161, 163
European Court of Human Rights 139–140, 150–153, 160, 189, 203
European Court of Justice 159
European Union: constitutionalisation of Europe 157–163; foreign policy, unified 163; as inter-statal institution 139; migration and 152; subsidiarity 163–164; transnational law 140, 149–150, 163–164; treaties, presence of human dignity in 9; treaty of 163
evidence 81
executive exceptionalism 16
executive power 85, 143
extra-national regulatory regimes 140

Fabre, C. 111–112, 120–121, 125–126
fairness 88
Feinberg, J. 22–23
force, use of 44, 83, 119–120, 122–123, 126–128, 131
Forst, R. 24
foundation, human dignity as 3–5, 7, 9–10, 12, 25, 50, 153
Fox-Decent, E. 180–181
freedom 45; of contract 46, 148; human rights and 51; innate right to 47; as a right 42–44, 46; as status principle 46; from superior authority 50
free expression 79
Fricker, M. 166
Fuller, Lon 9, 140–141, 178–179
functional differentiation 186–188
functionalism 173–174
functions, of human dignity 8, 25, 49, 60, 78
Furundzija, Prosecutor v. 125

general jurisprudence of human dignity 14–18
Geneva Conventions 122–124
genocide 129–131
German Constitutional Court 159
Gewirth, A. 113
global constitutional principles 109–114
globalisation 140–142; consequences of 166; human rights 149–153; multi-national entities 144–148
global justice 91–92, 144, 156
governance: demands of good 82; morality of 67, 82–83, 88–90, 102, 112, 188
governing authority, human dignity as 8
Griffin, J. 17–18, 52–53, 72, 194
Grotius 20, 40, 119, 126
Groundwork (Kant) 57–60
group rights 93, 116–119
Grundnorm 5, 9
guilt cultures 193
Gur-Ayre, M. 202

Habermas, J. 179–180, 186–187
hard law 129, 154
Harel, Alon 82, 84, 174, 176–177, 185, 202
harm principle 190–191
health, right to 155–156
Heath, J. B. 3, 105, 133
Hegel, G.W.F 196–198
Held, David 112
history of human dignity concept 19–20
Hobbes, T. 43, 72–73
hope, denial of 204–205
hubris 19
human condition 67–68, 74–81; action 75–76, 79–81; environment, relationship with 77–78; plurality 75–76, 78–80; public-private divide 77–80; sustainability 78
humanitarian intervention 8, 125–130
humanitarianism 109, 116, 122
humanitarian law 122, 124
humanity 35, 67
humanity's law 110–111
human ontology 32
human person, nature of 34–36, 45
human rights: agency 51–52, 54–55, 58; constitutional rights distinct from 172; criminal law and 189–190; democratic institutions 82; dependence on human dignity 57; emergency powers and suspension of 85; globalisation and 149–153; human dignity as status 50–57; human dignity function 60; human dignity linked to 26; indivisibility 119, 182–183; interest theory 54–55; language of human person 35; as moral rights 46; political conception of 34; sovereignty principle 50, 55; threshold 52; transnational law

149–153; violations 57, 122, 197; will theory 54–56; *see also* human rights law
human rights law 46–48, 56–57, 69–72, 74, 93; autonomy of 152–153; criminal law 189; evolution of 71; free expression 79; human dignity foundational relationship with 7, 48; human person and 34–35; international 102, 104–105, 111, 114–119, 114–120, 122, 124–125, 129, 203; presentism in 87; protection from state's power 70–71; public law 172, 178, 180–181, 183–184, 187, 189; sovereignty principle and 46, 69, 71, 93; subsidiarity 151; suspension of 122; transnational 139, 143, 147, 149, 151–153, 161; universal scope 52
Hume, D. 19, 33

ICC (International Criminal Court) 126, 128–130, 132, 150
ICCPR (International Covenant on Civil and Political Rights) 103
identity: malleability of human 33; public-private divide 77
immunity, sovereign 41
inclusive positivism 14–16, 175
indeterminacy, normative 4–5, 106
inherent dignity 8
innate right 31, 40, 42–46, 59–60, 69; criminal justice 194–195; entitlements 45; to freedom 47; human rights and 51; Kant and 31, 42–46, 73; presumption of innocence 194–195
innocence, presumption of 45–47, 194–195
institutional cosmopolitanism 112
institutional implications of human dignity 13–14, 26, 68–69
integrity 22, 83–84
interactionism 140–141, 146, 157
interest theory 54–55, 118
International Bill of Rights 107
International Court of Justice 106, 111, 122
International Covenant on Civil and Political Rights (ICCPR) 103
International Criminal Court (ICC) 126, 128–130, 132, 150
International Labour Organisation 147–148
international law 101–134; contradictions 103–109; cosmopolitan tradition 111; criminal justice 130–134; global constitutional principles 109–114; humanitarian intervention 125–130; human rights law 114–119; jurisdiction 94; overview 101–103; shifting between apology and utopia 108–109; sources of 106–107, 113, 131; space, relationship with 107; warfare 119–125
International Law Commission 111
International Monetary Fund 146
interstitial principle, human dignity as 12–13, 16–17, 26

judgment: category of human person and 36; law as a moral 18
judicial review 84
judiciary: counter-majoritarian power of 84; decision-making in hard cases 84–85; dignitarian reasoning in 182–183
juridical entitlements 31, 36, 66, 70–72, 194
juridical equality 41, 45, 51, 69
juridical necessity 31–32, 40–45
juridical status 40
jurisdiction 94, 107, 142, 173
jurisprudential problems: constitutional incoherence 5–6; normative indeterminacy 4–5; regulatory redundancy 5
jurisprudential questions 6–10
just cause 129
justice 3, 21, 25–26; artificial virtue 72; circumstances of 74–75, 77–79, 82; corrective 72, 78; criminal 193–200; difference from human dignity concept 67–74, 79, 161; distributive 78; as first virtue of social institutions 69, 75; global 91–92, 144, 156; intergenerational 86; international criminal 130–134; *lex permissiva* 73–74; limits of 69–74; natural 72–73, 196; need for 75; normative parity of human dignity and legal justice 17–18
Justice for Hedgehog (Dworkin) 61
justifiability, limits of 119
just war theory 120–121, 126

Kant, Immanuel 19–20, 87; criminal justice and 197; Doctrine of Right 57, 59, 175; innate right 31, 42–46, 59–60, 73; *lex permissiva* 73–74; presumption of innocence 45–47; on public right 177; punishment and 197, 201; on value 58–59
Kateb, G. 8
Khen, H. M-E. 125
Koh, H.H. 145
Korsgaard, C.M. 58
Koskenniemi, M. 108, 116, 129
Kreiger, H. 120
Kumm, M. 142

labour 139–140, 146–148, 185
Lacey, N. 195
Lagon, M.P. 58
Lasswell, H.D. 101
law: as action 81; hard 129, 154; judge-made 84; mediating function of 68; soft 111, 129, 154; synthetic character of 81; as work 81
law-breaking, legitimacy of 8, 12
League of Nations 107
legal pluralism 140–141
legal positivism 14, 59, 61, 74, 173
legislation, dignity of 83–84
lex mercatoria 142, 144–149
lex permissiva 16, 67, 73–74
liberties 69, 72, 88, 186–187, 190–191
liberty 15, 204–205
Life Imprisonment Case 204
Lindemann, G. 187–188
Linklater, A. 150
Locke, J. 43
loss of human dignity 38
Luban, D. 3, 178
Luhmann, N. 186–188

MacCormick, Neil 62
MacIntyre, A. 21
Macklin, Ruth 110
Maine, Henry 38
majoritarianism 82–83, 166
manifesto rights 15, 27, 115, 119
Margalit, A. 23, 35
margin of appreciation 151, 158
marketplace of ideas 79
Marmor, A. 184
Martens Clause 124–125
Marx, Karl 148, 186
materialism 78
McCrudden, Christopher 4, 7–8
McDougal, M.S. 101
means-end rationality 164, 178, 182
merchants, law of *see lex mercatoria*
Metaphysics of Morals (Kant) 57
Meyerson, D. 199
migration 139, 152, 161–162
Mill, J.S. 190–191
minority groups, protection of 117
monism 145
moral agency 55
moral commitment, human dignity as 5
moral cosmopolitanism 66, 90–95, 111–112, 188; social and economic rights 153; subsidiarity 139; transnational law and 151
morality: internal of law 178; limitation of law by 12, 16, 46, 132; limitation of morality by law 12, 46; limitation of politics by law and 13, 46
morality of governance 67, 82–83, 88–90, 188; international law 102, 112; subsidiarity 139; transnational law 139, 144
moral judgment, law as 18
Moral Law 20, 58–59, 63
moral liberty 69, 186
moral phenomena 18
moral progress 110
moral rights 46, 52–53, 69, 162
moral sentiment, theory of 62
moral status 37
MSS v. Belgium and Greece 152, 161–162
multi-national entities 144–148, 166
Murphy, J.G. 201

national law: international criminal law superior to 131–132; jurisdiction 94
natural equality 20, 46
natural justice 72–73, 196
natural law 48, 69; cosmopolitanism 67; human dignity link to 4, 9, 14, 16, 18, 20, 25–26, 80–81; international law and 104, 111, 119, 132; Kant and 59, 73–74; *lex permissiva* and 67, 73–74; limitation of law by morality and 12, 16, 26; natural sovereign 41; natural sovereign equality and 40–41; procedural 61
natural liberties 69, 186–187, 190
natural rights 14, 20, 25, 42–43, 51–52, 67, 72–73, 119

natural sovereign equality 40–41, 43–46, 49–50, 69
Neal, Mary 6
negation of human dignity 38–39
new beginnings (natality) 75–76
Nolte, G. 120
normative core of human dignity: as basic status of the human person 34; human dignity as status 32–36; philosophical anthropology 32–33; right to have rights 32–34; value 32–33
normative implications of human dignity 13, 17, 21, 26; human dignity as status 31, 45–40; human person, centrality of 34–36
normative indeterminacy 4–5, 106
normative parity of human dignity and legal justice 17–18
normative systems, governance of 11–12
norm entrepreneurs 107, 138, 145–146
nuclear weapons, legality of 111, 122

objectification 4
obligation principle 11–13, 46–47; criminal justice 193–194; institutional implications of human dignity 68; limitation of law by morality 12; limitation of morality by law 12; limitation of politics by law and morality 13; morality of governance 90; normative certainty across structures of obligation 47; rule of law contrasted with 179
obligations: corrective 74; distributive 74; generation from principles 48; human dignity as status 36–37, 41, 44, 46; morality and 68; permissive principle 47; personal practical reasoning 62; as status principles 46
Olsen, H. 141
Omega 159–160
O'Neill, O. 23
On Human Rights (Griffin) 17
open borders 162
open future 67, 86–87
orders, refusal to follow 8
outrages on personal dignity 123–124

participatory rights 61
paternalism 56, 62, 89–90, 165, 191
peace 116–117
Peace of Westphalia 107
peremptory force of human dignity 26
permission: human condition and 69; *lex permissiva* 16, 67, 73–74; strong 73; weak 73, 187
permissive liberalism 191–192
permissive principle 11, 13, 15–16, 46, 47; criminal justice and 195; institutional implications of human dignity 69; liberties and 69, 186, 190; morality of governance 90; public-private divide and 185
personality rights 177, 203
personal practical reasoning 62
philosophical anthropology 32–33, 38, 46
Pico 19–20, 31, 33–34
pluralism 102, 118–119; international law and 112–114, 132; legal 140–141; moral 181; qualified 113–114, 118
plurality 66–67, 75–76, 78–80, 93; in transnational law 140, 145, 147
political order 179–180
politics: agency and 76; future-orientated 76; limitation on by law and morality 13, 46–47; sustaining human plurality 76
positivism 14–16, 59, 61, 74, 153, 173
poverty 39–40
power: emergency 85; executive 85, 143; limitations on 8, 70–71, 175, 181; subsidiarity 164–166
practical rationality 164
presumption of innocence 45–47, 194–195
price 59
principles: human dignity as cluster of 57; obligations generation from 48; status 45–46; turned into judgments 16; use of 15–16
prisons, privatised 202
Pritchard, M.S. 20, 22
privacy 11, 184
private law, multi-national entities and 148
privatisation of the public sphere 185
procedural naturalism 61
progress, moral 110
proportionality of punishment 193, 197–198, 203
public expression 79

public law 171–205; criminal justice 193–200; criminal law 189–193; democratic accountability 144; jurisdiction 94; multi-national entities and 148; public-private divide 185–189; punishment 200–205; responsibilities of the state 172–178; rule of law and public reason 178–183; time and territory 94
public-private divide 77–80, 185–189, 191–192
public reason 10, 26, 80; public law and 172–174, 176, 181–183, 185–187, 193, 195, 200; transnational law and 155, 161–162, 167
Pufendorf, Samuel von 20, 40, 119
punishment 200–205; denial of hope 204–205; proportionality 193, 197–198, 203; protection from arbitrary 198; right to 197–198, 201–202

qualified pluralism 113–114, 118

Radbruch, Gustav 175–176, 200
rape 125
rational agency 62, 89, 178, 191
rationality, means-end 164, 178, 182
rational moral action 59
Rawls, John 34, 53, 181, 191
Raz, J. 179
rebellion, permissibility of 47
redundancy problem, human dignity as 27
refugee 162
regulation, private resistance to public 144
regulative incoherence, human dignity as 5
regulatory capture 146
regulatory redundancy 5, 17, 66
respect 23–24, 50, 199
respect-conferring practices in law 17
right(s): acquired 53; constitutional 54, 61; cultural 156; defensive 119; dignitarian 53–54; to dignity 48; economic 153–157; to education 156; of exit and entry 162; group 93, 116–119; to health 155–156; indivisibility 51, 102, 119, 182; innate right 31, 40, 42–46; interest theory 54–55; manifesto 15, 27, 115, 119; moral 46, 52–53, 69, 162; natural 14, 20, 25, 42–43, 51–52, 67, 72–73, 119; in non-ideal circumstances 51, 56; nonpaternalistic protection against paternalism 56; participatory 61; personality 177, 203; social 153–157; special 70; of states 40, 119; suspension of 85–86; waiving 55–56; will theory 43–44, 54–56; *see also* human rights
rightful standing/rightfulness 43–45, 47, 194, 205
right of entry 162
right of exit 162
rights-holder 34, 42, 45, 54
rights inflation 26–27, 116, 119
right to have rights 32–34, 45, 48, 152
Right to Protect 120, 128–129
Ripstein, A. 42, 45, 192
Rivers, J. 84
Roberts, Paul 198
Roman law 38
rule of law 9, 16–17; definition 13; indicators 115; international 102, 115, 132; limit of the political 46–47; obligation principle contrasted with 179; public law 178–183; public-private divide 183

scarcity 77
security 88
self-constitution 19, 21, 33, 39, 47, 56, 77, 156
self-creation 19, 21, 54
self-defence 119–120, 126–127
self-determination 19–21, 40, 44, 46, 60; of groups 118; human rights and 51; morality of governance 89–90
self-esteem 19, 22
self-respect 22–23, 39
shame cultures 193
Shapiro, S. 14–15, 141
Shue, Henry 123
Siliadin v. France 138
Singer, P. 91
Smith, Adam 62
social contract 40
social engineering 89–90
social existence: limitations and 75; need for justice 75
social institutions, justice as first virtue of 69, 75
social liberties 69, 186
social practices, human dignity and 61

social rights 153–157
social station 37–39
social systems, boundaries on governance of 11
soft law 111, 129, 154
solidarity 102, 112–113, 116, 117
Soobramoney v. Minister of Health, KwaZuku-Natal 171
sovereign immunity 41
sovereign inviolability of states 109
sovereignty: human rights as moral rights 53; of the individual 54, 93
sovereignty principle 13, 46–47; human rights and 50, 55, 69, 71; institutional implications of human dignity 69
speciesism 32–33, 35
state: criminal justice and 196–199; justification of 92, 173; lack of integrity 83; moral failures of 175; responsibilities of the 172–178; sovereign inviolability of 109; territory and 107, 173
status: basic status 37–40; historical context 37–38; juridical 40; moral 37; as society-specific 49
status, human dignity as 25, 30–63; entitlements 36–37, 43–44; equality and 25; human rights 50–57; juridical necessity 31–32, 40–45; natural law connection 25; natural rights connection 25; normative core of human dignity 32–36; normative implications of human dignity 31, 45–40; obligations 36–37, 41, 44, 46; value and 57–63
status poverty 39
status principles 45–46
subsidiarity 139, 163–167, 185–186
subversion, human dignity as 26
sustainability 78–79, 83

territory: bypassed by transnational chains 142–143; jurisdiction and 107, 173; public law and 173; rights of states 107
Third Party Effect 177
Tierney, B. 73
Toddington, S. 141
Torre, M. 87
torture 21
transnational law 138–167; constitutionalisation of Europe 157–163; defining 139–144; human rights 149–153; jurisdiction 94; *lex mercatoria* 144–149; overview 138–139; social and economic rights 153–157; subsidiarity 163–167
trials 193–195, 198–199
Tsagourias, N.K. 104–105, 109
Tuck, R. 119

Union Carbide 148
unions 146–147
United Nations: international law and 107, 111–112, 114–116, 120, 126–127, 129; transnational law and 147, 154, 162, 166
Universal Declaration of Human Rights (UDHR) 6–8, 20, 103–104, 115–116, 153
Universal Principle of Right 45
unjust law 12

value: human dignity as status 48–49, 57–63; Kant on 58–59; normative core of human dignity 32–33; rational moral action 59; self-constitution and 33
victims 196–198
violations of human dignity 38
virtue 19, 21–23, 63, 72
vulnerability 69, 78

Waldron, Jeremy 17, 37, 60–61, 70–71, 81, 83–84, 199
war crimes 130–131
warfare 119–125
Weinrib, Jacob 24, 43–44, 174–176, 178, 200
will theory of rights 43–44, 54–56, 118
work 148
World Trade Organisation 147, 154
worth 58